VOLUNTEER TOURISM

T0372545

New Directions in Tourism Analysis

Series Editor: Dimitri Ioannides, E-TOUR, Mid Sweden University, Sweden

Although tourism is becoming increasingly popular as both a taught subject and an area for empirical investigation, the theoretical underpinnings of many approaches have tended to be eclectic and somewhat underdeveloped. However, recent developments indicate that the field of tourism studies is beginning to develop in a more theoretically informed manner, but this has not yet been matched by current publications.

The aim of this series is to fill this gap with high quality monographs or edited collections that seek to develop tourism analysis at both theoretical and substantive levels using approaches which are broadly derived from allied social science disciplines such as Sociology, Social Anthropology, Human and Social Geography, and Cultural Studies. As tourism studies covers a wide range of activities and sub fields, certain areas such as Hospitality Management and Business, which are already well provided for, would be excluded. The series will therefore fill a gap in the current overall pattern of publication.

Suggested themes to be covered by the series, either singly or in combination, include – consumption; cultural change; development; gender; globalisation; political economy; social theory; sustainability.

Also in the series

Tourism Destination Development
Turns and Tactics
Edited by Arvid Viken and Brynhild Granås
ISBN 978-1-4724-1658-2

Planning for Ethnic Tourism
Li Yang and Geoffrey Wall
ISBN 978-0-7546-7384-2

The Dracula Dilemma
Tourism, Identity and the State in Romania
Duncan Light
ISBN 978-1-4094-4021-5

Emotion in Motion
Tourism, Affect and Transformation
Edited by David Picard and Mike Robinson
ISBN 978-1-4094-2133-7

Volunteer Tourism
Popular Humanitarianism in Neoliberal Times

MARY MOSTAFANEZHAD
University of Hawai'i at Mānoa, Hawai'i

LONDON AND NEW YORK

First published 2014 by Ashgate Publishing

Published 2016 by Routledge
2 Park Square, Milton Park, Abingdon, Oxon OX14 4RN
711 Third Avenue, New York, NY 10017, USA

First issued in paperback 2017

Routledge is an imprint of the Taylor & Francis Group, an informa business

British Library Cataloguing in Publication Data
A catalogue record for this book is available from the British Library

The Library of Congress has cataloged the printed edition as follows:
Mostafanezhad, Mary.
  Volunteer tourism : popular humanitarianism in neoliberal times / by Mary Mostafanezhad.
      pages cm.—(New directions in tourism analysis)
  Includes bibliographical references and index.
  ISBN 978-1-4094-6953-7 (hardback)—ISBN 978-1-4094-6954-4 (ebook)—ISBN 978-1-4094-6955-1 (epub) 1. Volunteer tourism. 2. Humanitarianism. 3. Neoliberalism.
I. Title.
  G156.5.V64M67 2014
  338.4'791—dc23
                                                                      2013049241

ISBN 13: 978-1-138-08252-6 (pbk)
ISBN 13: 978-1-4094-6953-7 (hbk)

Contents

For Isar

Chapter 1

Introduction: Sentimental Sojourns in Northern Thailand

With a burning cigarette in one hand and freshly printed color brochures in the other, Tom, a *tuk-tuk*[1] driver, elaborates on his newfound business plan. We are at a home for single mothers in crisis about 20km outside of Chiang Mai. Tom is showing me the brochures he made with the help of some of his English friends who stay at the hostel below his sister's apartment. A hand drawn map printed on the back and brief descriptions of six volunteer sites on the front, Tom keeps these brochures in the backseat pocket of his *tuk-tuk* so that they are easily noticed by his passengers. Tom is a former Thai soldier who recently acquired a *tuk-tuk* from his cousin. Since he began driving the *tuk-tuk* two years ago, Tom has noticed an increasing number of *Farang*[2] volunteers in Thailand. I ask Tom what he thinks about the increase in Western volunteers.[3] He pauses for a moment, takes a drag of his cigarette and explains: "Thailand can't help everyone." He continues, "[Volunteer tourism] is good because it helps Thailand to improve. It's better to have international NGOs and foundations than have no one to help solve the problems. So there are people to help. It helps improve the situation."

I surmise that most people would agree with Tom: "It is better to have international NGOs and foundations than have no one to help solve the problems." After all, it is the core ideology "of all western-based development—that the Global South is inevitably better off with ongoing interventions (in the name of development) than it would be without them" (Manzo, 2008, p. 652). Echoing this ideology, Sally Brown, founder of Ambassadors for Children, explains how, "If a kid can be held for a couple of days, you're able to make a small difference" (Fitzpatrick, 2007). It is around these small differences that volunteer tourism—travel for the purpose of volunteering time, energy and financial support to benefit environmental conservation and development oriented projects—is positioned. Volunteer tourism is now at the forefront of tourism

---

1   A *tuk-tuk* is a motorized rickshaw that is a commonly used as mode of public transportation in Thailand. It is especially popular among foreign tourists.

2   *Farang* is the Thai word for Westerner. It primarily refers to Westerners of European descent and can have various connotations, depending of the context.

3   When I refer to the "West" and "Westerners" I am primarily referring to Europe and its former colonies including the United States, Canada and Australasia. Tester, K. 2010. *Humanitarianism and Modern Culture*, University Park, PA, Pennsylvania State University Press.

development agendas and is the fastest growing niche tourism market in the world (Vrasti, 2012). The expansion of volunteer tourism is more than the latest trend in alternative travel; it is a cultural commentary on the appropriate response to global economic inequality. *Volunteer Tourism* examines this commentary through the lives of ordinary individuals who like their celebrity counterparts or the colonial explorers that came before them, have become key signifiers in the reorganization of international humanitarianism in the Global South.

The volunteer tourism experience complicates postcolonial readings of the tourism encounter. Existing stereotypes about the superficial sociality of tourism experiences is seemingly vindicated through intimate interaction with "host community members"[4]—often the foremost attraction in volunteer tourism. Ted, the founder of Chiang Mai Friends—one of the NGOs on which this research is based—explains on his website how meaningful cross-cultural experiences are and how volunteer tourism departs from mainstream tourism experiences (Ted, 2010, Founder of Chiang Mai Friends). In this way, volunteer tourists are able to escape the "tourist bubble" through intimate encounters with local people. Thus, the sentimentality of the volunteer tourism experience is at least in part what authenticates and differentiates volunteer tourism from mass tourism experiences.

Sentimentality intersects with humanitarianism and development discourse in volunteer tourism in ways that reflect an emerging transnational cultural logic. As Tester points out, "[T]he linkage between humanitarianism and culture is intrinsic and actually essential because humanitarianism means paying moral attention to others who are beyond one's immediate sphere of existence, and therefore it requires, and involves an imagination about the world, about the relationships between the near and the far, 'us' and 'them'" (Tester, 2010, p. vii). This cultural logic engages with neoliberalism as both a cultural ideology and economic practice that takes shape in distinctive ways in diverse geopolitical contexts. Rather than a monolithic force with undifferentiated characterizations, neoliberalism is manifest and is co-constituted within existing political and economic circumstances (Springer, 2010, Ferguson, 2010). Daley points out how "humanitarianism has become corporatised and professionalised at the same time that neoliberal economic restructuring has reduced state-provisioned social welfare" and that "Western humanitarian actors have become increasingly diversified, ranging from government agencies, Western militaries, multilateral organisations, international non-governmental organisations (INGOs), wealthy philanthropic individuals, ordinary citizens, and celebrities" (Daley, 2013, p. 375–6). Along with these actors is the increasingly conspicuous volunteer tourist who now makes regular appearances along the banana pancake trail in Southeast Asia.

---

4 Despite the sometimes ambiguous nature of the concept, I use the terms "host community members" in this book to refer to primarily Thai people living in the places where the volunteers work. I use the term "volunteers" to refer to the primarily Western international volunteer tourists.

In *Volunteer Tourism*, I consider the ways that neoliberalism mediates the volunteer tourism experience including 1) how neoliberalism is resisted as well as how this resistance is co-opted through the privatization of social justice agendas; 2) how individuals take on neoliberal subjectivities and identity formations; and 3) the ways neoliberalism is appropriated as a coping strategy in local struggles for economic survival. Despite its protean nature, I argue that there is a tie which binds these practices into a recognizable neoliberal project of humanitarian ilk. This project takes place within the contemporary moment "in which realms of culture and society once considered 'outside' the official economy are harnessed, reshaped and made legible in economic terms" (Mukherjee and Banet-Weiser, 2012, p. 1). Through ethnographic and theoretical mappings of these configurations in the context of volunteer tourism in northern Thailand, I offer a nuanced geography of neoliberalism as a cultural, political and economic ideology and practice that takes place, shifts and reconfigures within the transnational volunteer tourism encounter.

The "voluntary turn" which has progressively expanded since the mid-1980s and the corollary rapid expansion of NGOs—now key players in international development and the expansion of global civil society are illustrative of how the cultural articulates with the economic and political in neoliberalism (Milligan and Conradson, 2006b, Milligan and Conradson, 2006a, Hailey, 1999). The intensified focus on the individual as a moral consumer is one link in the broader chain of expansion of "moral economies"—most notably exemplified by fair, ethical and alternative consumer products—as well as global justice movements. In this way, volunteer tourism represents a growing consumer consciousness of global economic, social and political inequality. Today, "instead of the rational, calculating and cold-blooded American Psycho, the good neoliberal subject of the twenty-first century is the rather schizophrenic figure of the compassionate entrepreneur, the happy workaholic, the charitable CEO, the creative worker, the frugal consumer and, last but not least, the volunteer tourist" (Vrasti, 2012, p. 21). Ironically, within this commodity driven context, both supporters and critics of neoliberalism facilitate its expansion through their mutual commodification and privatization of development as well as their appropriation of sentimentality as the flag under which they compete for legitimacy.

A central question in contemporary scholarship on the Third World[5] "is how the linked processes of globalization, modernization, and transnational capitalism affect people's everyday lives" (Wilson, 2004, p. 8). This question is regularly debated in the public arena where audiences around the world are becoming increasingly mindful of the negative implications of neoliberal global capitalism. While local governments have been debilitated by the wake of neoliberalism's onslaught of structural adjustment programs, state pullbacks and privatization

---

5 I use the term Third World to highlight unequal access to resources, power and development as well as the ways in which the Third World has been discursively developed in the Western imaginary. Mowforth, M. and Munt, I., 2009, *Tourism and Sustainability: Development and New Tourism in the Third World*, New York: Routledge.

schemes—middle and upper class Western consumers have decided to take action into their own hands. Volunteer tourism has become an increasingly popular approach for people to participate in humanitarianism: as *TIME Magazine* reports, "[G]etting in touch with your inner Angelina Jolie is easier than it used to be!" (Fitzpatrick, 2007, also cited in Mostafanezhad, 2013). In myriad ways, celebrities like Angelina Jolie, Madonna and George Clooney have made international volunteering sexy! While most people cannot commit their lives or bank accounts to long-term volunteer projects, there has been a recent explosion of the range of humanitarian organizations and projects that are suited for first-timers.

The primary argument that threads through the pages that follow is that the volunteer tourism encounter is mediated by the cultural logic of neoliberalism which reframes questions of structural inequality as questions of individual morality. As a result, volunteer tourism—albeit inadvertently—contributes to the continued expansion of the cultural logic and economic practices of neoliberalism as well as contributes to the ongoing redefinition of humanitarianism and social activism. Additionally, I argue that the focus on sentimentality in the encounter obscures the structural inequality on which the volunteer tourism experience is based. Thus, while the small, and indeed sentimental changes that Brown notes above are meaningful in their own right, in *Volunteer Tourism* I illustrate how and why the sustainability of the accomplishments of volunteer tourism remain tenuous. This is, I argue, because the problems that volunteer tourism seeks to address are the outcome, rather than the cause of underdevelopment. The work of *Volunteer Tourism* traverses between anthropology of tourism and tourism geographies and extends into the interdisciplinary terrain of cultural, tourism and humanitarian studies. It engages with crucial questions regarding how the contemporary generation has transformed activism and social resistance in ways that articulate with the market. This widespread reorientation forces us to consider resistance in relation to, among others, the consumer-cum-volunteer tourist (Sturken, 2012, p. x).

The Media(ted) Humanitarian Gaze

The voluntary impulse in Thailand reached new heights in the aftermath of the 2004 Indian Ocean tsunami where more than 150,000 people were killed including more than 7,000 people in Thailand (Rigg et al., 2005, Jankaew et al., 2008). Ricky Martin and other high profile artists such as Madonna, George Clooney and Christina Aguilera took part in campaigns to raise funds for tsunami victims (Jeckell and MacNeil, 2004). In his week-long tour of the tsunami affected area of southern Thailand, Ricky Martin met with the Thai prime minister at the time, Thaksin Shinawatra and Foreign Minister Surakiart Sathirathai to discuss the extent of the devastation. He also toured Patong and Kamala beaches and several orphanages, where photographs of him holding and kissing children attracted international media attention. Media representations of the humanitarian and environmental devastation caused by the tsunami were inescapable. Coupled with widespread attention to celebrity humanitarians calling out for the help of their fellow global citizens, thousands of international volunteers rallied to Thailand and other affected regions in Asia. Notably, "the immediacy of the suffering and the extensive news coverage helped mobilize people in the countries that supply Southeast Asia with most of their tourists: Europe, Japan and Australia" (Hitchcock et al., 2009, p. 6). While many volunteers knew victims, "others had first-hand experience of the places and people struck by the tsunami, and had a feeling of solidarity as a result of visiting the region" (Hitchcock et al., 2009, p. 6). A consequence of the successful recruitment of Western volunteers was the growing identification among the public as potential humanitarian actors. Like the phenomena of volunteer tourism itself, the increasing visibility of celebrities in humanitarianism should not be taken for granted. Daley notes how "[S]ince the mid-1980s, celebrity advocacy has become more widespread; through its association with the technological developments in the social media, it is helping to reshape public engagement with politics in Western societies" (Daley, 2013, p. 376). Celebrity humanitarianism and volunteer tourism embody a different, yet related cultural politics that merge as mutual forms of popular humanitarianism which require a "moral sensibility demanding action on the part of the safe and secure toward the suffering and endangered" (Tester, 2010, p. vii). This sensibility was reinforced in the aftermath of the 2010 earthquake in Haiti where more than three million people were affected and at least 150,000 people were killed.

Sean Penn spearheaded celebrity contributions to the reconstruction in response to the humanitarian crisis. Penn told the press: "There's something that takes over and it's really an obligation because you see the strength of the people who have never experienced comfort, and the gifts that that can give to people like myself and to our country and culture. You see the enormous gaps" (Huffington Post, 2011). Celebrity rapper P. Diddy joined the effort on Twitter, where he wrote, "God Bless Haiti!!!! God please!!!," while Lindsay Lohan tweeted, "[A]nyone that may be listening's attention [sic]. Call 1884074747 State Dept for Haitian Relief Please help them … I know I will as much as I can … Please do all that you can." (Bull, 2010). Celebrities who responded to the event also encouraged citizens to contribute to the effort: "I hope I see you there," Penn commented to reporters (Bull, 2010).

More recently, a *People Magazine* article, "Christina Aguilera Takes Emotional Trip to Rwanda," quotes Aguilera, pop singer, global spokesperson for Yum! Brands World Hunger Relief effort and an Ambassador Against Hunger for the UN World Food Programme, as stating, "This trip came at a time when I really needed to step away and connect with bigger issues in the world, [and] this trip really touched me in a way I never felt before … The people of Rwanda touched me in a way I cannot express or put into words" (Leonard, 2013). Sentimental celebrity commentary such as Aguilera's is echoed throughout the industry that almost invariably obscures the broader structural causes of the issues that celebrities speak to. Yet, this is not to say that these events are without critique. For example, on the popular blog, *Africa is a Country*, an author sums up the *People Magazine* article with the comment: "Africa: helping white people who're a wee bit down-in-the-dumps feel better about themselves since 1884" (Nsabimana, 2013). Thus, as one link in this broader chain of events, celebrities have become interlocutors and spokespeople for myriad causes and as such, are reconfiguring the political economy of international humanitarian interventions. Tester asks why it is that we listen when celebrities "speak with the voice of humanitarian concern even though they have as much—and as little—knowledge as anyone else" (Tester, 2010, p. ix). I ask, how is it that the celebrity industrial complex has become such a powerful force in Western society? And in what ways is it linked to the growth of volunteer tourism and its corollaries? Commenting on the link between commodities, celebrities and activism, Sturken observes how:

> [C]ontradictions are inevitable here. Activism is consumerism. Celebrity humanitarianism. Commodity-driven social resistance. Neoliberal activism. Yet ... seeing it all as contradiction does not help us anymore, that a sense of contradiction is derived from reining in an outdated mode of thinking. We cannot dismiss these modes as simple hypocrisy, incorporation, or corporate appropriation. They demand a more complex, less cynical, less dismissive approach. Indeed, these very practices of consumer activism demand a recognition of the key relationship of consumerism and affect, the emotional content of consumer transactions. They thus demand new models for taking the emotional effects of consumer transactions seriously rather than seeing them as uncritical and acquiescent (Sturken, 2012, p. x–xi).

The emerging, if contradictory culture of popular humanitarianism is the context in which an estimated 3.3 million people volunteer abroad annually. Daley illustrates how through their advocacy, neoliberal subjects such as volunteer tourists, and their corollaries, celebrity philanthropists "serve to enhance consumer capitalism—thus helping firstly to commodify humanitarianism as a largely privatised concern that sits easily with neoliberal imperialism and secondly to divert attention from the structural inequalities associated with such forms of domination" (Daley, 2013, p. 376–7).With estimated annual growth rates of 10 to 20 percent for at least the next decade, volunteer tourism is a noteworthy contender in the broader redefinition of consumer driven humanitarianism politics (Washington University, St. Louis, 2009). While the Euro-American market continues to dominate, the growth of volunteer tourism of Asian origin is notable, especially regarding inter-regional volunteer tourism. For example, volunteer tourists of East Asian origin now regularly volunteer in Southeast Asia (Cochrane, 2008). While both domestic and international forms of volunteer tourism exist, I focus on international volunteer tourism of Western origin in northern Thailand.

Humanitarian Gaze

I use the concept of the humanitarian gaze as an organizing metaphor to describe the relational act of spectatorship in popular humanitarianism. The humanitarian gaze is not the act of an individual or solitary practice but a field of relations which is mediated by myriad institutions, cultural practices and actors (e.g. celebrity humanitarians, alternative consumers and volunteer tourists) and maneuvered by post-colonial power and political economic structures. In *Volunteer Tourism*, I focus on how the humanitarian gaze is enacted within volunteer tourism as well as how discourses of neoliberalism mediate the humanitarian gaze in ways that confine the relationship between the gazer and gazee to a market mentality. To develop the analytic of the humanitarian gaze I draw on emerging work on the geopolitics of emotion and assemblage theory as well as Urry's "tourist gaze" to describe how power mediates tourism experiences. As Berger famously notes, "we never look at just one thing; we are always looking at the relation between things and ourselves" (2008, p. 98). Like the tourist gaze, the humanitarian gaze is a relational act, not of an individual, but a field of relations that is mediated by discourses of institutions as well as cultural, political, economic, social and historical experiences of the gazer and gazee. Urry suggests that the tourist gaze emerged in 1840 along with "collective travel, the desire for travel and the techniques of photographic reproduction, becom[ing] a core component of western modernity" (Urry and Larsen, 2011, p. 12). Re-examining the tourist gaze in relation to the performance turn, Urry and Larsen highlight the multi-sensuous nature as well as the role of performance in the gaze. The gaze, they suggest, does not reflect the world so much as it shapes and classifies it through "skilled social practice" (Urry and Larsen, 2011, p. 12).

The humanitarian gaze is extended through pro-poor, social, responsible and sustainable tourism encounters, to name a few. Within this expansion, care and responsibility have become part and parcel of the personalization of development politics where private characteristics (e.g. responsibility, ethics, morality, empathy) have replaced public and political responses. This blurring of the public and private or the political and the personal in the humanitarian gaze extends geographies of care in new and particularly neoliberal ways. Thus, the humanitarian gaze is extended through a range of component actors that work to organize our understanding of popular humanitarianisms in the West. Through a spatialized field of care, our attention is extended through idealized, idolized individuals such as the celebrity humanitarian, the ethical consumer and the volunteer tourist. Identifying with these subject positions, the neoliberal subject seeks to participate in a spectacle of care where participation is reserved for those with sufficient cultural and economic capital. In the humanitarian performance, these actors participate in an intersubjective dialectical tango. The viewer (e.g. the celebrity, consumer or volunteer tourist) is hailed by overt images of humanitarian gestures. Interpellation facilitates the extension of the humanitarian gaze through images of friends and celebrities, for example, narratives and images of the pale skinned volunteer encompassed by darker skinned children on Facebook, Twitter and other social media outlets. In the foreground of these popular culture encounters stands the figure of the self-reliant individual as well as the individual aid worker. Through a totality of institutionalized market driven networks such as NGOs, packaged development experiences and the expansion of ethical consumer items, the humanitarian gaze is mapped on to a moral geography in the West.

While it may be hard to summarize the extent of the implications of celebrities on the motivations of volunteer tourists, a correlation is unmistakable. Today, "when most people think of the UN now they think of Angelina Jolie on a crusade, not the work that goes on in the field. Celebrity is at the heart of every UNICEF campaign these days and the association is being sold incredibly cheaply" (Manzo, 2008, p. 646). Backpacker Becki, for example, a 20-something British self-described around-the-world traveler and blogger describes her voluntourism experiences and comments under her photo—which closely resembles her celebrity counterparts— "If you can't look like Angelina, be like Angelina" (Becki, 2012). *Look to the Stars*, a website dedicated to celebrity philanthropists suggests: "We regularly receive requests from readers about stories featuring celebrities who have traveled to areas for humanitarian purposes ... Most of them ask how they can become involved on a firsthand basis—they see what their heroes are doing, and they want to help" (Vasquez, 2010). These celebrity and celebrated practices are part of the broader assembling of the humanitarian gaze. As Crouch et al. explain, while the tourist imagination may be affected by media representations, "equally, holiday images can feed back into the imaginative activity of the media" (2005, p. 1). The media and its institutions comprise core components of the humanitarian gaze. Indeed, "the media are heavily involved in promoting an emotional disposition, coupled with imaginative and cognitive activity, which has the potential to be converted into tourist activity" (Crouch et al., 2005, p. 1). The consistency of images in the media representing humanitarian encounters reflects broader trends in popular culture where the conscious consumer buys their way into cosmopolitan citizenship. A core aspect of these consistent messages is that of the sentimental Western savior, which like the celebrity humanitarian, reinforce "global power hierarchies in which hegemonic powers are depicted as humanitarian 'saviours' whilst enforcing 'accumulation by dispossession' in the periphery (Harvey 2003)" (Daley, 2013, p. 377).

Rather than a fixed entity, the humanitarian gaze is a collective assemblage. The analytic of assemblage highlights relations of exteriority of all socio-cultural formations and allows for a more focused examination of the intersection of social realities at various spatial scales and the ways in which they connect with exterior assemblages (Deleuze and Guattari, 1980). Indeed, "[P]art of the appeal of assemblages, it would seem, lies in its reading of power as multiple co-existences—assemblages connotes not a central governing power, nor a power distributed equally, but power as plurality in transformation" (McFarlane, 2009, p. 562). In the context of volunteer tourism assemblage theory helps us tease out the diverse elements of the humanitarian gaze that is co-constituted in part, by volunteers, host community members, NGOs, state organizations, universities, supranational organizations, media, celebrities and corporate sponsors, among others. These relationship are "linked not in a linear fashion but rhizomatically as 'reciprocal presuppositions and mutual insertions play themselves out,'" and emphasize "both temporality and spatiality: elements are drawn together at a particular conjuncture only to disperse or realign, and the shape shifts according to the terrain and the angle of vision" (Li, 2007, p. 265). In this way, assemblage is "a multiplicity that exceeds its component parts but which nonetheless retains elements of specificity" (McFarlane, 2009, p. 561).

Practices of assemblage in volunteer tourism demonstrate the collectivities, groups and varied agencies of the component whole as well as the incompleteness and continual emergence of the project. Assemblage is particularly useful here because it helps "us disassemble bordered thinking in terms of, at least, desire, territory, philosophy, bodies and movement" (Legg, 2011, p. 128). We can think of the humanitarian gaze as a composite of disparate elements drawn together at various moments of intersection such as that between humanitarianism, popular culture and tourism. Undoubtedly, these composite parts are not unified in a coherent whole, yet together they represent a broad networked assemblage. Li notes how a key aspect of an assemblage is "its potential to finesse questions of agency by recognizing the situated subjects who do the work of pulling together disparate elements without attributing to them a master-mind or a totalizing plan" (Li, 2007, p. 265). This is also a key aspect of the humanitarian gaze, where the individual volunteer tourist perpetuates—albeit perhaps unknowingly—the humanitarian gaze.

Cultural Politics and Volunteer Tourism

The cultural politics of the humanitarian gaze as assemblage in volunteer tourism has tangible political, economic and cultural dimensions. Tourism is the largest industry in the world and employs one out of every 12 workers worldwide, making it a highly political, although often overlooked platform from which local, national and global development politics are played out. Tourism is an often neglected indicator of global politics and how we engage with other people and places. A cultural politics perspective allows us to interrogate and denaturalize the normative truths that are perpetuated through seemingly mundane experiences. For example, Vrasti illustrates how volunteer tourism tells us much about how "white women ... use charity and philanthropy towards colonial subjects and the domestic poor as a way to carve out a space for themselves in the public sphere and assert their equality vis-à-vis white men" (Vrasti, 2012, p. 10). Volunteer tourism in Thailand embodies a very complex and often times contradictory cultural politics. Like the phenomena of volunteer tourism itself, the increasing visibility of celebrities in humanitarianism should not be taken for granted. Thus, it is not so much "the novelty or magnitude of volunteer tourism that should trouble us, but the virtuous place it occupies in our collective imagination, from self-righteous participants, enthusiastic parents, educators, employers, all the way to the congratulatory coverage in popular and scholarly publications" (Vrasti, 2012, p. 4).These cultural practices embody a different, yet related cultural politics.

Following Hall, cultural politics refers to the relationship between culture—or signifying practices—and power (Hall, 1996). In this vein, it is suggested that "meanings and practices—particularly those theorized as marginal, oppositional, minority, residual, emergent, alternative, dissident, and the like, all of them conceived in relation to a given dominant cultural order—can be the source of processes that must be accepted as political" (Alvarez et al., 1998, p. 7). These opposing tendencies are a core aspect of contemporary popular culture and create tension within society. In the context of 9/11, Sturken comments on how "much of the culture of comfort functions as a form of depoliticization and as a means to confront loss, grief and fear through processes that disavow politics" (Sturken, 2007, p. 6). For example, she shows how a patriotically decorated teddy bear exists within what she describes as "comfort culture" in the United States. These kinds of objects and associated meanings are at least in part how "an American public can acquiesce to its government's aggressive political and military policies, such as the war in Iraq, when that public is constantly reassured by the comfort offered by the consumption of patriotic objects, comfort commodities, and security consumerism" (Sturken, 2007, p. 6).

Frequent images of impoverished and marginalized peoples in developing countries has encouraged the development of new geographies of compassion as well as a restructuring of cultural politics around global inequality in the West. What I refer to as an emerging cosmopolitan empathy—or empathy for "humanity at large"—is the result of the growing influence of humanitarianism in the West. For volunteer tourism operators, this emerging cosmopolitan empathy has contributed to new and commodifiable emphases on sentimentality in tourism. As a consequence, NGO practitioners call upon these sentiments in their recruitment of "global citizens" in Western countries where nearly 80 percent of the respondents are women (Mintel, 2008). In this way, volunteer tourism reinforces the stereotype of the sentimental, care-giving Western woman (Wexler, 2000, Berlant, 2011). Volunteer tourism—as a corollary of the shifting geographies of compassion and an emerging cosmopolitan empathy—depends on the media which emphasizes sentimentality in its production of international humanitarianism. Media depictions of global inequality mediate the volunteer tourism experience and facilitate the ability of volunteer tourism advocates to capitalize on this burgeoning transnational moral landscape.

Angelina Jolie, Sean Penn and George Clooney are not the only individuals encouraging this movement; popular travel and reference guides are increasingly important mediators of the volunteer tourism experience (Ausenda and McCloskey, 2006, Hindle, 2007, Collins et al., 2002). The recent publication of Frommer's *500 Places Where You Can Make a Difference* (Mersmann et al., 2010), Earthscan's *The Ethical Travel Guide: Your Passport to Exciting Alternative*

Holidays (Pattullo and Minelli, 2006), the Rough Guide's *Ethical Travel: Make the Most of your Time on Earth* (Dunford, 2007) and Lonely Planet's, *A Traveler's Guide to Making a Difference Around the World* (Hindle, 2007) are testament to the growth and potential of the volunteer tourism industry. The increased "demand for [volunteer tourism programmes] has been paralleled by an increase in sending organizations, which promote, sell and organize programmes for volunteer tourists" (Raymond and Hall, 2008, p. 531). Mainstream tourism enterprises have also joined the volunteer tourism bandwagon. In 2007 Cheap Tickets, in partnership with United Way, created a way for its customers to book volunteer activities with their vacations online (Fitzpatrick, 2007, Ruiz, 2008), and Travelocity partnered with the Dave Matthews Band to promote environmentally responsible tourism through carbon offsetting:

> As concern grows about the prospect of global climate change, more and more travelers are searching for ways to build awareness of carbon impact into their travel plans. In particular, the Dave Matthews Band has taken a proactive role in fighting global warming by offsetting the CO2 pollution that touring activities such as transporting gear, powering stages, and air travel generate. Since 1991, the band has offset 100% of their tour's carbon dioxide emissions. If you'd like to follow their example and offset your own travels, Travelocity now offers a way to help. Travelers now have the option to purchase "carbon offsets" when booking on Travelocity, the first major online travel agency to take this step (Travelocity.com, 2007).

Similarly, MTV notes that while "student activism and volunteerism are hardly new concepts ... now more than ever, students are forgoing the revelry of traditional spring-break hot spots and finding deeper gratification in helping others" (MTV, 2007). Clearly, the similitude of Jolie, MTV and Travelocity indicates that something big is going on here. These emergent discourses play a powerful role in redefining activism in the contemporary period. A new kind of "commodity activism" is at work here that has critical implications for the way we think about cultural resistance (Mukherjee and Banet-Weiser, 2012). Reflecting on the role of commodity activism in the contemporary era, Sturken asks: "[W]hat does cultural resistance aim to do—empower, expose ideological frameworks, change the culture industries, make us feel better? Can resistance be pragmatic, instrumentalist, and embedded in consumer practices? ... Clearly activism is not what it used to be. Resistance was never what it was understood to be. And, capitalism is always reinventing itself" (Sturken, 2012, p. x). Volunteer tourism is just one of many examples of how capitalism has cleverly accommodated social resistance.

Volunteer Tourism and Development in Southeast Asia

Tourism in Southeast Asia emerged during the late nineteenth and early twentieth century. Despite this early emergence, mass tourism did not materialize until the mid-1970s. By 1990 tourism was one of the most important sectors of the economy for Thailand, Singapore, Malaysia, Indonesia and the Philippines. As a result, "the tourist" became an increasingly present figure that punctuated anthropologists' narratives in Southeast Asia. The merging of the anthropological gaze and the tourist gaze in places like Bali, Bangkok and Manila is well represented in the anthropology of tourism and anthropologists who study tourism continue to be drawn to Southeast Asia (Teo, 2001, Hitchcock et al., 2009, Hall, 2000, Adams, 1997, Bruner, 2005, Bruner, 1995, Bruner, 1989).

Over the past decade, Southeast Asia has experienced the highest global growth rates for international arrivals. While the tourism industry in Cambodia, Laos, Vietnam and Burma are relatively smaller in scale, in the past decade they have also similarly experienced unprecedented growth in tourism revenues (Hitchcock et al., 2009). Additionally, in the next decade, the Asia Pacific region—including Southeast Asia—is expected to continue its position as the fastest growing tourism region in the world (Singh, 1997). This growth is the result of "increases in economic growth, disposable income and leisure time, political stability, and aggressive tourism campaigns, among other factors, have fueled the significant growth of tourism" (Singh, 1997). Burma is particularly notable for the current and potential growth of its tourism industry. This growth is primarily due to political developments including the release of pro-democracy leader and chairperson for the National League of Democracy, Aung San Suu Kyi from house arrest in 2010 and her subsequent election to parliament in 2012. The consequential unprecedented international investment and rapid development has been matched by a substantial growth in tourism with an estimated 1.5 million international tourists expected to travel to Burma in 2013—nearly doubling the 791,505 international arrivals in 2010 (Feng, 2011). Increased political stability and economic growth in countries like Burma will contribute to the expansion of tourism as the most important sector of the economy in many Southeast Asian countries. As Graburn predicts, "[B]efore long, Asia will dominate tourism due to the region's growing economies and populations" (Graburn, 2010, p. 4).

Thailand—a core player in the region—attracts 22 million tourists annually and this accounts for more than six percent of its gross domestic product (GDP) (UNHCR, 2013). The beginning of the expansion of international tourism in Thailand is marked by the establishment of a "recreation and rest" destination in southern Thailand for US soldiers during the Vietnam War (Nimmonratana, 2000). In 1997, the Amazing Thailand campaign—in which the Tourism Authority of Thailand (TAT) invested nearly four billion baht—intended to make Thailand the tourism hub of the region as well as brand the country as a cultural, historical and ecotourism destination (Higham, 2000). This rebranding was an attempt to overshadow some of the devastating environmental, social and cultural consequences of unbridled tourism development, as spectators increasingly note how "there is little doubt that Thailand's tourism sector has been over-promoted and under managed" (Higham, 2000, p. 138). Rebranding was also an attempt to detract attention from Thailand's infamous sex tourism industry and replace low-budget backpacker tourism with family tourism. In line with this agenda, the TAT recently began promoting the "Little Big Project" in 2013 (http://www. thelittlebigprojectthailand.com/). As the first government sponsored volunteer tourism program in Thailand, it is the only legitimate competition to NGOs which spearheaded the expansion of volunteer tourism as a seemingly more ecologically, socially and culturally appropriate form of tourism development for more than a decade in Thailand.

Created in opposition to the perceived negative implications of mass tourism, volunteer tourism emerged in Thailand around the perception of the continued need for "development" among NGOs, local people and tourists, among others. In this context, the capacity of Western NGOs and volunteer tourists to "bring development" to Thailand frequently goes unquestioned. While Bangkok has experienced substantial economic and social development over the past three decades, the decline in poverty as well as the severity of poverty varies between regions. Three quarters of Thais who live in extreme poverty live in the North and Northeast region and nearly 85 percent of the poor live in rural areas (Shetty et al., 1996). This economic inequality is among the highest in Southeast Asia where the richest 20 percent earn nearly 60 percent and the lowest 20 percent earn only four percent of the total national income (Chaitrong, 2012, Yuthamanop, 2011). Widening economic inequality is a cause of the longstanding friction between the urban and rural provinces (Phongpaichit and Baker, 2002, Keyes, 1987, Costa, 2001). The widely held perception that "country people" in northern Thailand are still "developing" continues to mediate Thai politics. Manop, a manager at a small orphanage just outside of Chiang Mai city explained to me how:

> The country people and the city people are very different, completely different. And speaking from the perspectives of the development officers, they should turn more of their attention to the country people because as long as average people in the country are not developing in the same way as the city people, the differences will only widen. And when there is so much difference, different ideas in different fractions of society, eventually they become the problems of the country.[6]

---

6 Notably, on November 25, 2008, two months after Manop made this statement, Don Mueang and Suvarnabhumi International Airports were blockaded by the People's Alliance for Democracy (PAD) in what was referred to as Operation Hiroshima which resulted in a loss of more than US $100 million per day.

The context in which this perception has materialized is central to a critical understanding of Thailand as the hub of tourism in Southeast Asia. The rice paddies and thatched roof houses of the North and Northeast are in sharp relief to the glittering shopping malls and luxury sky rises that canvass the crowded streets of Bangkok. This disparate landscape is indeed one of the draws to Thailand where tourists are able to experience the luxury of urban decadence as well as the simplicity in rural living. The well-developed tourism infrastructure is central to the destination image of Thailand as a relatively safe, geographically diverse, yet still developing country within the region. Indeed, volunteer tourists in Thailand are primarily first timers who chose Thailand because they wanted to volunteer in a so-called developing or "Third World" country, but wanted to have a familiar standard of accommodation. For these reasons, Thailand is widely seen as an ideal volunteer tourism destination.

Thailand's highly developed tourism economy as well as its position as the hub of tourism and NGOs in mainland Southeast Asia are also key factors in the rapid expansion of volunteer tourism in the country (Tirasatayapitak and Laws, 2003). Volunteer tourism has exploded onto the NGO scene as a seemingly ideal form of alternative development in Thailand and Southeast Asia more broadly. In Cambodia, for example, there has been a rapid expansion of volunteer tourism in orphanages—also known as orphanage tourism (Guiney and Mostafanezhad, 2015).[7] In Thailand, volunteer tourism is not a fixed category, as it refers to a broad range of humanitarian and development experiences. Observing the burgeoning volunteer tourism market in Chiang Mai, Tom, the *tuk-tuk* driver who frequently brings volunteers to a women and children's shelter describes the diversity of the industry: "I think that there are more [volunteers]. [The type of volunteering] depends on the person. Because some people only come for a short time and some people come and work, as well as sightsee. There are many projects. Elephants, taking care of children and teaching English are common examples." Tom's observations are corroborated in the tourism literature where "sending organizations now offer a large variety of options depending on volunteer tourists' preferred activity, location and duration (see Callanan and Thomas, 2005)" (Raymond and Hall, 2008, p. 531). There are both short- and long-term volunteer tourism opportunities. Short-term opportunities, which have been called volunteer vacations by industry professionals, usually involve a payment to the organizing agency and may only be a small part of a longer vacation. Long-term volunteer tourism experiences are between one to 12 months in length.

Despite the range of experiences that volunteer tourism refers to, it is commonly claimed by the industry that volunteer tourism experiences facilitate

---

7   It is notable that in Cambodia orphanage tourism has been singled out as one type of volunteer tourism that may have deleterious effects such as making children vulnerable to sexual predators. UNICEF and other organizations have started "anti-orphanage tourism" campaigns in the country. To my knowledge, this kind of resistance to volunteer tourism or specifically orphanage tourism has not occurred in Thailand to the same degree.

positive social and economic impacts to host communities (Sin, 2009, Wearing and McDonald, 2002, Wearing, 2001, Raymond and Hall, 2008, Zahra, 2007, Brown and Lehto, 2005). Thus, "volunteer tourism is ... seen to provide a more reciprocally beneficial form of travel in which both the volunteer and the host communities are able to gain from the experience" (Raymond and Hall, 2008, p. 530). While this is often the goal, there are many factors on which its realization depends. For example, volunteers often have preconceived notions about work, development and schedules that prevent them from learning from local people. Similarly, local people often have preconceived ideas about the tourists and "it is worth remembering that the images and stereotypes locals have of tourists can be as distorted as the tourists' ideas about them" (Gmelch, 2010, p. 14).

In Thailand and especially Chiang Mai, tourist–host relations are complicated by the high levels of international migration and international marriages between Thais and Westerners (Cohen, 1986). Chambers speculates on how:

> [A] Western visitor to a remote Hmong village in northern Thailand might ... find himself or herself entranced by the sense of visiting an enduring and decidedly different, clearly mysterious place. But closer familiarity with the community provides an entirely different context to such an adventure, particularly as the visitor discovers that a fifth of the 'villagers' are currently living in Canada and the United States. Consider then the possibility that the 'exotically' dressed woman that the visitor just photographed only recently returned from visiting her sister in Los Angeles, where she was a tourist in her own right (Chambers, 2009, p. 3).

Volunteer tourism is one of many agents of the changing social landscape in Chiang Mai. For example, Anchali, a Thai host community member at Orchard Home became the manager in 2009:

> Before this I lived with my husband. But then we split up and I ran away from him and came to Orchard Home with my two children. But before that I used to wash and iron clothes. But after I left my husband I came to Orchard Home. Orchard Home has helped me get a job here.

Anchali is the mother of two boys, five and ten years old. When I returned to Orchard Home in 2012 I learned that she had married a longtime volunteer and former lawyer from Norway. They now live together in Chiang Mai and are expecting a child.

Anthropology and Tourism Encounters

While the presence of colonial administrators, government officials and missionaries were excluded from ethnographies, today they punctuate what may have previously been an untainted picture of an ostensibly isolated cultural whole.

Over the past 30 years the range of Others from the West working in the "field" has broadened. Today anthropologists are now routinely in contact and, indeed, collaboration with NGO workers, expatriates, and tourists. By the same token, these "others" increasingly find a place in ethnographies from the so-called Third World (Bruner, 1995, Asad, 1986, Clifford, 1989, Clifford, 1986, Nash, 1981, Nash, 2001, Nash, 2007). The crisis of representation in the 1980s encouraged this reflexive anxiety within anthropology. Gmelch points out that "[I]n anthropology, research on tourism began to flourish at the same time a major paradigm shift was taking place (Gupta and Ferguson 1997), that is anthropologists ceased treating cultures as bounded in place and time, cut off from outside influences and change. They became more interested in process and in the encounters that link people" (Gmelch, 2010, p. 7). Despite this turn, there is a continued reluctance among anthropologists to draw attention to the touristic elements of their research. It has been suggested that anthropologists may avoid this conversation because of the superficiality connoted by the "touristic" and thus the threat of de-authenticating the fieldwork experience—the traditional rite of passage for novice anthropologists who seek to enter anthropological adulthood (Errington and Gewertz, 1989, MacCannell, 1999, MacCannell, 1992, Stronza, 2001).

At least since the time of Malinowski, ethnography has involved active participation in people's lives for extended periods of time in order to gain an emic or insider perspective. These experiences are translated into written expressions of authentic local culture (Clifford, 1988). The connection between the intimacy of fieldwork and ethnographic truth was long taken for granted within the ethnographic experience (Clifford, 1989, Marcus, 1998, Gupta and Ferguson, 1997). Margaret Mead noted how rather than only observe local culture, the anthropologist participates in the intimate life of the people, which is a precondition for ethnographic truth: "the anthropologist not only records the consumption of sago in the native diet, but eats at least enough to know how heavily it lies upon the stomach; not only records verbally and by photographs the tight clasp of the baby's hand around the neck, but also carries the baby and experiences the constriction of the windpipe; hurries or lags on the way to a ceremony; kneels half-blinded by incense while the spirits of the ancestors speak, or the gods refuse to appear ..." (Mead quoted in MacCannell, 1973, p. 592).

In an effort to distinguish between the professional identity of the anthropologist and the tourist, anthropologists argue that, in contrast to the tourist, the anthropologist has a theoretical lens through which they are able to gain a deeper understanding of the culture (Nash, 2001, Galani-Moutafi, 2000, Bruner, 1989, Errington and Gewertz, 1989). Cohen attempts to redeem the ethnographer's role when he suggests that while the tourists' "experience may ... be fuller and more spontaneous, they also lack the professional attitude and critical capacity necessary to determine whether the traits by which they determine the 'authenticity' of an object or an attraction are genuine or false" (Cohen, 1988, p. 377). Like tourism, anthropological fieldwork is based on the distinction between front and back stages; the ethnographer gains access to the "back stage" to participate in authentic cultural experiences (MacCannell, 1973, MacCannell, 1976). It is through the intimate backstage experience that ethnographic truth reveals itself. Foreshadowing these broader shifts nearly four decades earlier, MacCannell notes how tourists and ethnographers have much in common as they are both criticized for having a superficial view of their experiences (MacCannell, 1973, MacCannell, 1976, Galani-Moutafi, 2000, Wallace, 2005). In a noteworthy comparison between tourists and anthropologists, Cohen suggests that there exists a positive correlation between alienation and the quest for authenticity; the more alienated the subject, the more seriously they seek out authenticity in other peoples and places (Cohen, 1988, Cohen, 2001). Anthropologists, he argues, "like curators and ethnographers, even if paradigmatic of the modern tourist, appear to entertain more rigorous criteria of authenticity than do ordinary members of the traveling public. They belong to the wider category of modern, alienated intellectuals—indeed, their alienation from modernity often induces them to choose their respective professions" (Cohen, 1988, p. 376). There is a clear linkage between the "search for authenticity" in tourism and the anthropologists' similar concern for authenticating their fieldwork experience through close "real" contact with local people (Culler, 1981, MacCannell, 1973, MacCannell, 1976, Cohen, 1988). Commenting on this distinction, between the "authentic" ethnographer and "superficial tourist," MacCannell writes:

> ... the Greyline guided tours of Haight Ashbury when the hippies lived there cannot be substituted for the studies based on participant observation that were undertaken at the same time: the intellectual attitude is firm in this belief. The touristic experience that comes out of the tourist setting is based on inauthenticity, and as such it is superficial when compared with careful study; it is morally interior to mere experience (MacCannell, 1973, p. 599).

Social researchers and volunteer tourists tend to have similar socio-economic backgrounds, values and education (Vrasti, 2012). Social researchers distinguish themselves from their tourist counterparts through "sabbaticals, 'research' work, the presence of friends, colleagues and relatives, the emergence of work brigades and the visits promotion by international development charities—a range of work—and activity-centered holidays, all used by the new middle classes to signal that this is more than just a holiday" (Mowforth and Munt, 2009, p. 139). With the expansion of alternative and niche tourism experiences which foreground the intimate, authentic cross-cultural experience, the structure of tourism increasingly resembles that of anthropology in that both actors seek out the same other (Goss, 2010). Indeed, the common goal of volunteer tourists to gain "a deeper understanding of the culture" is not unlike that of anthropologists, as "underlying volunteer tourism is a multiculturalist appreciation for cultural diversity, romantic reverence for nature and tradition and what seems to be a genuine desire to help but also learn from other cultures and people" (Vrasti, 2012, p. 1). Echoing these desires, an anthropology field school in Malta notes how the experience is "Off the Beaten Track" and emphasizes the authenticity of the experience (Expeditions Research in Applied Tribe, 2009).

Chiang Mai Friends, a volunteer tourism NGO, describes how its volunteers will have intimate, authentic interaction with elephants, "primitive living" and ethnic minorities in northern Thailand: "[B]athing elephants, shadowing mahouts and interacting with Thailand's ethnic minorities—frame it just right, and it's hard to believe you're actually *working*. Oh, and did we mention the tree house you'll be living in?" (Chiang Mai Riina, 2009). Historically, these types of experiences have been the content of the anthropologist's fieldnotes. Goss (1993) points out how the desire to get past the tourist bubble and into the "real" heart of the culture through intimate, sincere interaction is a common touristic narrative. For example, destination advertisements for Hawaii have long captured this desire through the promise of an intimate, intersubjective experience. Tourists are regularly offered the opportunity to learn about the culture, language and feel the *real* Aloha and ultimately "realize the ultimate dream of the Western cultural anthropologist" (Goss, 1993, p. 672). Similarly, anthropologists commonly adopt local names and develop new "families" during fieldwork. In many ways, this involvement with the intimate lives of the host community is not unlike that of the long-term volunteer tourist who may have similar familial experiences. Comments such as "they made me feel like family" and "I feel like I have a second family in Thailand" are frequently echoed throughout the volunteer tourism experience. Reflecting on her fieldwork on volunteer tourism in Guatemala and Ghana, Vrasti writes: "I was not the only ethnographer in the field: all volunteers are anthropologists eager to understand the local culture without spoiling it" (Vrasti, 2012, p. 18); I identify with this feeling in many ways.

While conducting research on volunteer tourism, it became impossible to ignore the similarities between myself and the volunteers who were my "informants." Like the anthropologist, the volunteer tourist seeks to "gain cultural capital through the collection of knowledge and experience in volunteer tourism, and to perform desired identities that will in turn secure 'entry to the privileges of work, housing and lifestyle' (Desforges 1998: 177)" (Sin, 2009, p. 489). International fieldwork experiences help anthropologists to gain professional credentials that are often a prerequisite for a successful academic career. Yet, while there are significant similarities between volunteer tourists and anthropologists, there are also many crucial differences. For example, my long-term commitment to the communities that I was worked with significantly affected my relationships with host community members. Unlike tourists, anthropologists are increasingly held responsible for the effects they have on local communities in which they conduct their fieldwork. This has resulted in new ethics, methods and outcomes of research: collaborative research being a notable example (Lassiter, 2005). In comparison to the anthropologist, it is noted that "tourists are not made personally responsible for anything that happens in the establishments they visit" (MacCannell, 1973, p. 598). This is because international tourists generally do not share a history or a responsibility to maintain long-term commitments to local people (McLaren, 2003).

Anthropologists are also critically cognizant of the power dynamic of the encounter, especially in the Global South. Wilson notes how "[T]here is the bare fact that the United States' great financial and political power underwrites U.S. citizens' ability to conduct research in less wealthy nations such as Thailand" (Wilson, 2004, p. 27). There is a similar power dynamic among tourists from wealthy nations who have the economic power and political privilege to cross international borders, often without going through the sometimes painstaking process of gaining visa permissions. While I argue that there are indeed important differences between tourists and ethnographers, the tourist/researcher dichotomy is increasingly obsolete and should be replaced by more nuanced kinds of identities that take into account the full complexity of ethnographic research within what Bruner refers to as "liminal borderlands" (Bruner, 2005). Rather than isolated places of pristine, untainted culture, attention to liminal borderlands highlights the fluidity and dynamism of encounter as it breaks down illusory boundaries of "us" and "them." Clifford similarly emphasizes contact approaches which are "not sociocultural wholes subsequently brought into relationship, but rather systems already constituted relationally, entering new relations through historical processes of displacement" (Clifford, 1997, p. 7). Ethnographic practice inevitably takes places as a contact approach within liminal borderlands where "fieldwork as a travel practice highlights embodied activities pursued in historically and politically defined places. This worldly emphasis contributes to an opening of current possibilities, an extension of complication of ethnographic paths" (Clifford, 1997, p. 8). It is to these complicated roads of ethnographic inquiry that I now turn.

Fieldwork

Volunteer Tourism is based on 16 months of ethnographic fieldwork between 2006 and 2012 in Chiang Mai, Thailand. Initial research was conducted during the summers of 2006 and 2007. Primary research was conducted between October 2008 and June 2009. Follow-up research was conducted in the summers of 2010 and 2012. Through this research I investigated how Thai host community members, NGO practitioners and international volunteers experience volunteer tourism. From the inception of this research I have been interested in what volunteer tourism, as a unique cultural practice, can tell us about contemporary transnational social, political and economic trends. I concur with Vrasti who argues that "the effectiveness of volunteer tourism should not be assessed in terms of the goods and services it delivers to the global poor or the emancipatory alternative it presents to liberal modernity, but in terms of how well it helps (re)produce subjects and social relations congruent with the logic of capital in seemingly laudable and pleasurable ways" (Vrasti, 2012, p. 4). This book is framed by theories from economic anthropology and political geography, tourism and cultural studies; cultural and feminist political economy are my cardinal points of origin, while theoretical insights from geographies of responsibility and emotion, critical humanitarian and celebrity studies are indicative of my interdisciplinary approach. Methodologically, I draw from ethnographic research including participant observation, 90 semi-structured interviews, content analysis and questionnaires (Bernard, 2006, Creswell, 2009). I analyzed data from my fieldwork using grounded theory approaches. I also conducted discourse analyses of relevant materials such as volunteer tourism brochures and websites.

This book is primarily based on research among three NGOs which have adopted volunteer tourism as a social and economic development strategy in the Chiang Mai Province of northern Thailand. Chiang Mai is located 750 km north of Bangkok and is the second largest city in the country, yet it is 10 times smaller than Bangkok. The province itself is 20,170 square km. It has 19 districts including the district of Chiang Mai City. Approximately 150,000 people live in Chiang Mai City. The metropolitan area and province as a whole have a population of one million and two million, respectively. Chiang Mai attracts more than two million foreign visitors per year and according to the TAT, it is considered the cultural center of Thailand (Tourism Authority of Thailand, 2008). It is also the most popular tourism destination in the north for both foreign and domestic tourists. Major attractions include trekking, ethnic minority villages, temples and handicraft shopping. Chiang Mai is particularly known for its large expatriate population. Tourists, development and NGO workers, educators and retirees, among others have been an increasingly conspicuous part of the reorganization of the social fabric of Chiang Mai since at least the early 1970s (Cohen, 2001).

The NGOs that I worked with and form the substance of *Volunteer Tourism* include Borderless Volunteers (BV), Traveling Teachers (TT) and Chiang Mai Friends (CMF) (to protect the privacy of research participants, all individual names as well as names of NGOs in *Volunteer Tourism* are pseudonyms). All three organizations have volunteer sites outside of the Chiang Mai city center: BV volunteers go to Mae Nam Village in the Huey Kaew sub-district, 50 km northeast of Chiang Mai City; in addition to other locales, CMF volunteers work at Orchard Home, the young, single mothers' and children's home in Bo Sang, 20 km outside Chiang Mai and TT sends volunteers to various schools including a rural minority school in San Sai, 10 km outside Chiang Mai and Dok Mai Orphanage for Hmong children[8] in the same area. Beyond the sites addressed here, each NGO is additionally involved in a range of activities at numerous project sites.

---

    8   Hmong are an ethnic minority group from the highlands of northern Thailand. Hmong are also referred to as "Hill Tribe" people which collectively refers to more than 13 different ethnicities including Karen, Lisu and Akah groups. The term "hill tribe" is a derogatory term and is increasingly being faded out for the seemingly more subtle term, "ethnic minority." As Dok Mai Orphanage makes clear, "The Hmong are one of the ethnic groups of Thailand. But most Thai people, even government officials, see the Hmong only as a hill tribe. 'Hill tribe' in Thai is a word meaning 'others' not 'us.' This means that they are different from the Thai lowlanders, leading to discrimination and neglect." CATON 2012. Taking the Moral Turn in Tourism Studies, *Annals of Tourism Research*, 39, 1906–28.

I explore the volunteer tourism experience from the perspectives of Western volunteers, Western and Thai NGO practitioners and primarily Thai host community members[9] to address the varied interests of participants as well as the relation between experiential encounters and larger structural realities. My critical phenomenological perspective "combines concern with lived experience and subjectivity with political economy perspectives that highlight the historical and structural production" (Mattingly, 2010, p. 39). Critical phenomenology links the phenomenal with the political (Good, 1994) and attends "to the many, and often highly charged political, social, and discursive forces that contribute to life in particular settings" (Desjarlais and Jason Throop, 2011, p. 93). Moreover, this interpretive framework "recognizes the macro structural dimensions of our social existence (the way discursive regimes are embodied and played out in everyday social practice)" while also "foreground[ing] the personal, intimate, singular, and eventful qualities of social life" (Mattingly, 2010, p. 7). This framework, combined with an ethnographic lens, allows me to examine volunteer tourism as an individual and social practice embedded within broader socio-spatial cultural, political and economic entanglements.

Importantly, a significant proportion of host community members were children who I did not formally interview. Additionally, many "host community" members did not have regular interactions with the volunteers. Throughout the book, my attention oscillates between participants—although in places, the focus is perceptibly turned towards the volunteers. This focus is in part because I seek to draw out connections between what is observable in the volunteer tourism experience and the broader political, economic and cultural implications of this local level encounter. I am conscious of how, as Clifford notes, "one must bear in mind the fact that ethnography is from beginning to end enmeshed in writing. This writing includes, minimally, a translation of experience into textual form. The process is complicated by the action of multiple subjectivities and political constraints beyond the control of the writer"(Clifford, 1988, p. 120). The process of translation, both literal and metaphorical—for example between Thai and English and from experience to the written word—ensures the impossibility of an unequivocal representation.

While, as a multi-sited ethnography, I had the opportunity to examine a range of volunteer tourism experiences and participants, this study did not begin multi-sited. Originally, I planned to conduct the majority of my research in Mae Nam Village, a small, 40 household community in the Huey Kaew sub-district. I was to stay in the vicinity of Mae Nam Village for the duration of my fieldwork. Despite years of preliminary fieldwork and the optimism of the residents and NGO operators, when I commenced my primary fieldwork in October of 2008, Mae

---

9 While many of the women at the single mothers' and children's home were decendents of ethnic minority groups from the highlands such as Hmong and Lisu, the women identified as Thai. This self-identification as Thai has many social, legal and economic implications that are beyond the scope of this book.

Nam Village was unprepared for volunteer tourists. Moreover, there was little, if any interaction between the host community members and the infrequent volunteer tourist. Additionally, I found that some of my earlier assumptions underestimated the complexity of volunteer tourism in Chiang Mai. My experience was not a smoothly traveled path from proposal to the monograph that you hold in your hands. As Clifford reminds us, "[T]here is … a myth of fieldwork, and the actual experience, hedged around with contingencies, rarely lives up to the ideal. But as a means for producing knowledge from an intense, intersubjective engagement, the practice of ethnography retains a certain exemplary status. Moreover, if fieldwork has for a time been identified with a uniquely Western discipline and a totalizing science of 'anthropology,' these associations are not necessarily permanent. Current styles of cultural description are historically limited and undergoing important metamorphoses" (Clifford, 1988, p. 119–20). During my fieldwork I found there to be a range of players in the volunteer tourism industry—many of which are linked through complicated networks of NGOs, religious organizations, tour operators and public/private partnerships. Additionally, "host communities" are often comprised of children and temporary communities: elementary schools, temple schools and homes for women and children are common sites for volunteer tourism. Moreover, host community members have various intensities of interaction with the volunteers. A lack of interaction can at least in part be explained by language barriers, (in)frequency of volunteers or personality.

NGOs and Host Communities

Borderless Volunteers (BV), Chiang Mai Friends (CMF) and Traveling Teachers (TT) are the primary NGOs on which this research is based. These NGOs were chosen, in part, because they vary in size, structure and volume of volunteer tourists. For this reason, they illustrate the diverse nature of volunteer tourism in Chiang Mai. A relatively new form of alternative tourism, the range of volunteer tourism experiences is still emerging. Despite the differences in NGO structure, it is notable that the Western NGO practitioners at all three NGOs were former international volunteers. Each of the NGOs sent their volunteers to several different host communities. As such, the host community members also vary by age, sex, class, and mobility.

Borderless Volunteers (BV)
BV is the non-profit arm of Wild Adventure Chiang Mai, a for-profit organization. The founder, Eric moved to Thailand from South Africa. His wife, Annie, is Thai and they have two sons. Wild Adventure Chiang Mai develops outdoor and environmental education activities for tourists, international students and corporate groups. The non-profit arm BV recruits volunteers to help create an ecotourism destination in Mae Nam Village. The sub-district is composed of eight villages. There are 55 families and 164 people (20 out of 164 are children under 15 years) in Mae Nam Village. The community was established over 100 years ago.

Originally attracted to the area because of the fertile land that is suitable for tea crops, they produce "Cha-Miang" or "pickled tea leaves," which is a traditional crop of northern Thailand. They recently began cultivating coffee beans. On average, people collect 10.5 kilos of Cha Miang per day (8am–5:15pm) which is worth approximately 63 baht. Tea is picked from May to October (six months). They earn six baht per kilo of tea in its natural state. From January to May they clear and prepare the fields for the harvest and stock wood. Out of the 55 families (two to four people), 48 cultivate tea. Each family also grows fruits and vegetables for personal use and raises chickens. Almost every household in the community has family members working outside of the village in Chiang Mai or Bangkok. The average monthly income is 7,000 baht (USD $230). The local community is based on strong community ties and a partial barter economy.

Mae Nam Village became involved in volunteer tourism because their land was seen as an ideal space for ecotourism development. Mae Nam Village community members were approached by Eric and his partner in 2002 about developing an ecotourism lodge on their land and in exchange, they are to become the beneficiaries of the ecotourism trails that were to be built in the village in ten years' time—although at the time of writing the trails were not yet complete. Besides the village headman and his close family, most of the community members do not interact with the volunteer tourists. The ultimate goal of BV is to prepare the village community members to manage the emerging ecotourism destination. The role of the volunteers is to contribute to the realization of this goal through various activities including teaching English, building nature trails, developing agro-forestry, building an environmental education program and creating activities for future ecotourism participants. At the time of this research BV hosted approximately eight volunteers per year and was the least financially successful organization in this study. Eric and the volunteer coordinator, Jen, a 28-year-old American woman from Los Angeles were the only employees working exclusively for BV. In addition to Eric and Jen, several employees from the for-profit arm of the organization contributed to BV including several long term international interns.

Traveling Teachers (TT)
TT is an international volunteer organization that recruits volunteers to teach English to children in developing countries. It has operations in 14 countries including five operations in Thailand and runs more than 50 projects in 30 locations. TT Chiang Mai had two volunteer coordinators at the time of research. The first branch of TT was opened in 2002 in Nong Khai, Thailand. It is a non-profit organization which connects volunteers "with grassroots community projects in the developing world" (Traveling Traveling Teachers, 2010). Through the use of budget and low-cost destinations in developing countries, TT can "maintain a closer contact with the visiting volunteers, the local people, and the projects" (Traveling Traveling Teachers, 2010). TT currently has programs in more than ten

developing countries. A core value of TT is to benefit local communities through remaining small and connected with the host community.

During the first few months of my research Helen, a 32-year-old Scottish woman and Lek, a 26-year-old Thai woman, were managing the program. Helen later took a job in England as a fair trade consultant for a transnational retail firm and Lek was transferred to TT, Nong Kai in the Northeast. They were replaced by Ronny, a 42-year-old Dutch man and his boyfriend, Aek, a 22-year-old Thai man. Both Helen and Ronny were TT volunteers prior to working for the NGO. This experience is not uncommon, as TT suggests, it "has always been very lucky in that several of their volunteers have wanted to stay on, help and get involved with the organization ... [and] these volunteers continue to work for Traveling Teachers today, in the head office or as in-country coordinators around the globe. Other ex-volunteers are promoting from their home countries as representatives of Traveling Teachers" (Traveling Teachers, 2010). TT volunteers primarily teach English. Yet, recently it has "expanded from teaching English and computer studies into other areas such as art, sports, restoration and wildlife" (Traveling Teachers, 2010). While TT has expanded into other volunteering arenas, "the element of teaching and learning has continued to be the main objective and core of all of [their] projects" (Traveling Teachers, 2010). TT works with various schools throughout the year in order to offer a diversity of experiences for the volunteer tourists. Thus, the volunteers usually spend from one to two months at one site and then move to a new school. In addition to teaching English, volunteers also contribute to the reconstruction of schools and building libraries. In 2009 TT Chiang Mai hosted approximately 250 volunteers per year.

Chiang Mai Friends (CMF)
CMF is a Chiang Mai-based organization which was founded in 2006 by Ted, a 32-year-old American and former US Peace Corps volunteer. While CMF offers various opportunities for its volunteers, the sites which are most frequented by volunteers include an elephant camp, temple schools and Orchard Home (a women and children's shelter). The elephant camp is located in an "ethnic minority village" that cares for elephants and gives elephant rides to tourists. The temple schools educate and house novice monks. The novice monks at the temple schools are often orphans or children of parents who cannot financially support them. Orchard Home is an NGO that was founded by Mic and Leslie, American lay missionaries. Mic is a Vietnamese refugee who was granted asylum in the United States several decades earlier. He holds a Master's degree in architecture from a university in Texas. Leslie is a native Texan who holds a Master's degree in religious studies. Orchard Home primarily hosts young pregnant and new single mothers who are victims of physical and sexual abuse. The staff at Orchard Home seek to help the women become self-sufficient. The amount of time each woman spends at the home varies from a few months to seven or more years.

International Volunteer Tourists[10]

Volunteer tourists in this study are short term volunteers (less than six months) who travel for the purposes of volunteering in social, environmental or economic development projects at any point during their holiday in Thailand (Wearing, 2001). While I did not intend to focus exclusively on international volunteers from Western countries, all of the volunteers that I encountered were from the West except for one female volunteer from Japan. While I met Thai volunteers during my fieldwork, they were never directly involved with the volunteer tourism organizations. Instead, many were involved with different NGOs in the area. Most of the volunteer tourists in this study were university students, recent university graduates or "gappers" (gappers are recent high school graduates who take one year off before college to travel abroad) between 18 and 30 years old. In addition to the student volunteer tourism market (between 18 and 25 years), volunteer tourism organizations are increasingly targeting several niche markets including 50+, families, teens, gappers, working professionals and groups (Cross Cultural Solutions, 2010). It is notable that after students and gappers, the 50+ sector is the fastest growing market in the industry. While still marginal, approximately eight percent of the volunteer tourists in this study were of the 50+ crowd. It is also noteworthy that women, who make up approximate 80 percent of all volunteer tourists, comprised 74 percent of all respondents in this study. The predominance of female volunteers has also been highlighted, and in some cases lamented by the adult host community members in this study who were primarily women.

The Book's Chapters

In the chapters that follow I examine how volunteer tourism articulates with sentimentality, neoliberalism and popular humanitarianism through every day experiences of its participants including Western volunteers, NGO practitioners and primarily northern Thai host community members.[11] I explore these articulations ethnographically and consider how they are reflective of broader cultural, political and economic shifts in contemporary neoliberal times. Tourism is first and foremost a commodity, albeit an intangible one. As one of the newest niche products within this commodity formation, volunteer tourism takes on existing characteristics of alternative, moral and ethical consumer practices. In *Volunteer Tourism*, I examine how these practices intersect with sentimentality, neoliberal ideology and social activism.

Indeed, "[T]he range of questions marking the ethical practices of commodity activism ... deny clear distinctions between modes of social action that appear to have collapsed into co-optation and others that seem to operate 'outside' the

---

10   Throughout the remainder of this book, I refer to volunteer tourists as volunteers.

11   I also included the voices of Burmese and Vietnamese refugees who identify as Thai for political reasons that are beyond the scope of this book.

logics of neoliberal capitalism" (Hearn, 2012, p. 3). To this end, I ask: what
role does sentimentality play in motivating and mediating the volunteer tourism
experience?; how do participants co-produce the humanitarian gaze?; and what are
the broader implications of the cultural politics of the volunteer tourism encounter?
In addition to the theoretical significance of these questions, they also have critical
implications for the realization of development and humanitarian goals among
volunteer tourism participants. As Vrasti explains, "[W]here usually critical theory
will erase the white middle-class subject from the picture, claiming it is already at
the centre of cultural value and knowledge production (which is true), and try to
replace it with the voice of the oppressed and marginalized, it seems to me it is still
important we understand the conditions, both symbolic and material, that make the
bourgeoisie the norm-setting class" (Vrasti, 2012, p. 23). Through ethnographic
insights from white, middle-upper class Western volunteers, I contribute to the
emerging "anthropology of home" literature.

This book is organized into seven chapters. In Chapter 2, *"Making a Difference,
One Village at a Time": Volunteer Tourism and the Peace Corps Effect*, I situate
volunteer tourism historically, charting its progression to the contemporary era.
To begin, I chronicle the historical precedents of volunteer tourism including
religious missionaries, Thomas Cook's health tours and the US Peace Corps and
highlight the converging trajectories of these movements and the contemporary
expansion of volunteer tourism. This expansion is part of what I call the "Peace
Corps effect," which helped lay the ground work for the development of volunteer
tourism in the West.

In Chapter 3, *The Seduction of Development: NGOs and Alternative Tourism
in Northern Thailand*, I am concerned with global inequality, neoliberalism,
and NGOs in the context of volunteer tourism and "alternative" development
in Thailand. The intensified interest in the individual and the community as the
primary agents of change has shifted the capacity and goals of development
practitioners. The theoretical and applied implications of this shift are critical:
under this political-economic ideology, NGOs act as coping strategies that
fill in gaps left by the rollback of state-based social services (Mosse, 2013). In
this way, I critically examine what is alternative about alternative development.
I argue that NGOs are contradictorily positioned as both ideological opponents
and active agents of neoliberalism. Additionally, I address how theories and
discourses of development highlight the binary opposition between "developed"
and "developing" or "First" and Third World countries. Building on these
observations, I ethnographically illustrate how volunteer tourism participants
negotiate development discourse through their everyday interactions and reactions
to each other and their experience.

Morality and sentimentality are core themes that mediate the volunteer
tourism and Western humanitarian encounter. I address these themes in Chapters 4
and 5. In Chapter 4, *Cosmopolitan Empathy, New Social Movements and the Moral
Economy of Volunteer Tourism*, I argue that the expansion of humanitarianism in
the West contributes to an emerging "cosmopolitan empathy"—a product of and

reaction to the growing influence of the privatization of humanitarianism in the West. I situate these emerging sentiments within the broader expansion of moral economies, which emerge within the context of neoliberalism and the voluntary turn (Goodman, 2005, Goodman, 2004). Additionally, I illustrate how several strands of the loosely articulated global justice movement and its corollaries—anti-neoliberalism, anti-globalization and antipoverty movements—in the West have been co-opted by the market and have materialized in alternative tourism. This political-economic backdrop, I argue, laid the cultural groundwork for the rapid expansion of volunteer tourism's popularity, especially among middle- and upper-class Euro-American youth.

In Chapter 5, *The Cultural Politics of Sentimentality in Volunteer Tourism*, I explore how the overwhelming focus on the sentimental in volunteer tourism deflects attention from the structural inequality on which the encounter is based. As illustrated in Chapter 2, the US Peace Corps and its related international counterparts set the standard in international development and humanitarian agendas. Intimacy, love and compassion in these historically similar cross-cultural experiences depoliticize the expansion of Western political, economic and cultural hegemony.

The interests of volunteer tourism participants including international volunteers, NGO practitioners and host community members are addressed in Chapter 6, *Converging Interests? Cross-Cultural Authenticity in Volunteer Tourism*. Several key questions are explored: what motivates participation in volunteer tourism?; how is volunteer tourism experienced?; and how do participants benefit from the experience? These questions are examined not to develop a typology of the volunteer tourism experience or to make a statement regarding whether it is a "good" or "bad" practice—as I have so often been asked in seminars and conference presentations. Rather, it is to examine how answers to these questions are illustrative of broader transnational political-economic and cultural trends. I argue that intimacy is a core aspect of these trends as it is through close cross-cultural encounters that a counter-narrative punctuates dominant development discourses. As a result, within the intimate spaces of the volunteer tourism encounter "authenticity" and "development" are reconstituted by (inter)personal experience. In this way, the interests of the volunteers and host community members seem to converge around different yet mutual interests in an authentic, cross-cultural encounter. Insights from this chapter shed light on the broader reconfiguration of governmentality in the West and how it is enacted within volunteer tourism encounters in the Global South.

In the concluding chapter, *Re-mapping the Movement: Popular Humanitarianism and the Geopolitics of Hope in Volunteer Tourism*, I reflect on the personal and political implications of volunteer tourism. The possibility for volunteer tourism to become a platform from which to gain support for the social justice agendas should not be overlooked. Rather, volunteer tourism may be one strand in a broader movement for more radical structural change. While I am optimistic about this possibility, I also highlight the challenges that the current political-economic order places on the realization of this movement. Most notably, I argue that neoliberal modes of development and resistance increasingly co-opt the alternative visions of NGOs and other social movement facilitating organizations. For example, like Hearn, I consider how "radical imaginaries of social critique seem to falter under the seductive force of neoliberalism" (Hearn, 2012, p. 11). In this way, I lament that while volunteer tourism is often identified as an alternative development strategy, it faces many of the same challenges as mainstream tourism development. Yet, I also contend that the extent to which social movements articulate with the market is no longer a valid measure of their legitimacy. Rather, volunteer tourism gestures towards new trends in social activism, the full implications of which have yet to be fully worked out in popular or academic circles.

Chapter 2

"Making a Difference One Village at a Time": Volunteer Tourism and the Peace Corps Effect

> Thinking historically is a process of locating oneself in space and time. And a location … is an itinerary rather than abounded site—a series of encounters and translations (Clifford, 1997, p. 9).

On March 1 1961, American President John F. Kennedy established the US Peace Corps. The Peace Corps was founded to promote world peace through international goodwill and understanding between nations in the aftermath of WWII and throughout the Cold War period. Intended to establish the US as a benevolent nation, the Peace Corps quickly became one of the most potent signifiers of Western humanitarianism and was instrumental in setting a global agenda of international development and aid. Similar organizations were founded in Japan and almost every country in Western Europe. Between 1958 and 1965, young people throughout the Global North were packing up and heading south. Having shed the religious overtones of its predecessors such as colonial missionaries, the Peace Corps became the most visible symbol of institutionalized Western secular volunteering, putting a human face to discourses of development (Hoffman, 1998, p. 8). The Peace Corps continues to attract young, idealistic Americans who represent international goodwill on behalf of the US and its mission, structure and ideology have been widely adopted both domestically and abroad. Contemporary international volunteering programs offer experiences similar to those of the Peace Corps.

A mutual outcome of volunteer tourism and the Peace Corps is what is broadly referred to as cross-cultural understanding. Indeed, the largest international volunteer organization in the US, Cross-Cultural Solutions explains:

> Both CCS and the Peace Corps now have many years of experience in operating highly successful international volunteer programs, and they share similar missions and philosophies. We are both dedicated to creating opportunities for people of different cultures to share perspectives and foster cultural understanding. We also share a commitment to provide volunteers and service in the local communities, rather than financial aid or material contributions (Cross Cultural Solutions, 2010).

The goal of cross-cultural understanding rather than financial or material contributions echoes the Peace Corps' three core goals:

1. Helping the people of interested countries in meeting their need for trained men and women.
2. Helping promote a better understanding of Americans on the part of the peoples served.
3. Helping promote a better understanding of other peoples on the part of Americans (US Peace Government, 2010).

Whether or not the Peace Corps helps "the people of interested countries in meeting their need for trained men and women" continues to be hotly debated among academics and development workers (Guthrie and Zektick, 1967, Searles, 1997). The second and third goals focus on intercultural exchange and enhanced mutual understanding and are echoed in various institutions.

Today, volunteer tourism embodies many of the ideals and objectives laid out by the Peace Corps. Ted, the founder of CMF and a former Peace Corps volunteer in northeastern Thailand explains:

> As you probably noticed the Peace Corps has 3 goals. One is assisting an organization or a group in need of labor or development or whatever. Second, being teaching host country citizen about the behavior of Americans and vice versa; teaching Americans about the host country. The first part was somewhat flawed in terms of actually fulfilling the objective of our project but the second two were really good. I would say connecting with a lot of people and letting them know about me and what I'm all about. Western culture, stuff like that and vice-versa; letting people in Thailand know about my home. Those are probably part of the most productive aspects of the experience ... When they are able to connect with someone is probably more important than the actual teaching in the classroom.

TT similarly states that their mission is to help improve education in the Third World and facilitate multi-cultural understanding between people from diverse backgrounds. Research on volunteering shows how the friendships that are developed through the intimate work atmosphere that volunteering facilitates are deemed to be more important than the project itself (Wearing, 2001). As one blogger writes:

> Every single person I know who joined the Peace Corp [sic], half dozen or so, and the ones that joined through other organizations said that they felt like they contributed very little when they thought about it. But what they did contribute was 'emotional support,' i.e. [sic] making people believe that others cared about their condition which was encouraging to them (Yoda17, 2007).

Reporting on Cross-Cultural Solutions, the *New York Times* writes: "[F]or those who want something different, something akin to a mini-stint with the Peace Corps, there is Cross-Cultural Solutions" (Cross Cultural Solutions, 2010). Reflecting the close relation between the Peace Corps and volunteer tourism, more than a quarter of the volunteers who participated in this research considered joining the Peace Corps or a comparable organization in their home country, but did not want to commit to long-term service. Volunteers often suggest that volunteer tourism offers all the perks of the Peace Corps—such as gaining intercultural competence, hands on experience in the development and having an authentic experience with locals—all without the long-term commitment.

The Peace Corps Effect

While cross-cultural understanding is the mutual goal of the Peace Corps and international volunteering, this goal is not always realized (Mowforth and Munt, 2009, Zavitz and Butz, 2011). Instead, as Vrasti notes, "research on aid workers in the developing world confirms that the aim of transnational philanthropy is not to spread development and cross-cultural understanding, but endow Western subjects with the 'cultural competencies' (tastes, values, sensibilities and experiences) necessary to perform a 'white,' 'bourgeois' and 'enlightened' type of subjectivity" (Vrasti, 2012, p. 10). What these cultural practices have also given rise to is what I call the "Peace Corps effect."[1] I define the Peace Corps effect as the collective effect of an assemblage of cultural practices (e.g. Peace Corps, volunteer tourism, CSR and ethical consumption) that produce a myopic focus on an individual object of concern. These assemblage components are part of the broader assemblage of the humanitarian gaze (see Chapter 1) that identifies not the broader political, economic, and structural causes of chronic poverty and systemic violence against the poor—but the individual child, household or village and their immediate concerns. In late capitalism, the Peace Corps effect has been at the center of contemporary international development initiatives where there is a focus on making a difference one person or village at a time through the purchase of ethical chocolate, fair trade coffee and volunteer vacations. Taking its cues from the Peace Corps, volunteer tourism tends to attract likeminded participants who are keen consumers of products that "give back" to society (Butcher, 2003, Freidberg, 2003, Goodman, 2004, Mostafanezhad, 2013a, Mostafanezhad, 2013b).

A historical perspective offers signal insights into how the contemporary discourses of "giving back" in volunteer tourism are at least in part a legacy of the Peace Corps and related development initiatives in the West. The emergence of volunteer tourism over the last decade is not only a legacy of the Peace Corps—its self-proclaimed predecessor—but illustrates a cultural impetus in the West that is linked to neoliberal economic trends in late modernity; this impetus includes entrepreneurialism, self-development and privatized social and economic development (Vrasti, 2012). While the Peace Corps as well as the volunteer

---

1   The term "Peace Corps effect" was originally expressed by Krisna Suryanata in a personal communication at the University of Hawai'i at Mānoa.

tourism experience are meaningful in their own right, the sustainability of their material accomplishments remain mutually tenuous because the problems they seeks to address are the outcome, rather than the cause of underdevelopment.

Drawing from Foucauldian archaeology, I chronicle volunteer tourism since the mid-twentieth century in order to understand the root of its seduction (Foucault, 1970). A Foucauldian archeology perspective is crucial for a more nuanced perspective of volunteer tourism beyond whether it realizes its goals or is "good" or "bad." Rather, I argue that volunteer tourism encounters, like Clifford's "crossing, tactics of translation, experiences of double or multiple attachment … reflect complex regional and transitional histories which, since 1900, have been powerfully inflected by three connected global forces: the continuing legacies of empire, the effects of unprecedented world wars, and the global consequences of industrial capitalism's disruptive, restructuring activity" (Clifford, 1997, p. 6–7). The experiences of the Peace Corps and the more recent growth of volunteer tourism, corporate social responsibility (CSR) and ethical consumption contribute to a collaborative project of Western international hegemony. Volunteer tourism is situated within these broader economic and cultural practices. It is also a key site from which to examine how culture shapes economic behavior as "frequent cross-cultural interactions are rich sites from which to examine ideas about authenticity, the globally inequitable distribution of money and leisure time, the nexus of economic development and indigenous-rights politics, and the points of agenda articulation between capitalists, governments, and local people" (West, 2008, p. 599). The historical legacy of missionaries, colonialism and development encounters of the nineteenth century inform contemporary forms of volunteer tourism. A chronicle of these precursors of volunteer tourism shows that there are significant points of historical disjuncture as well as continuity between them.

From Colonial Missionaries to Alternative Spring Breakers

The practice of sending Western citizens abroad for humanitarian and charity purposes is much older than its contemporary successors would suggest. Colonial missionaries and the Grand Tour of the sixteenth century precede contemporary movements for similar purposes of spreading the word of God, enhancing bourgeois wellbeing, and civilizing—or in contemporary terms, developing—distant parts of the world. As perhaps the earliest historical predecessor of volunteer tourism, missionaries continue to play an important role in international development in contemporary times with some of the largest international volunteering organizations such as World Vision and Habitat for Humanity having connections to the church (Lyons et al., 2012). As Hoffman points out, "missionaries like the poor, have always been with us. Even before the Crusades, Christians went off to foreign continents to convert, uplift, or if necessary beat into submission native peoples. But in the middle of the twentieth century there appeared the secular volunteer" (Hoffman, 1998, p. 13). Referred to as mini-missions or "mission lite," volunteer tourism is also widely compared to the Grand Tour (Brown and Lehto, 2005, Brown and Morrison, 2003). The main "purpose of the Grand Tour was one of education, exploration and sensibilization to the manifold realities of the growingly interconnected world. It was also a way for young men from the upper classes to gain social status and demonstrate a certain sense of maturity and masculinity" (Vrasti, 2012, p. 7). Recognized as a possible medium for philanthropic acts[2] since its inception, Thomas Cook's original package tour in 1850 was motivated by a "broad social agenda" and philanthropic goals. Cook saw the railway as social force that would advance human progress through opportunities for travel and expanded networks of philanthropy (Higgins-Desbiolles, 2005, Turner and Ash, 1975). In this way he reinvented the Grand Tour in the nineteenth century for the middle classes through democratizing access to tourism. For example, in 1861 he organized an excursion of 1,500–1,600 people to a working man's protest (Higgins-Desbiolles, 2005, p. 1194). During this period "Cook made a loss of 120 pounds and described the venture a 'labour of love minus profit.' Nevertheless, a similar excursion was organized in the following year (1975, p. 53)" (Higgins-Desbiolles, 2005, p. 1194). Thus, Thomas Cook's tours inaugurated mass tourism which was intended to be a secular, social mission for the goodwill of its participants as well as for the destination communities. The Grant Tour and social missions of the colonial and Thomas Cook era gave rise to the contemporary experience of "'going-round-the-world' or 'taking a year off to travel'" which have "become a latter-day equivalent of the Grand Tour and an important component of the culture of travel" (Mowforth and Munt, 2009, p. 129).

Study Abroad, Service Learning Projects and Alternative Spring Breaks

Today, study abroad and service learning programs, including anthropological field schools are common and often mandatory educational experiences (Brown and Lehto, 2005, Sin, 2009). A primary goal of these programs is to encourage students to think critically and become responsible global citizens as they are "an attempt that 'speaks to our sense of duty and fairness in the world: those who can support those who cannot, giving opportunities to those left behind' (Butin 2005: vii)" (Sin, 2009, p. 482). These programs intersect with volunteer tourism in varied ways such as the now regular inclusion of volunteering as part of study abroad trips (Wearing, 2001, Hoffman, 1998, Brown and Morrison, 2003, Hailey, 1999).

Earthwatch was established in 1971 as the first institutionalized volunteer tourism organization. This program is primarily educational and focuses on teaching its participants about environmental conservation through overseas

---

2   I focus on Western travel traditions in this book, while recognizing that other travel traditions in non-Western contexts have also contributed to contemporary travel within their own countries as well as the West and may have even preceded Western forms of tourism. Chambers, E. 2009. *Native Tours: The Anthropology of Travel and Tourism*, Long Grove, Illinois, Waveland Press, Inc.

volunteering trips. Yet, prior to the early 1990s volunteer tourism was virtually unmappable. In the 1990s we also witness the widespread intensification of neo-liberal global capitalism. The corollary "voluntary turn" of the late 1990s furthered the ability for volunteer tourism to succeed (Milligan and Conradson, 2006a). The demand for volunteer tourism has been attributed to "an increased sense of global awareness among the baby boom generation, along with a growing willingness to make a contribution to other societies while on holiday" (Brown and Morrison, 2003, p. 73). This demand extends to the children and grandchildren of the baby boom generation who are now the participants of alternative spring breaks. Instead of "partying like its 1999" like the artist formerly known as Prince might suggest, or nursing a hangover on the beach in Cancun, they are building houses, teaching English or caring for children in developing countries (Rhoads and Neururer, 1998, McElhaney, 1998, Brumbaugh, 2010). Together, these contemporary cultural practices play an important role in promoting Western ideology and hegemonic power.

Growth of the Volunteer Tourism Industry

Clearly, the volunteer tourism industry is growing is size and shape. My interest is not so much on the implications of this growth for the industry, but the implications of what this growth says about broader cultural trends in contemporary society. While alternative spring break and service learning abroad programs are still marginal compared to mass tourism experiences, they are "significant in terms of both the claims that are made about them and the rate at which they are growing" (Mowforth and Munt, 2009, p. 2). The expansion of volunteer tourism is observed by host community members, tour operators and international volunteers alike. Manop, a Thai orphanage worker, has perceived growing numbers of volunteers in Thailand: "I don't have any information to support my answer but from what I have seen, there are probably more than before." Tom, the local *tuk-tuk* driver similarly observes this growth and suggests how NGO practitioners should develop ways to reach the mainstream tourists, many of which, he notices, are interested in volunteering during their vacations:

> It needs to be publicized. They need to put the brochures in the tour company because sometimes the tourists want to book a tour. Sometimes the tourists work in social services already. Some people want to help Thai children or Hill Tribe children who have problems. I show them the brochure and people think, okay, I think I will go there. So I put the brochure in the back seat. Like these customers, they asked if I knew of any children that they could go see and help. They can take out the brochure to take a look and see if they want to go.

The expansion of volunteer tourism is also evidenced by the sheer number of organizations oriented towards this market. As the NGO Tourism Concern (2007: 6) describes, there is now "a rapidly growing industry champing at the bit to create placements to fulfill this new market" (Mowforth and Munt, 2009, p. 126). Euromonitor International reports that young single travelers are increasingly moving towards volunteer vacations (Fitzpatrick, 2007). This movement is in part evidenced by the attention volunteer tourism has received by mainstream media over the last five years. A *TIME Magazine* article reports that "[A]s the industry grapples with how to make money without compromising the results of the volunteer work, one thing is clear: more and more private citizens are ready to roll up their sleeves and lend a hand. 'I was just so sick of just donating a gift at the end of the year,' says Yates of his decision to spend a week volunteering in Costa Rica. 'I worked my butt off'" (Fitzpatrick, 2007). Similarly, CNN's Humanitarian Travel report explains how volunteer vacations are an increasingly popular way to spend one's vacation and highlights the predominance of women, retirees and newlyweds (Palk, 2010, Clothier, 2010, Vasquez, 2010). Travelocity reported that approximately 40 percent planned to take a trip for charitable reasons in the next 12 months and Rob Lovitt's MSNBC/ Conde Nast 2008 survey suggests that "… more than half (55 percent) of the respondents expressed interest in taking a volunteer vacation. The survey polled more than 1,600 people and found that approximately 20 percent had taken at least one volunteer vacation. Of those who hadn't, nearly two-thirds (62 percent) said they'd be very likely or somewhat likely to take one'" (Clemmons, 2010) and in June 2009, the University of California, San Diego suggested that "'[T]wo-thirds of high school students and about half of college students surveyed say they have participated in discussions in the past year related to traveling to other regions to provide volunteer service, whereas less than half of the adult population, and only one-quarter of retirees, say they have done so'" (Clemmons, 2010). This growth in the volunteer tourism industry echoes the broader expansion of the voluntary turn in the West.

The "Voluntary Turn"

In his 1999 address to the National Council for Voluntary Organizations (NCVO), former British Prime Minister, Tony Blair described the increasing importance of the voluntary sector:

> In the second half of the century we learnt that government cannot achieve its aims without the energy and commitment of others—voluntary organizations, business, and, crucially, the wider public … history shows that the most successful societies are those that harness the energies of voluntary action, giving due recognition to the third sector of voluntary and community organizations (Macmillan and Townsend, 2006, p. 16).

Two years later, the United Nations dedicated 2001 to the International Year of Volunteering—which helped to usher in what is broadly referred to as the "voluntary turn." The concomitant reduction in government spending on social welfare and services in the United States and several European countries has also been met by the "community turn" (Macmillan and Townsend, 2006). It is suggested that, "[T]he 'community turn' ... is fundamentally part of this relentless search for more effective, costless solutions 'beyond-the-state.' As such, it is appropriate to think of this 'turn' as part of an 'institutional fix,' designed to achieve social and economic ends in a period marked by the unraveling and reshaping of the guideposts of the relatively comprehensive (social democratic) welfare settlement" (Macmillan and Townsend, 2006, p. 26). This call for the expansion of the voluntary sector and community turn is echoed by US President Barack Obama and was backed by his 2011 budget request to the Corporation for National and Community Service for $1.4 billion dollars. It is expected that this expanded budget will "improve the lives of tens of millions of our most vulnerable citizens—reducing the number of high school dropouts, expanding economic opportunity, increasing energy efficiency, mentoring at-risk youth, combating hunger and homelessness, providing health services, caring for veterans, supporting independent living, and responding to disasters" (Scott, 2010).

With more than six million Americans expected to partake in the "volunteerization" of America, this growth of the voluntary sector is meant to help solve some of the nation's most pressing problems. It is explained that the 1.4 billion dollar request "represents increasing national consensus among elected officials, business and nonprofit leaders, and ordinary Americans that service isn't secondary or separate from achieving national priorities; it's essential to achieving them" (Scott, 2010). In Chapter 4 I discuss how these sentiments of individual responsibility, civic engagement and commodity activism have been echoed in related movements toward the expansion of global civil society (Hearn, 2012). Compassionate conservatism captures these sentiments most explicitly in its call for personal responsibility for the self, the nation and increasingly, the world. As one of its advocates argues:

> Telling the poor that they are mere passive victims, whether of racism or of vast economic forces, is not only false but also destructive, paralyzing the poor with thoughts of their own helplessness and inadequacy. The poor need the larger society's moral support; they need to hear the message of personal responsibility and self-reliance, the optimistic assurance that if they try—as they must—they will make it. They need to know, too, that they can't blame "the system" for their own wrongdoing (Magnet, 1999).

As a hallmark of the cultural logic of neoliberalism, the *individual* volunteer becomes the focus of attention. Comaroff and Comaroff explain how within the shadow of neoliberalism "emerges a more radically individuated sense of personhood, of a subject built up of traits set against a universal backdrop of likeness and difference" (Comaroff and Comaroff, 2005, p. 183). This advancement of organic solidarity and the emergence of the individual intensified the contemporary expansion of the voluntary sectors in the US and Europe.

The Volunteer Tourist as Neoliberal Subject

Postmodern tendencies towards individualized, niche consumer markets and the progressive privatization of social services under neoliberal policies of the past three decades have given rise to the expansion of the neoliberal subject. Vrasti describes the neoliberal subject as simultaneously "strongly individualized and keenly socialized. It is a subject expected to make a difference while also making a profit out of it" (Vrasti, 2012, p. 132). The volunteer tourist as neoliberal subject has emerged at a unique historical conjuncture where social dissent has become increasingly accommodated for by the market and civil society has become part of international development agendas. Within this atmosphere of commoditized concern, "radical leaders of the past, iconic figures like Che Guevara and Malcolm X, deployed within mainstream culture as little more than fashion statements" (Hearn, 2012, p. 2). The continuity between the old and the new forms of popular humanitarianism contribute to localizing and globalizing processes in both unique and familiar ways that hail the neoliberal subject-cum-humanitarian. This subject position has emerged out of a longer history of soft power and corporate social responsibility strategies.

Soft Power, the State and Corporate Social Responsibility

In January of 2006 US "Secretary of State Condoleezza Rice underscored the move toward soft power ... that highlighted the State Department's plan for a new 'transformational diplomacy'" (Rieffel and Zalud, 2006). This policy shift was a response to a widespread skepticism around "hard power" as a result of its failure in the Iraq war (Rieffel and Zalud, 2006). Coined by Joseph Nye, "soft power" refers to the power to persuade rather than coerce cooperation and is widely considered an economical yet effective mechanism to intensify national influence globally (Shrestha, 2002: 273). International volunteering programs are a core aspect of this strategy as "[T]he face of America that has been welcomed most enthusiastically in the rest of the world for decades has been the face of a volunteer: assisting with disaster relief, building houses for poor families, teaching English to university studies, and so much more" (Rieffel and Zalud, 2006). Government documents note how these programs contribute to US security and well-being and "represent one of the best avenues Americans can pursue to improve relations with the rest of the world" (Rieffel and Zalud, 2006). A 2006 Brookings Policy Brief Series report explains how:

> Overseas volunteer work is a form of soft power that contributes measurably to the security and well-being of Americans. Volunteers working in other countries develop life-long relationships and promote cross-cultural understanding in ways that few other federally funded programs can do. They bring home to the US an understanding of foreign cultures that enriches our country and informs our policy choices. Volunteers also contribute to institutional capacity building,

social capital, democratic governance, and a respect for human rights, all of
which help to make the world a safer place for Americans both at home and
abroad (Rieffel and Zalud, 2006).

Assani examines how American international volunteer programs primarily
targeted "the heart and mind of the elite of these countries in order to raise soft
power, and that US cultural policy was foremost conditioned politically by the
ideological inclinations of the beneficiaries of American assistance" (Assani, 2010,
p. 1). Examples of cultural practices associated with soft power include Hollywood
movies, music, news and educational international exchange programs such as the
US Fulbright program. These programs are "used as part of the strategy to project
the ideals democracy and freedom in these countries while simultaneously proving
the capacity of America as a global leader" (Assani, 2010, p. 3). Vrasti argues
that in addition to CSR, ethical consumption and social entrepreneurship, these
programs play a central role in providing "capital with the 'forms of sociality and
subjectivity' it needs to reproduce itself. It does so by cultivating emotional and
communicative competencies required from adaptable workers and transgressive
entrepreneurs" (Vrasti, 2012, p. 119).

While government sponsored international volunteer programs have grown in
the US, private international volunteer programs have far exceeded the number and
geographic scope of the government backed programs. Privatized international
volunteer programs' values and ideals are in sync with neoliberal capitalist values
where "the exigencies of neoliberal capital are such that individuals need to treat
all areas of life, even leisure time, like work or an investment in one's future
ability to work" (Vrasti, 2012, p. 124). The fastest growing sector of overseas
volunteer programs is the private sector where corporations are now using
international volunteering as an international CSR strategy as a "large number of
multinational corporations now encourage their employees to engage in volunteer
work in their local communities or in places where there is a high demand for
their skills, including foreign countries" (Rieffel and Zalud, 2006). While
the concept of CSR emerged around 50 years ago (Carroll, 1999, p. 268), the
contemporary use of the term can be traced to the early 1990s. Contemporary CSR
is associated with the related growth of sustainable business, the triple bottom
line and environmental responsibility (Broomhill, 2007, p. 6). The expansion of
neoliberal policies in the 1980s was met with a "significant shift away from state
intervention in both developed and developing countries. The increased mobility
of capital enabled TNCs to exploit regulatory differences between states by (re)
locating (or threatening to relocate) their production facilities in countries with
more favourable regimes, a phenomenon that has been referred to as 'regulatory
arbitrage.' These trends were reflected in developing country policies towards
TNCs, which shifted dramatically from regulation of their activities to intense
competition to attract foreign direct investment (FDI)" (Jenkins, 2005, p. 527).

Yet, these deleterious practices did not go unnoticed and "[B]y the 1990s the
heyday of neo-liberal policies had passed in the North, and corporations started to

attract criticism for their global environmental and labor practices. The growth of global 'value chains,' in which northern buyers control a web of suppliers in the South, led to calls for them to take responsibility not only for aspects such as quality and delivery dates but also for working conditions and environmental impacts" (Jenkins, 2005, p. 527). Importantly, this was also during the period of expansion of the internet and other communication technologies and public awareness and protest were more easily organized (Jenkins, 2005, p. 527). In efforts to reduce brand devaluation through the exposure of unethical corporate practices, many companies began their own CSR campaigns. Jenkins notes how "Levi Strauss was one of the first companies to do so, adopting its Business Partner Terms of Engagement in 1992 after its overseas contractors were accused of treating their workers as indentured slaves" (Jenkins, 2005, p. 527–8). Other companies such as Gap, Nike and Disney followed suit as part of their public relations campaign to save the brand image and 1995/6 was described as the "Year of the Sweatshop" (Jenkins, 2005, p. 528). Within CSR there is a widespread focus on environmental sustainability and restrictions against child labor but "these priorities lead to a tendency to see CSR in negative terms, in other words, with an emphasis on things that companies should not do, such as employing children or violating human rights, rather than on seeking positive development outcomes, such as helping to eradicate poverty," thus "[T]he current CSR agenda is as significant for what it does not include as for what it does. Corporate practices such as transfer pricing, tax avoidance or the abuse of market power are not part of the CSR mainstream" (Jenkins, 2005, p. 528). Therefore, critics of CSR argue that "[C]ompanies are concerned largely with the potential damage to their reputations that may accrue as a result of media exposure of corporate malpractice" (Jenkins, 2005, p. 528). For example, Sheldon and Park explains that CSR is important to the industry precisely because not being socially responsible will affect destination image and therefore the bottom line (Sheldon and Park, 2011). CSR is widely seen among the development community as an inadequate response to the sometimes devastating implications of private corporations, especially in developing countries.

Jenkins notes how "Development NGOs have, for the most part, been extremely critical of the voluntary initiatives undertaken by the corporate sector. In a recent report Christian Aid stated that 'CSR is a completely inadequate response to the sometimes devastating impact that multinational companies [have]', while a recent Oxfam study highlights the way in which the supply chain purchasing practices of retailers in the garment and horticulture sector undermine their professed aspirations to social responsibility as set out in their corporate codes of conduct" (Jenkins, 2005, p. 525). These concerns echo critiques of moral consumption and the neoliberalization of development through consumerism. Sin examines CSR and ethical consumer activism as two sides of the same coin and explains how "[C]orporations have an incentive to take on CSR as a means to create value and brand loyalty through attempts at aligning themselves with what they deem to be consumer perspectives (e.g. carbon offsetting programs to show consumers that they are equally conscious of their environmental footprint); on the other hand, 'consumers use the commercial value of their brand loyalty to lobby corporations for a variety of goods and services, the delivery of which was once presumed to be the obligation and function of elected governments in promoting social welfare' (Foster 2008: xvii)" (Sin, 2012, p. 163). These practices illustrate the growing turn towards corporate social responsibility and ethical business models (Vrasti, 2012, p. 1). They also foreshadowed the emergence of volunteer tourism that Wearing describes as the poster child of ethical tourism programs (Wearing, 2001).

Commodification and Authenticity

Like the Peace Corps, contemporary forms of volunteer tourism are in part a reaction against Euro-American political, economic and military hegemony. Hoffman observes how "as much as Americans enjoyed … power, it sometimes disturbed them as well. Embedded in the nation's history was a recognition of the corrupting effects of power on political virtue" (Hoffman, 1998, p. 1). The US hoped to show that it would use its power to bestow benevolence and goodwill onto all nations. Observing Peace Corps volunteers in his home country of Nepal, Shrestha observes:

> … [Peace Corps volunteers] were going overseas … to "exotic" countries, some in search of cheap marijuana and hashish and in search of cultural relief from the material opulence of stale suburban life. Nepal was viewed as a mecca for such relief. How ironic that many volunteers, sent to promote American values and materialistic development were themselves yearning for reprieve from that very same material life in a culture that was described as backward and poverty (Shrestha, 2002, 273).

Volunteer tourism attracts a similar array of young participants, many of whom possess alternative ideals and have become disenchanted with capitalist society. McLaren observes how "[M]asses of young people dissatisfied by US imperialism … afflicted by the postmodern malaise of alienation, no sense of grounding, no redemptive identity, can be manipulated by cultural strategies that offer Otherness as appeasement, particularly through commodification and travel to rural and indigenous cultures which is increasing at a rate never seen before as the world becomes globalized and we lose our cultural identities and ties with community" (McLaren, 2003, p. 47). What motivates volunteer tourists is a widespread romanticization of peoples and places perceived to be beyond the realm of capitalist modernity and therefore living more authentic and community oriented lives. These motivations are not unlike the motivations of other so-called alternative tourists such as backpackers or eco-tourists (Muzaini, 2006, Hampton, 1997). For example, West explains how "[T]he touristic primitive is also 'uncontacted' or only 'contacted slightly,' and for Stasch's tourists this notion of 'isolation' encompasses all of the other attributes that he examines" (West, 2008, p. 599).

Within this context the discourses of environmentalism, poverty reduction and sustainability are increasingly appropriated in institutionalized contexts such as the World Bank, regional banks, and bilateral aid donors. These same discourses are appropriated by volunteer tourism organizations and are echoed by alternative tourism participants including NGOs which have become key players in the alternative tourism market and who tend to emphasize a more dialogic, individualized and globally conscious alternative to mass tourism (Mowforth and Munt, 2009, Poon, 1989, Uriely et al., 2003, Stronza, 2005, Stronza, 2001). Volunteer tourists often seek to have intimate, mutually beneficial encounters with the host community and contribute to the host community's social, natural or economic betterment. These aspects of the volunteer tourism experience are lauded for the positive implications they have for its participants (Broad and Spencer, 2008, Brown and Morrison, 2003, Gray and Campbell, 2007, Campbell and Smith, 2006, Halpenny, 2003, McIntosh and Zahra, 2007, Scheyvens, 2010, Wearing, 2003, Wearing, 2001). As a 22-year-old German volunteer suggests, people are interested in volunteering abroad: "[B]ecause many people want to do more—to have a different experience, rather than just traveling." This desire to do "more than just traveling" is a core motivation of volunteer tourists. Within participatory forms of tourism such as volunteer tourism, tourists seek out dialogical encounters with host community members. This desire is partly based on the assumption that the "transpersonal" experience or being able to communicate with and have reciprocal interaction with the Other is the ultimate signifier of the authentic traveler (as opposed to the tourist). According to the volunteer tourists that I talked with, the difference between tourists and travelers is primarily that travelers have intimate, "real" interactions with local people and tourists do not.

With the ability to link the financial capital of environmental and socially conscious individuals from the West to their economic, social and environmental goals, volunteer tourism is a seemingly ideal form of alternative tourism development that has exploded onto the international NGO scene, marketing itself as an authentic, decommodified experience (Gray and Campbell, 2007, Wearing, 2005). For example, TT explains that it "was founded in opposition to the large western corporations who use volunteering to make a profit" (Travel to Traveling Teachers, 2010). In addition to tourists, NGO practitioners and tourism academics discursively position volunteer tourism outside the mainstream market. For example, Wearing asks whether "a philosophy and practice of volunteer tourism exists outside the market priorities defined and sustained in the global market place of tourism" (2001, p. 12). Volunteer tourism, Wearing argues, departs from other forms of tourism in its profit objective, which is secondary to the desire to help communities (Wearing, 2001). Questioning this alternative identity, Wearing and Lyons ask "whether volunteer tourism is an example of a niche product in the broader arena of tourism or whether it is an alternative social phenomena that challenges the commodity-intensive underpinnings of tourism" (Lyons and

Wearing, 2008, p. xiii). While advocates suggest that volunteer tourism falls outside mainstream capitalist relations, critics argue that it reproduces traditional capitalist structures of exchange. Despite claims of a decommodified experience beyond the realm of capitalist modernity, volunteer tourism reinforces neoliberal subjectivity by hailing the new moral consumer to become an active participant in international development agendas. Opposition to inauthentic experiences materializes in alternative modes of travel such as volunteer tourism which is seen to exist outside market mentality. In volunteer tourism this desire for the unmediated, decommodified, authentic experience is in constant tension with host community members' widespread interest in further market integration—the topic of the following chapter.

Chapter 3

The Seduction of Development: NGOs and Alternative Tourism in Northern Thailand

As I jump into the hatchback of a rusty, white pick-up truck, Lek, a 26-year-old Thai volunteer coordinator from Isan[1] reminds me to grab the construction paper off the counter. Still recovering from last night's farewell party for one of the volunteers at the local Reggae Bar in downtown Chiang Mai, seven European volunteers wait in the back of the truck while I grab the paper from inside the house. Emma, a blonde, robust German volunteer, is holding her head in her hands as she tries not to vomit while we ramble down the dusty road to the elementary school just outside of Chiang Mai. We are going to teach the children animals and colors today. We stop at the shop near the school to make copies of the lesson plans. Lek asks me to run into the store since I can speak Thai and she is still going over the day's lesson. As I jump out of the hatchback and walk into the shop, the children stare at me with a slight sense of confusion. "The foreigner can speak Thai!" they exclaim before giggling and running away. They hide behind the shelves stocked with expired candy and peer through the gaps. When we make eye contact they giggle and proceed to the back of the aisle where they cannot be seen. "Forty baht" the woman at the copy machine says as she slips the warm photocopies into a clear plastic folder. Noticing the time, I rush back to the truck. "Okay," I yell, "let's go." The driver, Lek's cousin, starts the truck, and we take off.

As we drive up to the elementary school, a large group of students run to the truck. Hardly able to catch their breath from the excitement, they scream, "Hello teacher!" in English, laugh and run away. They return with another exclamation of "hello teacher!" and "my name is ..." and bang the sides of the truck for effect. Helen, a 32-year-old TT[2] coordinator from Scotland, picks up Nid, a six-year-old Burmese-Thai boy. The snot dripping from his nose has saturated his torn red t-shirt. Helen swings Nid in circles for a minute. She then puts him down and walks him to the outdoor sink where she wipes the snot from his face. Lek yells, "Okay, everyone inside for class" in Thai, and the children obediently shuffle inside where they sit in five uniform lines on the cement floor. Most of the students are dressed in colorful outfits, which work well for our lesson on colors. The students are not wearing their normal school uniforms this week because it is

---

1   Isan is the northeast region in Thailand.

2   As noted in Chapter 2, Traveling Teachers is an international NGO with three programs in Thailand as well programs in seven other developing countries. Traveling Teachers primarily teaches English to underprivileged children.

summer break and we are at an optional English camp sponsored by TT. As I walk into the cement room I notice the assortment of tiny flip flops outside the main entrance. We begin by reviewing yesterday's lesson: "head, shoulders, knees and toes, knees and toes ..."

This experience is increasingly common in Chiang Mai—a city where everyday hundreds of primarily Western volunteers load into the beds of pick-up trucks and make journeys to rural and impoverished schools to teach English. Volunteers from across the West arrive in Thailand seeking to contribute to its social and economic "development." While the scale of international volunteering in Thailand continues to grow, skeptics ask, is this really "development"? And to what kind of "development" can these young Westerners ultimately contribute? Defenders of international volunteering suggest that at the very least, these experiences contribute to cross-cultural understanding and respect—which, they argue, is a fundamental aspect of social development (Brown and Lehto, 2005, McGehee and Santos, 2005b, Wearing, 2004, Wearing, 2001, Chen and Chen, 2011). The host community members that I conversed with about this point generally agree that Westerners *can* bring development. But what they mean by development is not altogether clear. While there is not a unified voice regarding what kind of development they hope the volunteers will facilitate, there is widespread consensus that "development" is needed and one of the surest ways to realize development is through Western influence. This observation illustrates how while academic theories of development such as post development, alternative development and alternatives to development criticize the development project for its linear, teleological, and Western-centric associations, conventional development discourse remains a powerfully seductive force, which has not lost its appeal to most of the world's population (Crush, 1995).

The expansion of neoliberal development in Thailand and the concomitant rise of volunteer tourism raises a number of questions about international development and how it articulates with popular humanitarianism: how does volunteer tourism fit into broader transnational popular humanitarian discourse(s)?; how have neoliberal policies and practices encouraged the rapid adoption of volunteer tourism by NGOs in northern Thailand?; how do volunteer tourism participants discursively construct development as both a practice and discourse?; and how does volunteer tourism reflect the concerns of development and humanitarian agendas? Collectively, answers to these questions illustrate some of the contradictions and ironies of the expansion of neoliberalism and its social, economic and political corollaries. Recurrent themes in participants' conversations of the binary oppositions between "developed" and "developing" or "First" and "Third" World countries form a core part of volunteer tourism discourse. These articulations "make the practice of international development doable, knowable and accessible to young travelers" (Simpson, 2004, p. 681) as well as to Thai NGO practitioners and host community members. Yet, I argue, these discourses do not go undisputed. The contestations of these categories punctuate the experience in ways that challenge development discourse in sometimes unforeseeable ways.

As a result, the way volunteer tourism intersects with history, politics and economic rationalities of development can be seen as a prism through which to examine the broader re-articulation of humanitarian oriented development in the contemporary neoliberal era.

Development Practice and Development Discourse

On January 20, 1949, President Harry Truman inaugurated more than 60 years of development when he discursively split the world between developed and under-developed, with two thirds of the world sitting "on the wrong side" of the new world order:

> We must embark [President Truman said] on a bold new program for making the benefits of our scientific advances and industrial progress available for the improvement and growth of underdeveloped areas. The old imperialism—exploitation for foreign profit—has no place in our plans. What we envisage is a program of development based on the concepts of democratic fair dealing (Esteva, 2007, p. 6).

Truman's introduction of the concept of underdevelopment "changed the meaning of development and created the emblem, euphemism, used ever since to allude either discreetly or inadvertently to the era of American Hegemony" (Esteva, 2007, p. 6). Following Truman's lead, President John F. Kennedy declared the 1960s the decade of development (Mowforth and Munt, 2009). Development theorists sought to understand this practice in the face of growing disparities in global wealth (Adams, 2008, Bebbington and Bebbington, 2001, Escobar, 1995, Escobar, 2002, Escobar, 2005, Estava, 2007, Ferguson, 1994, Ferguson, 2002, Shrestha, 2002, Smith, 1984, Thomas, 2000).

Since the "textual turn" in the social sciences in the late 1980s, neo-Marxist, poststructuralist, feminist and postcolonial theorists have focused on development as a discourse, often at the expense of consideration of development as a practice (Crush, 1995). This turn resulted in academics questioning of the meaning of development and progress (Crush, 1995). Development discourse creates powerful constellations of ideas about the ordering of the contemporary world. Since the mid-1990s, development discourse has emerged as one of the most important units of analysis in what is broadly defined as post-development studies. Escobar (1995) urges a critical analysis of the ways in which development is discursively constructed and advocates the production of new terms and ways of thinking which go beyond "development." Following WWII, the West defined itself and others through the discursive construction of the First, Second and Third World: "notions of underdevelopment and Third World were the discursive products of the post-World War II climate. These concepts did not exist before 1945. They emerged as working principles within the process by which the West—and, in different ways, the East—redefined itself and the rest of the world" (Escobar, 1995, p. 31).

In contrast to "alternative development" approaches, post-development ultimately rejects development altogether. Post-development is based on the critique of three related postures including "the problematization of poverty, the portrayal of development as Westernization, and the critique of development" (Pieterse, 2000, p. 175). While many of the critiques that post-development scholars make regarding the project of development are recognized as valuable, they have also been accused of throwing out the baby with the bath water. Rather than contribute to a progressive politics, this maneuver has been described as an anti-politics (Ferguson, 1994). For Pierterse, an important distinction arises between alternative development and "alternatives to development." He points out how there is an anarchist tone in post-development literature that in many ways works to depoliticize the discourse of development by rendering it to a mere discourse among other implicitly equally legitimate discourses (as there is no single truth, only multiple discursive formations). Corbridge (1994) and Pieterse (2000) argue that "'an unwillingness to speak for others is every bit as foundational a claim as the suggestion that we can speak for others in an unproblematic manner' (quoted in Kiely, 1999: 23)" (Pieterse, 2000, p. 182). In this way post-development positions are blamed for depoliticizing and disengaging with academic discussions of development from lived, everyday realities. Furthermore, critics argue that dichotomous thinking fails to account for the complexities of development agendas and that rather than being a unified voice, are constantly engaged in internal contradictions and temporal rearticulations.

Thailand and the West

Despite the fact that Thailand has never been officially colonized, its position as an economic colony is widely noted as "since the mid-nineteenth century, Thailand has been profoundly influenced and constrained by Europe (England and France in particular), Japan (which occupied the country during World War II), and later the United States" (Wilson, 2004, p. 16). Thailand avoided colonization through the strategic mapping of Siam into a seemingly coherent and homogenous nation state (Thongchai, 1994). The King of Siam secured its borders from the ensuing encroachment of French and British colonizers through the establishment of its boundaries and turned Thailand into a buffer zone between France and Britain (Costa, 2001, Thongchai, 1994, Wyatt, 1982). While Thailand effectively resisted colonization it was not as successful in resisting economic subordination. Thailand was forced to accept several unfavorable economic treaties with the West over the past two centuries. For example, "[I]n the nineteenth and early twentieth centuries, Europeans used the political clout to force Siam to adopt economic treaties and political arrangements that were favorable to their corporate and colonial enterprises in the region, and they dominated the Thai import-export business" (Wilson, 2004, p. 16).[3]

The 1885 Bowring Treaty with Britain may represent the most decisive moment in Thai history. Costa explains that "this event, like the crisis of 1893, rendered Siam politically and (more importantly for the future), economically weak, placing it in a compromised structural and categorical position" (Costa, 2001, p. 120). Anderson explains how "'The Bowering "treaty" of 1855 essentially deprived the Thai sovereigns of a key element of their sovereignty (i.e., control over foreign trade) as well as of the traditional royal commercial monopolies' (1978: 209)" (quoted in Costa, 2001, p. 120). Thus, the Bowering treaty effectively opened the doors for foreign investment and trade, destroyed monopolies and promised minimal taxes on foreign trade (Costa, 2001, p. 121, Wyatt, 1982). The global market increasingly directed local production and trade in Thailand. The increasing integration into the global capitalist system resulted in Thailand's emergence as a global leader in rice exports (Wilson, 2004, Wyatt, 1982, Costa, 2001, Thongchai, 1994). This role put Thailand in the subordinate position of supporting the imperial nations' economic interests. While "Siam, and in particular, the port cities of Ayutthaya and Bangkok, had been involved in international trade for centuries, integration within the world capitalist (and categorical) system was given a hearty shove by this new treaty and others that followed soon after" (Costa, 2001, p. 121). The Bowering Treaty as a landmark event continues to have implications for Thailand's position on the international stage today.[4]

By the early 1990s, Thailand was widely expected to join the ranks of its neighbors as the fifth Asian Tiger, as it maintained some of the highest annual gross domestic product growth rates in the world (Hewison, 2003, Wilson, 2004). This was in part because Thailand's manufacturing, service and financial sectors

---

3 Almost a century later, similar political-economic arrangements between Thailand and the West exist. The familiar arrangement of open borders, limited state interference, and the facilitation of a favorable business climate for Western investors is currently referred to as neoliberalism. This begs the question, when did neoliberalism emerge? Is there a longer history of neoliberal-like relationships that existed in Thailand prior to the late 1970s? And, what is the historical significance of neoliberal-like, colonial encounters between Thailand and the West? Moreover, it complicates neoliberalism. While the basic tenets of neoliberalism remain the same, following McCarthy and Putnam, I suggest that we should refer to neoliberalism in the plural because of the complex interests of neoliberalism (McCarthy and Putman 2004).

4 It is beyond the scope of this book to go into greater depth on the recent history of Thailand. There are many excellent sources that offer a compelling account of Thailand's history over the past 300 years: Anderson, B. 1978. Studies of the Thai State: The State of Thai Studies, in Ayal, E.B., ed., *The Study of Thailand: Analyses of Knowledge, Approaches and Prospects in Anthropology, Art History, Economics, History, Political Science*, Ohio University, Center for International Studies; Wyatt, D. 1982. *Thailand: A Short History*, New Haven, Yale University Press; Thongchai, W. 1994. *Siam Mapped: A History of the Geo-Body*, Honolulu, University of Hawaii Press.

experienced unprecedented expansion. Yet, this celebratory culmination of growth was short lived as the Economic Crisis of 1997 soon followed. As Costa points out, "the excesses of the private sector in borrowing and lending for property and capital investment, combined with the government's disinterest in monitoring or curbing unsound fiscal practices resulted in an economic meltdown, not only in Thailand, but in other Asian countries as well (Montes 1998; Pasuk and Baker 1998: 315–320)" (Costa, 2001, p. 149), and the poor were disproportionally affected by the bursting of the economic bubble (Nations, 2010). Workers from the provinces in Bangkok left the city in masses as unemployment crippled its economy. While "the average rate of poverty declined during the boom years (1988 to 1996) at a rate of 2.7 percent of the population per year, between 1996 and 1999 'the crisis reversed 28 percent of the poverty reduction that had occurred during the eight year period of economic boom which immediately preceded the crisis' (ibid.: 6)" (Costa, 2001, p. 150).

Following the 1997 Economic Crisis, Thailand became further confined by its position within the global political economy. This remarkable growth was facilitated by "Asian Capitalism," which its most virulent critics, neoliberal economists, suggest contributed to "market distortions" that ultimately led to the crash of 1997 (Hewison, 2003). Thus, following the Crisis, international policymakers and orthodox economists at the IMF and World Bank were partly relieved that the flaws of Asian Capitalism, and the corollary dominance of neoliberal capitalism, had finally been revealed (Hewison, 2003, p. 2). Neoliberal reformers in Thailand were ultimately empowered by the 1997 Crisis because it "proved" that Asian Capitalism and its policies of state interventionism contributed to corruption and irrational economic governance. The IMF and World Bank bailed out Thailand with a $17 billion loan in exchange for substantial economic and bureaucratic restructuring. Market liberalization and the reduction of the state in the economy were both central to the massive structural adjustment plans. At this point the IMF and its allies "diagnosed Thailand's problems as deriving from too much government intervention in the economy, too much corruption, and a lack of transparency" (Hewison, 2003, p. 3). Thus, as a reaction against these obstacles, the IMF and other agencies demanded Thailand follow the neoliberal development policies of the West (Hewison, 2003, p. 2). Hewison observes that:

> ... in essence, this reorientation involved the following: keeping wages low; privatisation of state enterprises (especially targeting communications, transport and energy); civil service reform of the regulatory environment; an easing of restrictions on, and an increase in foreign investment; improvements to corporate governance; and increased private sector participation in infrastructure projects. All of this reform was to be supervised by the IMF (14 August 1997) (Hewison, 2003, p. 3–4).

Through the bursting of the economic bubble, the US and other Western countries were seen as the expert advisors and "[T]hrough structural adjustment programs which demand liberalization of markets and the internationalization of myriad laws and standards from the environment to labor, social welfare to taxes, countries like Thailand encounter a modern version of nineteenth century colonial 'civilizing mission'" (Costa, 2001, p. 150). Within this neoliberal climate NGOs and community-based organizations became key players in Thai development initiatives. Costa shows how the Eighth Social and Economic Development plan (1997–2001) prioritized sustainable economic growth and replaced top down administration with bottom up development schemes (Nations, 2010):

> Promoting popular participation in regional and rural development will provide opportunities for local people to improve their potentials for independently finding solutions to problems which benefit individuals, families and communities ... The private sector, NGOs and people's organizations should be encouraged to cooperate with the public sector so as to combine their efforts in the interests of development (NESDB 1997: 59) (Costa, 2001, p. 153).

The plan also suggests that policies will be made to "[E]ncourage NGOs to collaborate in development projects with communities, local organizations, government agencies and private business, by providing support in the form of necessary information and financial contributions (ibid.: 63)" (Costa, 2001, p. 153). The challenges presented by the burst of the economic bubble effectively opened the floodgates for the intensified neoliberalization of the Thai economy.

While the Thai economy continued to grow at unprecedented rates between 1950 and 1975, intense social unrest in Bangkok began to surface. On October 6th, 1976 this unrest reached an apex during the military coup d'état where 46 people were wounded during the Hok Tula, a student protest at Thammasat University in Bangkok. After the coup, foreign investors quickly fled the country leaving Thailand with a volatile political and economic situation (Costa, 2001). By 1979 Thailand was in such economic turmoil that it was forced to borrow millions of dollars from the World Bank and IMF, and conform to the structural adjustment policies of its lenders. While this resulted in the opening up of trade barriers and increased foreign investment and benefited Thailand's elite, it also deepened the gap between the rich and the poor. This deepening ultimately contributed "to a 'national culture' that pit the village (ba:n) against the city (mu' ang) (Pasuk and Baker 1995: 75; Keyes 1991)" (Costa, 2001, p. 139). The massive inequality between the "city people" and the "country people" continues to be a core of political tension in Thailand. To help alleviate this disparity, in the mid-1980s alternative development paradigms were increasingly applied in the north and northeastern regions as community participation became an important aspect of Thailand's Fifth National Development Plan (1982–86). Subsequent plans continued to depart from earlier top down models and promoted community participation in development. The sixth plan (1986–91), for example, explicitly acknowledges the role of NGOs in social and economic development (Costa, 2001, p. 159). In the North, "the introduction of community development interventions ... can be understood as a mechanism through which the Thai state sought closer governance of the borderlands" (McKinnon, 2006, p. 24).

Inequality in Thailand is perhaps best illustrated by what is commonly referred to as the "Hill Tribe problem." Following WWII (1939–45) and the onset of the Cold War (1947–91) Thai authorities were pressured by the US and its allies to deal with the Hill Tribe problem which revolved around three related issues including environmental degradation, opium production and national security among ethnic minority groups who live in the mountainous areas of the northern region—most notably in the Chiang Mai Province. This problem opened up new spaces of development in the 60s and 70s "as international funding became available to remedy these 'problems,' foreign development professionals began arriving to work on multilateral development programmes, often focused around opium crop replacement" and "between the late 1960s and 2000, highland villages were the focus of activities for approximately 20 internationally funded multilateral development projects, with a total budget of approximately US $185 million between them (Rendard 2001, 70–1); at least 158 registered ... NGOs if not more (Kampe 1995, unpublished data); and an indeterminate number of researchers—including 101 foreign researchers who registered with the Tribal Research Institute between 1968 and 1992 (Tribal Research Institute 1992)" (McKinnon, 2006, p. 23).

The Thailand government worked to unify the country into a homogeneous State; it also became increasingly self-conscious of its geopolitics as it was surrounded by communist countries. By allowing Western development professionals entrance into the highlands of the north, Thailand was able satisfy "multiple geopolitical agendas surrounding Cold War concerns with the spread of communism and the desire of the Thai state to actualize a vision of total governance within its borders (McKinnon 2004)" (McKinnon, 2006, pp. 23–4). Western researchers were inevitably implicated in Cold War politics as it became clear that funding for social research in the highlands was made available as a geopolitical maneuver by the US which worked to assist the Thai state in controlling the seemingly uncontainable and vulnerable population (McKinnon, 2006, p. 26). Additionally, as a pre-emptive defense against accusations of Thailand going red, it "pursued a laissez-faire capitalist path to economic growth that encouraged foreign investment, industrialization, and tourism, with relatively few regulations (including little protection for peasants, workers, or the environment)" (Wilson, 2004, p. 19).

Alternative Development in Northern Thailand

President Ronald Reagan's 1981 "Magic of the Market" speech at the North-South Conference in Mexico unofficially ushered in this neoliberal period and what is generally referred to as the "lost decade of development" (Mowforth and Munt, 2009, Esteva, 2007). Neoliberalism was introduced in a period of crisis during the Ronald Reagan and Thatcher era which helped it to gain support as a more efficient mode of economic development (Harvey, 2005). Structural adjustment programs were key aspects of this economic plan which were expected to rectify more than 30 years of inefficient development practice. While the concept of neoliberalism refers to a range of ideas, policies and practices, Ferguson notes how it invariably refers to "a valorization of private enterprise and suspicion of the state, along with what is sometimes called 'free-market fetishism' and the advocacy of tariff elimination, currency deregulation, and the deployment of 'enterprise models' that would allow the state itself to be 'run like a business'" (Ferguson, 2010, p. 170). Neoliberalism is both an economic practice and a philosophy that incorporates "a set of power relations that extends the logic of market relations across the entire social field. This means that, rather than mediating the tensions of the market, neoliberal government intervenes in society to create the necessary conditions for competitive markets and entrepreneurial conduct. The explicit task of governmental programs and strategies is to align social and ethical life with economic criteria and expectations" (Vrasti, 2011, p. 1). Hence, neoliberalism is characterized by free market principles including decentralization and privatization schemes, trickle down growth, the weakening of state interventions, and mergers between business and philanthropy. Moreover, "The central tenets of neoliberalism include the primacy of economic growth, the importance of free trade to stimulate growth, the unrestricted free market, individual choice, the reduction of government regulation, and the advocacy of an evolutionary model of social development anchored in the Western experience and applicable to the entire world" (Steger, 2009a, p. 10). This neoliberal logic has ushered in more than three decades of intensified decentralization and commodification schemes. Decentralization is a strategy that uncouples "'technical' questions of economics from the ideological concerns of 'politics' so that the logic of the market is presented as natural" (Mohan and Stokke, 2000, p. 251).

While NGOs contributed to social and economic development in Thailand well before neoliberalism took hold, their participation in development has become increasingly prevalent since the early 1980s. Rather than being institutionalized in foreign policy (such as the Peace Corps), contemporary international development volunteering is primarily carried out through NGOs and the private sector. NGOs symbolize the retreat of the state because they work to fill in where the state left off (Mosse, 2013). Essentially taking on the role of the state, NGOs are often welcomed by governments who see them as cost-effective development workers (Fechter and Hindman, 2011). Yet, as experience has shown, when NGOs expand and become "political," the state often feels threatened or becomes skeptical of the motivations of the NGOs and support quickly wanes. Additionally, while NGOs are lauded for their ability to work at the local or "grassroots" level, they are also critiqued for being inefficient and lacking the capacity to take over for state services. Thus, NGOs continue to work at the local level through privatized development and humanitarian schemes. As "Yudice asks: [might not] the effervescence of NGOs [be] cut two ways: helping to buttress a public sector evacuated by the state and at the same time making it possible for the state to steer clear of what was once see as its responsibility?" (Alvarez et al., 1998, p. 17).

While it is suggested that NGOs fill in the gaps left behind by state roll backs in developing countries, it may be argued that civil society institutions such as NGOs enable a state to function which otherwise would not have had the capacity to support its citizens (Dolhinow, 2005). In Thailand, civil society essentially bypasses the state and moves from non-performing development to civil society led development. Edelman and Haugerud observe how the budget cuts on social welfare, education and government agencies and the emerging importance of civil society organizations have contributed to the expansion of NGOs around the world (2005). Similarly, Kaldor suggests how "[I]n the absence of a global state, an army of NGOs … perform the functions necessary to smooth the path of economic globalization. Humanitarian NGOs provide the safety net to deal the casualties of liberalization and privatization strategies in the economic field" (Kaldor, 2003, p. 9). Thus, the shift to small scale, community development initiatives seems to emerge from the recognition that broader development initiatives have not only failed, but in many cases exacerbated poverty. As a result, the shift to "pro-poor" tourism development strategies is most aggressively pursued through NGOs.

NGOs become invested in "tourism with the aim of achieving socially appropriate tourism, which is defined as having community support and involving the host community in decision making (Hall, 1991). They aspire to benefit local (or host) communities directly and assist in providing real benefits that are ongoing within those communities and that can also be controlled at the local level" (Lyons and Wearing, 2008, p. 7). The growing trend of NGOs' involvement in tourism development is well noted (Broad and Spencer, 2008). These organizations tend to be at the center of development initiatives in developing countries and are often involved in a range of activities including "environmental education, the fostering of attitudes and behaviors that are conducive to maintaining natural and social environments and empowering local communities to operate and maintain sustainable approaches to industry such as tourism" (Lyons and Wearing, 2008, p. 7). Because NGOs are forced to compete for funding, they are often compelled to adhere to the agendas of donor agencies rather than the needs of the local community. As a result, NGOs are pressured to work within the market rather than against the market. Dolinhow shows how neoliberal agendas are perpetuated by a focus on individual needs, which ultimately limits the range of debate regarding collective action towards structural change. She explains how "as NGOs take on the provision of many services that previously existed in the domain of the state, they enter into a contradictory relationship. As they work to improve these communities abandoned by the state, they can become the conduit whereby neoliberal state policy enters marginalized communities" (Dolhinow, 2005, p. 558). The result of neoliberalism without state support does not work because it cannot contribute to the greatest good for the greatest number of people; it only has the capacity to help the community or the individual; this focus on the individual or community is the cornerstone of alternative tourism development agendas.

Thus, within neoliberal globalization, non-state actors such as NGOs "provide the safety net to deal with the casualties of liberalization and privatization strategies in the economic field" (Kaldor, 2003, p. 9). In recent years, governments themselves have been siphoning money towards NGOs, which have become increasingly responsible for the welfare of state citizens. While global civil society is a move away from state-centered to individual development schemes, it often depends on government support.

NGOs in Thailand face a number of difficulties because they are often not trusted and are actively criticized by the government and media. According to Viravaidya, the chairman and founder of the Population and Community Development Association (PDA), one of the longest running and most respected NGOs serving the rural poor in Thailand, government officials continue to be suspicious of NGOs and because of this suspicion, the government has set up multiple obstacles for the official institution of NGOs, such as limited tax incentives which are capped at two percent of their profits and impossible constraints on budgets which require only 30 percent or less to be spent on administrative expenses as well as forcing NGO spend at least 90 percent of their yearly income (Miller, 2009). For these reasons, most NGOs in Thailand are not officially registered with the state (none of the NGOs on which this research is based were officially registered in Thailand). Indeed, "Popular representations of NGOs and their members found in the press stress the radical, unruly and undisciplined nature of NGO members, most clearly defined in the image of the 'mob'" (Costa, 2001, p. 178). This may be in part because NGOs in Thailand are seen to be taking money from abroad (Miller, 2009). Despite limited participation from Thais and critiques from the Thai government, NGOs play an important role in Thailand as defenders of the environment and marginalized groups, especially in the provinces.

There are also several points of convergence between the transnational dimension of NGOs and the local articulation in Thailand. As Juree Vadit-Vadakan, the chairperson of the Center for Philanthropy and Civil Society (CPCS) of Thailand notes, "the transnational dimensions of NGOs constitutes a strength that equips them to promote international cooperation and popular support for a more ethical and caring world" (Miller, 2010, p. 125). While northern environmentalism seems to have monopolized the movement, the values and ethics of environmental concern that it is aligned with are conducive to Buddhist values and peoples' livelihood dependence on the environment in Thailand (Broad and Spencer, 2008). The relationship between global justice concerns and Buddhist values in Thailand is a notable symbiosis.

Alternative development can be understood as a critique against the modernization paradigm which advances an evolutionary and uni-linear approach to development as well as a neoliberal coping strategy. Its proponents suggest that locally managed and culturally specific development projects are more appropriate alternatives to state-led, trickle down policies which prefigured the development project. Yet, critics of alternative development ask what is alternative about alternative development (Bebbington and Bebbington, 2001,

Friedmann, 1992, Pieterse, 1998)? While alternative development used to mean "small is beautiful" and was led by the state, neoliberal versions of alternative development are primarily led by NGOs. Volunteer tourism is a materialization of this trend and presents itself as a remedy for the failures of earlier development paradigms, presenting a more locally based and culturally appropriate model. Late capitalist market trends including neoliberal policies that focus on privatization and decentralization and the end of the Euro-American Welfare State have ushered in what are seen as alternative development theories and practices intended to improve upon the dominant modernization and dependency theories.

In the late 1980s NGOs expanded in Thailand as a result of increased foreign assistance for various social, cultural and environmental causes including AIDS and environmental conservation (Rigg, 1991). In 1995 it was estimated that there were 2,547 NGOs in Thailand (Costa, 2001). Today there are more than 10,000 NGOs with thousands more unregistered organizations (Riska, 2010). NGOs first emerged in the late 1960s and were "gaining momentum in the 1980s and popular attention, both nationally and internationally, in the 1990s" (Costa, 2001, p. 162). The "father" of Thai NGOs, Dr Puey Ungpakorn, founded the Thai Rural Reconstruction Movement and the Graduate Volunteers Service at Thammasat University in 1967. NGOs have also been identified with Buddhism in Thailand and "constructed in this way, NGOs appear to exhibit what is often heralded as a 'core essence' of Thai culture (wathana: tham thai) and Thainess (khwa: mpenthai), i.e. merit-making through kindness and giving to others" (Costa, 2001, p. 176). While, in the 1980s and 90s, community based, small-scale initiatives were considered more effective than state sponsored development projects, the relative ineffectiveness of these development strategies have been brought to light (Bebbington et al., 2008). This is in part because NGOs usually provide practical, while obscuring strategic needs. Rather, the focus on "localism" seems to be most productive when it is coupled with and supported by both civil society and market-based relations (Bebbington and Bebbington, 2001). Without support from either of these arenas, an exclusive focus on the local is insufficient in making substantial changes, even at the "community" level. As Bebbington and Bebbington's study in highland Bolivia illustrates, alternative development paradigms tend to understate "the potential importance of the local state" (Bebbington and Bebbington, 2001, p. 7). Mohan and Stokke argue that what seems to be "required is 'a global sense of place' rather than conceptualizations of the local as discrete communities" (Mohan and Stokke, 2000, p. 264). When a balance between the civil, state and market is met, the participatory approach to environment and development planning opens up the possibility for more democratic and culturally appropriate development initiatives.

Catching up to the West ... Step by Step

While alternative and post-development interventions are popular among Western academics, teleological development paradigms that reflect modernization theory have retained their place in Thai development discourse. Modernization theory, the dominant development paradigm in the West until the late 1960s, is critiqued for promoting "a Western model of capitalist development which requires continued economic growth despite enormous costs to the environment, natural resources and human social life" (Costa, 2001, p. 153). The first National Development Plan paid little attention to the local community and instead suggested that development would be administered to the villages in a top down model. Essentially, modernization theory[5] was to be adapted to the Thai context where it was suggested that it was only a matter of time until the rural provinces would "catch up" with Bangkok and the country would "catch up" to the West. Echoing this widespread sentiment, Manop, the Thai orphanage worker, for example, believes that volunteer tourism is becoming increasingly popular because foreigners are realizing that Thailand is not yet "developed" in the North: "I think one reason [that more volunteers are coming] is about development. We must accept that Thailand is underdeveloped in this aspect. If the international volunteers come to help, it can help a lot." He suggests that the foreigners come to help Thailand develop: "We don't have self-development to the level that we should. When the foreigners see that certain changes need to happen, they come here to help with that ... They help make us modern like the West."

The seduction of the hegemonic discourse of development has had a continued presence in Thai identity and conceptions of self-worth. Shrestha demonstrates how in Nepalese society there had previously not been a distinction between the "developed" and "undeveloped" world. Yet, with the introduction of *Bikas* (modern things) like roads, airplanes and education, many people of his generation began to look down upon their parents' more traditional ways of life (Shrestha, 2002). Nepalese began to see how Westerners, such as Peace Corps volunteers, had material items that they too wanted to enjoy; today tourists can have a similar effect. This is at least in part because of the conspicuous economic differences between tourists and local people. As a result, it is often uncritically assumed by host community members that *Farang* can contribute to development because of their privileged economic and social positions. Additionally, some host community members believe that *Farang* have a responsibility to contribute to Thailand's development. For example, Tom, the *tuk-tuk* driver in Chiang Mai who frequently brings volunteers to a woman's shelter explains:

> ... [the volunteers] come from the basis that they have a secure job and surplus of money already and so they have enough surplus so they can help others. Suppose that you didn't have any money, and then you couldn't help anyone. And your family too. First everything else must be okay before you can help others. That is for the *Farang* they are okay with money and jobs so it is their turn to help Thailand catch up.

---

5   For more on modernization theory, see above.

Thai host community members involved in volunteer tourism tended to perceive Thailand as "under-developed," demonstrating how the discourse of development is internalized by host communities. This discourse is also negotiated within volunteer tourism, which is often seen by host community members as an encounter between the "developed" and "underdeveloped" world. As Manop comments:

> Thailand is developing step by step, but meanwhile, we must accept that our country Thailand is not a developed country. We are a developing country.

The discourse of Thailand "catching up" and developing "step by step" echoes modernization theory predictions about the end point of civilization which in part includes the separation of nature and culture. Shrestha shows how the discourse of development worked in his home country of Nepal as a second wave of colonization. He explains that so-called development came at the price of self-pride and self-reliance. Through development initiatives, people became increasingly estranged from the environment and development began to be "measured in terms of the distance between humans and nature. The greater the distance between the two ... the higher the level of development" (Shrestha, 2002, p. 274). This separation between nature and development is less clear in northern Thailand where environmental consciousness is deeply ingrained in society, partly as a result of Buddhist perspectives on the relationship between people and the natural environment.

Development Discourse and Popular Humanitarianism

Development discourse is critical to development practice as "dominant ideas about acceptable, normal, natural social relationships have profound implications for poverty" (Bebbington, 2007, p. 806). As Glynn, 26-year-old English volunteer suggests, the discourse of development and humanitarianism is becoming an increasingly popular among the current generation of college students.

> I think this international aid concept became popular recently. There have been studies for this subject for a long time, but the one, the concept of developing countries, it really—it's become popular recently ... and everyone wants to be a humanitarian these days ... and when people talk about development they want to show how worldly they are. Like talking about where they have traveled and for how long, especially in the Third World.

While the concept of the Third World is criticized within academia it continues to be a powerful semiotic operator in popular vernacular. Dirlik points out how the "continued use of the term also points to the persistence of the assumptions of modernisation discourse, which first gave birth to the Third World concept, and continues to shape thinking in both the everyday as well as the academic and political realms, even if it is no longer able to contain the forces at work in shaping the contemporary world" (Dirlik, 2004, p. 132).

The popularity of development and humanitarian discourse among young people in the Global North contributes to the ongoing discursive construction of the Third World. In what way does the so-called "Third World" exist? For many Westerners, the concept of the Third World conjures up images of poverty, starvation and disease, which often simultaneously evokes sympathy and fear (Mowforth and Munt, 2009). While these images are called upon in the popular media to represent the Third World, when Western volunteers come to Thailand, they often suggest that the images do not match their experience and that Thailand does not seem like a "real" Third World country. For example, Carol, a 68-year-old Canadian volunteer exclaims: "I really went to a Third World country!" Yet, she goes on to say, "I mean I never really considered Thailand the Third World." For Carol, Thailand did not match up to her expectations about what a Third World country would be like. What experiences like Carol's suggest is that preconceptions of the Third World are sometimes contested through lived experience. Tourism in developing countries can play a powerful role in helping to dissolve misguided preconceptions—often an indirect outcome of alternative tourism development. Like other ideological concepts such as globalization, development and modernity, the Third World is actively negotiated at the local and interpersonal level where the "reality" of the experience often comes into stark contrast to one's expectations. As Glynn, a 24-year-old English volunteer explains, common perceptions of "underdeveloped" countries can also deter potentially unworldly volunteers. When asked why he thought his friends who were interested in volunteer tourism did not volunteer abroad, he explained that in addition to commitments at home, people were often not willing to go to "underdeveloped" countries:

> It's a lot of things. You got work, you friends, you got family. If you are volunteering, you are choosing an underdeveloped country which some people didn't like that. But it is not really dangerous, maybe unclean, dirty and really long hours.

The geographical imaginations of volunteer tourists are often remapped through their experience in Thailand where the Third World begins to look very different to what they had imagined. Volunteers often spend their first couple of weeks in Thailand adjusting to the cultural, economic and social differences. These differences tend sometimes to result in "culture shock" which is gradually overcome with time and increased familiarity with Thai culture. Discussions of these differences are commonplace among volunteers who suggest that, while Thailand is a developing country, in many ways the "Thai" way might actually be better than the "Western" way. For example, one 24-year-old Danish volunteer comments on the differences in the transportation system and the Danish ethic of being "on time":

Just the way the buses run in Denmark that is so much different than they run in Thailand. [In Denmark] it's so much more scheduled and planned. And if the bus is five minutes late [in Thailand], you just wait. And if it's five minutes late, this is not even late, there isn't any bus schedule and you are just late. And if you are five minutes late to an appointment, the other one you are meeting with is probably 10 minutes late. This is really how it is and that's definitely a Danish culture thing that you are on time. And if you are not, you are going to call and it's always planning, it's always on time.

Noticing differences in the educational system was often a culture shock to the volunteers, who usually came from upper-middle-class backgrounds and were working towards or had completed at least a bachelor's degree. Many volunteers were surprised at how interested their students were in school and compared this to their own culture, where they suggested students often take their education for granted. Ann, a 19-year-old Dutch volunteer explains:

They are so willing to learn. They really appreciate school. It's really different in Thailand. They love education. That's all they have. It is a cultural thing I guess. But they have a more authentic lifestyle. That is what makes them happy.

Yet, they simultaneously vented their frustration about the difference in education styles. Alex, for example, a 22-year-old American volunteer and Ann observe what they perceive as substandard education and describe how they would like to contribute to its improvement:

Alex: They are smaller schools, so they don't get their funding so it's pretty bad.

Ann: Makes me want to do something about it.

Alex: Its maybe the Thai culture. In most of my classes, like my English teacher showing up an hour late to class, I mean it's weird. And they don't say anything.

Ann: It doesn't matter. I could not show up and they won't do anything. I volunteered there for to 2 weeks. It's phenomenal. I mean people come in 20 minutes late and people are talking in groups at the back. It's definitely different.

Alex: I learned about the differences in the world. What I have and what they don't have. And that's really the educational part.

These contradictory emotions around the superiority of Thai culture and the need for development were constantly negotiated throughout the volunteer tourism experience (see Chapter 6 for more on these contradictions).

English as the Lingua Franca of Global Capitalism

While host community members' interests around volunteer tourism vary by level of interaction, knowledge and experience with the volunteers, "development" is a common theme that seems to permeate descriptions of their experience. This focus on "development" by host community members is reflective of the structural inequalities on which the encounter is based. Development is understood in its economic and social connotations. Reference to economic development in terms of employment and financial benefits is a major interest of host community members who have the opportunity to benefit financially from their involvement. Understood in this way, English language education is also an important aspect of "development" that straddles the different, yet related schemas of "social" and "economic" development. This is at least in part because English language proficiency is perceived to be both a symbol of "modernity" as well as a skill that opens up employment opportunities—most notably in the tourism sector. Moreover, the emphasis on English—the lingua franca of global capitalism—is symbolic of the ways that economic structural inequalities mediate and are reflected in social and cultural worlds.

For example, interactions between volunteers and host community members depend significantly on their ability to communicate. It is notable that none of the volunteers that I conducted my research with spoke Thai except for a few phrases generally limited to "thank you," "hello," "bathroom," "spicy," "I don't want," "yes," "no" and "photo." The extent of verbal communication between the host community members and volunteers depended, to a large extent, on the English language abilities of the host community members—the majority of which did not speak English except for common phrases such as "hello," "what is your name?" and "where are you from?" For example, when I asked Anchali, a Thai NGO practitioner at Orchard Home how often she talked with or met international volunteers she responded: "Well, we don't really talk that much. We introduce ourselves and then talk a little bit. We greet each other. If I wanted to talk a lot, I don't think I could because I can't really speak English." The inability to speak English was interpreted by both host community members and volunteers as an inability to engage with modernity.

English as Social Development

The concept of social development and its most common referent—English language education—demands further analysis (see Chapter 6). For most volunteers, the value of learning English is clearly understood. It is seen as a way to realize well-paid employment, join the educated class and advance socially among one's peers. For example, Glynn explains:

> The easiest way to take people out of poverty is to teach them English. In most countries tourism jobs require English. Maybe, in addition to their education, that could help them and their family in the long run.

Similarly, John, 19, from Ireland notes:

> Well they get, I mean they get to learn a different language, English, which can actually help them in the future help them better their lives, maybe start a business. They can learn English. They can get a business while interacting with other English speakers. It can help, I mean for one, a lot of these villagers and the children are moving out and they need a future generation and by the children moving out, they are actually, they will make the village collapse in the future. Look, I am actually doing this all to get the kids interested to stay [in the village] by opening up job opportunities and teaching them job skills so they'll want to stay here and want to get involved and maybe carry out businesses of their own or make programs such as this, or get involved in future programs. So, overall benefit, the village as whole benefits, especially this generation now, because their knowledge of surrounding lands and the vegetation and animals benefits us and we can work together that way. Otherwise the kids might move away, they'd rather, maybe they want to stay here, learn this knowledge from the older people in the village and put it to use in these programs and also benefit them and give them jobs.

While many NGOs have goals that are global in scope, their strategies of realizing these goals are limited by economic and infrastructural capacities, which is one reason many organizations focus on teaching English as their primary "development" strategy. TT comments that "Teaching English as a foreign language is one of the most challenging and rewarding experiences we can offer our volunteers. For this reason English teaching remains our most popular programme" (Hale, 2004). The organization further observes that their English language programs have been well received in host communities such as Buddhist monasteries, orphanages or schools for underprivileged children. They believe that the best help that the volunteers can give a country is an English education. BV similarly offers opportunities for volunteers to teach English to local village children:

> Teach rural Thai students English and help contribute to an education that will provide them with the experience and skills necessary to become managers of this maturing ecotourism business. You will have the opportunity to teach English to village children in nearby village classrooms and/or as an Eco English camp facilitator at the ... Lodge Outdoor Education and Research Center (Borderless Berry, 2009).

English is widely perceived as a "passport to development" by volunteer tourism participants. Cindy, a 19-year-old volunteer from Holland notes how volunteer tourism "will definitely internationalize other countries. For instance the children learn English all day, and the women learn English. It is the language they should speak to communicate." Similarly, a 23-year-old volunteer from England explains: "In most developing countries the easiest way to take people out of poverty is to teach them English. In most countries tourism jobs require English. It might be an addition to their education that could help them and their family in the long run"

Fluency in English is representative of Western modernity and development for most Thai host community members. All of the host community members who participated in this study suggest that the most important contribution that *Farang* can offer them is English. For example, Pom, a 27-year-old housekeeper at an ecotourism village that hosts volunteers explained to me how the most important change she would like to see in five years is her ability to speak English. If she can speak English she will be able to talk with the international volunteers and may even be able to become a trekking guide. In a similar vein, Noi, a 40-year-old Thai host community member at the women and children's home explained:

> I think that [the volunteers] want to help Orchard Home to improve and develop and to help the women learn and to help them learn how to speak English. Before, some people didn't know how to speak anything. Now they know some English. We are learning to develop like the Westerners. We can talk to them now. Step by step we develop and catch up.

I have known Noi since 2007 and every time I see her she is delighted to demonstrate her improved English language proficiency. She tells me about her experiences, especially about how and where she speaks English. For example, in 2010 Noi explained to me how learning English has allowed the women to sell stuff at the market:

> Before there wasn't anyone to teach English. They didn't know how to sell stuff at the market. But now they know how to sell stuff at the market and they have started to like selling stuff at the market. They can earn money. Now they know that if they invest their money they can make a profit. English is what allows us to develop so we can earn money to buy nice things like the *Farang*.

This observation seems to concur with her assumptions about English and its development potential.

English language as development is an under theorized observation given its centrality in volunteer tourism. The widespread understanding of English as development has critical implications in Thailand and beyond. For example, in Nepal, Shrestha shows how Peace Corps volunteers motivated local young people to learn English as it was an important signifier of *Bikas* (Western modernity). In the context of Thailand Wilson shows how English names are used in shopping malls in Bangkok where "preference for English points to its hegemonic role in signifying modernity" (Wilson, 2004, p. 48). She further explains how "English reflects the orientation of elites in the multicultural city of Bangkok. Thais often convey this appeal by saying the English term sounds 'nice'" (Wilson, 2004, p. 48). The power of English fluency to demonstrate full acceptance into modernity and access to the West and Westerners is hard to overstate. NGOs, volunteer tourism and other non-governmental aid organizations have focused on English education as a core signifier of development in Thailand. Yet, as many of the NGO practitioners suggest, the capacity for volunteers to effectively teach English is questionable. Despite this, they have observed that the interactions between the host community members and the international volunteers are substantial contributions to cross-cultural understanding—which they perceive as an important aspect of volunteer tourism.

"Pro-Poor" and "Pro-Local"

NGOs' role in social and economic development has renewed interest in local grassroots development in Thailand as well as created new possibilities and limitations for development practice. McKinnon observes "how the development community in northern Thailand where these organizations embraced a 'pro-local' discourse in response to the challenges presented to development through a critique informed by post-colonialism. In the process, development professionals have contributed to significant changes in the landscape of development practice in northern Thailand" (McKinnon, 2006, p. 23). Pro-localism in Thailand has had simultaneously enabling and disenabling implications for local people. The current generation of development professionals in northern Thailand has almost uniformly adopted a pro-local position which is a reaction against postcolonial and post-structural critiques of the modernization paradigm. McKinnon explains how "[D]evelopment professionals in northern Thailand have engaged with post-colonial debates, and emerging participatory development approaches, to reconfigure their role within development in the highlands. In doing so, they draw on longstanding discourse of the professional as an emancipatory agent, emerging post-colonial critiques of 'First World'—'Third World' relations and recent movements towards participatory approaches in development practice" (McKinnon, 2006, p. 24).

Pro-local development in northern Thailand articulates with "pro-poor development" in ways that make development in Chiang Mai a unique blend of both local and transnational development discourses. Spencer explains that "pro-poor growth is defined as that which allows poor people to actively participate in and benefit from economic activity. It theoretically represents a significant departure from the trickle-down development concept as economic growth forms only part of the development process along with social factors such as everyone having access to minim basic capabilities" (Smith, 1997, p. 42). It is notable that volunteer tourism, in particular, seems to "channel tourism dollars to places that aren't usually featured in glossy travel brochures and don't have the infrastructure to support three-star, let alone four- or five-star, hotels" (Fitzpatrick, 2007). Additionally, "[F]or scenic places desperately in need of economic development, 'this kind of tourism is an easier sell,' says Kristin Lamoureux, director of the International Institute for Tourism Studies at George Washington University" (Fitzpatrick, 2007). As a consequence, organizations like the World Bank actively support pro-poor tourism development projects through institutions such as the International Finance Corporation and the Multilateral Investment Guarantee Agency (Babu, 2008, Pryce, 1998).

While alternative approaches to development can be seen as a response to the failed promises of modernization, they also speak to the increasing recognition of the different experiences between the First and Third World and within the Third World itself. They also show how localized political, economic and cultural specificities need to be reexamined as crucial to the potential successes of the development project. Yet, an overemphasis on the local presents its own challenges as McKinnon's study of three projects in northern Thailand shows, the pro-local position also runs the risk of being closed off to international development professionals and aid which could assist local communities in their struggles (McKinnon, 2006). Additionally, such risks include the tendency to ignore local political struggles, contribute to the further disengagement of local communities from global networks and the inability to realize structural change. Consequently, Thailand's renewed focus on the local has been criticized for weakening links between the state, civil society and the market. Yet, despite these critiques, the pro-local stance has also had many positive implications in Thailand. For example, "increased political liberalism, along with the growing participatory orthodoxy in northern Thailand and worldwide has allowed what was in the late 1980s a very small movement of highland activism, supported by a handful of pro-local professionals, to emerge as a significant and independent voice in national level debates" (McKinnon, 2006, p. 30).

The Ninth National and Social Economic Development Plan (2001–06) responds to these critiques through the application of the King's philosophical principles related to the "sufficiency economy." The sufficiency economy is guided by reference to the middle path or the Buddhist eight fold path to achieve Nirvana and foregrounds the importance of moderation and sustainability. As both a policy and way of life, the sufficiency economy is to be realized through balanced development and "was to be achieved through a combination of patience, perseverance, diligence, wisdom and prudence. The four pillars of this holistic approach of the ninth plan are social protection, competitiveness, governance, and environmental protection" (Nations, 2010). The Tenth National Development Plan (2007–11) advances the King's Sufficiency Economy philosophy and the explicit preference for middle path and sustainable development. The goals are also in line with the "Green and Happiness Society" and people-centered development schemes. As an "alternative" development paradigm, it focuses on civil society and accommodates Thai cultural precepts. For example, four main objectives of the Tenth Plan include: "1) developing the people to be knowledgeable and to have good moral standards, 2) promoting equality and strengthening the society, 3) reforming economic structure for sustainability and fairness, and 4) developing good governance as a norm at all levels" (Foreign Office, 2006). These goals reflect growing concerns for the environment and sustainability. The Eleventh Plan (2012–16) is strongly influenced by "pro-poor" initiatives that are based on the philosophy of the sufficiency economy and the "Happiness Society." Civil society and the private sector are considered key aspects of social and economic development for this period.

Over the past 15 years, NGOs have become the primary actors in alternative and sustainable tourism development in Thailand. NGOs are especially notable players in volunteer tourism because it fits within their current organizational structure of volunteered labor. Lyons and Wearing argue that NGOs are best able to include indigenous and host community participation in volunteer tourism development (Lyons et al., 2012). Neoliberal emphases on local management and the corollary rapid increase of NGOs contribute to the growing economic and social importance of ecotourism development. NGOs in Thailand tend to embrace what Costa refers to as culturalist approaches to development. Implicated in culturalist approaches to development are the assumptions that "1) a gap continues to exist between the global poor and scholar/critics now heralding the 'post-development' era (ibid.), 2) that power in local Thai contexts is understood differently than in the West, and 3) that the discourse of development is more powerful than is typically understood" (Costa, 2001, p. 192). Thus, CAD explicitly resists Western development schemes that fail to consider the local cultural context. This may, in part be because of the "widespread concern among NGO members that development based on Western models of aggregate growth and capital accumulation had caused environmental degradation, social disintegration and mass poverty particularly among farmers. Similarly, these models of development were also thought to be grounded in Western cultural models which favored capitalism, individualism and secularism" (Costa, 2001, p. 189). Yet, there remains a simultaneous confidence in development that is generally perceived to come from outside Thailand.

While social and economic development is often the unambiguous goal of volunteer organizations, there is often a fear by the volunteers that this development can all too easily slip into a form of Westernization. This fear that Thailand may be becoming too Westernized is described by many volunteers who observe that Thai people have adopted Western technologies, attitudes and styles. For example, when asked how she thought Thailand benefited from international volunteers, Carol, the 67-year-old volunteer from Canada commented that she and her husband, Sam were worried about Thai people adopting some of the negative qualities of Western culture:

> The only thing that scares me about this is like … we're talking to a Thai person and they were saying that some of the Western ideas are being taken over here.

Oh, my God, like I don't want that to happen. Take some of the positive that we have to offer, yes but this man was talking about some of the rudeness that the Westerners have are being adopted by Thai people. Sam and I are going like, "Wow! We don't want that to happen." Let them get our good qualities that we have to offer, but certainly not negative ones ... you see them with the cell phones and the computers, I guess they want to become modernized but I hope not so much so where they want to lose their culture. So I wouldn't like to see it becoming too Westernized because I think our values suck in many ways, right? There's bigger and better things and toys and many, many, many ... and we don't see that here. People are hard workers, they work for very little. They appreciate what they have and what they're doing.

Similarly, noting that while she wanted to see the education system improve, Ann stated: "I hope they don't become too Westernized with iPods and video games and stuff." Mather's account of American study abroad volunteers in Africa suggests that this simultaneous fear of the Third World becoming to Westernized while still needing development is not isolated to Thailand but instead may be a more general way Westerners discursively negotiate their relationship to the Third World. Mathers describes how:

The stories that Americans tell about travel to Africa all follow a similar trajectory. First, Africa is a mess, people are devastated, AIDS is killing them, and economic hardship seems to control their lives. Second, despite this poverty (or maybe because of it), there is so much good. People are working tirelessly to overcome the awfulness; there is kindness, laughter, smiles, all apparently so unlikely amid the mess (Barnett, 2005, p. 155).

This perception was not altogether disrupted by host community members who generally suggested that they had culture but the Westerners had development and could bring development to them. For example, when asked why she thought *Farang* like Thailand, Pim, a 32-year-old Thai mother explained:

I think it is because they are bored with their lives in the city. The traffic jams, or other life obstacles. Their lives are comfortable but here there is nature. There aren't any traffic jams or pollution. We have culture and nature and even though life is simple we can enjoy our lives. Farang have fancy things and electronics but we have Thai culture.

Culturalist models of development emphasize "going 'back to the roots,' to 'core' Thai culture and values and taking control of a development process which has spun terribly out of control" (Costa, 2001). There is a widespread belief among northern Thais that "'the solution is in the village' (Suthy 1995; Jaturong 1995; Nonaka 1993)" and "CAD supporters criticize development projects in which villagers are allowed no role in decision making and planning" (Costa, 2001, p. 192).

Even interaction with *Farang* was seen as development by many host community members. Making friends with Westerners has become an important symbol of modernity. Many host community members mentioned how their social status was buttressed by their new *Farang* associates. They also suggested that their newfound friendships with Western volunteers contributed to their communities' overall social development. For example, one host community member suggests that once the volunteers started coming to her village, the village became more "developed." By this she means that she and several of the other villagers and the children were now able to mingle with the Westerners. Manop:

> They are not scared anymore. The villagers talk with *Farang* and are friends with *Farang*. They are not scared of *Farang* anymore. In the past they were frightened but now we are more developed. More brave like the *Farang* ... Because they help encourage the children to get used to foreigners and so they won't be self-conscious. If they can develop these skills they will benefit. It is good for them. They will be able interact with foreigners like other people. Normally, Thai children or average Thai children, when they are around foreigners, most of them will be scared. Being close with them is enough for them to get used to it. It is natural.

When further asked if he thought that this interaction with the foreigners was as important as learning English, he commented:

> I think that maybe it is even more important because when the children have a close relationship with the foreigners the children will become brave and interact with the foreigners (by speaking), they will naturally gain their English language skill. But if they are not confident enough to speak, not get to know the foreigners, they will not dare [to speak English]. When they are familiar enough with the foreigners, it is easier for them to communicate [in English].

Manop's comments suggest that the opportunity to learn English, become comfortable around Westerners and in some cases, befriend them are all important aspects of host community members' discourse of "development."

Whether volunteer tourism ultimately contributes to development practice continues to be debated by researchers who highlight "[Q]uestions around long-term strategy, along with questions on the appropriateness and impact of volunteers, appear to be missing for the majority of ... programmes" (Simpson, 2004, p. 685). What is certain is that volunteer tourism contributes in unique ways to contemporary development discourse for all participants. It is also a site for the rearticulation of development discourse where the meaning of "development" does not go uncontested by its participants who sometimes engage with contradictory development discourses within development practice. In the following chapter, *Cosmopolitan Empathy, New Social Movements and the Moral Economy of Volunteer Tourism*, I expand on this discussion by examining what I refer to as an emerging cosmopolitan empathy in volunteer tourism. This empathy is a corollary of the cultural logic and economic policies of neoliberal global capitalism where structural inequality is met with individual sentimentality rather than state-centered development schemes. I show how the active participation of globally conscious individuals has contributed to increased support *and* commodification of new social movements which unassumingly contribute to the continued expansion of neoliberal capitalism through the progressive privatization of humanitarian development.

Chapter 4

Cosmopolitan Empathy, New Social Movements and the Moral Economy of Volunteer Tourism

In 2006, Time Magazine named 'YOU' person of the year. Arguing that the Internet and social network sites had facilitated the emergence of 'community of collaboration on a scale never seen before,' the magazine went to celebrate Web 2.0's revolutionary political possibilities, suggesting that the new Web demonstrated 'the many wresting power from the few,' which might lead to 'a new kind of international understanding' (Hearn, 2012, p. 23).

This YOU is regularly called upon in volunteer tourism where consumers are metaphorically and literally asked: "Feel like saving the world this week?" (Let's Go Publications, 2010). Western tourists now regularly respond to this question in their engagement with chronic poverty, literacy challenges and climate change as international volunteer tourists in the Global South. Popular media outlets such as guidebooks, magazines and online blogs identify volunteer tourism as an important player in this emerging "community of collaboration" where there is a conscious effort by participants to engage with ideas like world peace, human rights and fair trade.

In this chapter I examine the connection between what I call cosmopolitan empathy with new social movements and volunteer tourism. The alternative, moral, or ethical consumption industry has become an increasingly potent, if sometimes contradictory force in global justice that "can be understood as opening up ethical and political considerations in new combinations" (Barnett et al., 2005, p. 23). I explore these navigations by situating volunteer tourism and its participants within the broader expansion of what Mukherjee and Banet-Weiser refer to as commodity activism. The concept of commodity activism:

> helps provide the means for understanding how economic relations and the workings of capitalism have transformed public life, concepts of citizenship, social movements, and the nature of political action itself ... thus engaging with the crucial and ever difficult question of what gets to count as activism, and constitutes social and cultural resistance (Sturken, 2012, p. x).

I engage with "new theoretical frameworks that refuse the traditional and nostalgic binaries that position politics in opposition to consumerism" and consider how "neoliberal capitalism both enables and confounds modes of social activism at the present moment" (Hearn, 2012, p. 13). Volunteer tourism, I argue, is a specific kind of product within emerging moral economies in the West that stretches our imagination about the possibility of how neoliberalism articulates with new social movements as well as how it simultaneously limits the radical horizon of our activism.

Cosmopolitan Empathy

Cosmopolitan empathy refers to an emotional response to the plight of the poor in the Global South. Today, this ambiguously defined focus of commoditized concern is largely acted upon through consumer choice. While there is nothing new about suggesting that people feel empathetic for those beyond their own borders, there *is* something decidedly new about the broadening range and increasing intensity at which these motivations materialize within increasingly transnational commodity landscapes (Mostafanezhad, 2013a). To that end, volunteer tourism is a unique form of commodity activism that brings together the producer (host community members) and the consumer (volunteers). The globalization of the media as well as new transportation technologies have encouraged people to feel intimate with, compassionate towards and responsible for the well-being of people in countries in which they are not citizens. Coupled with neoliberal policies and practices including the privatization and commodification of global justice agendas as well as Western humanitarian discourse, these experiences gave rise to cosmopolitan empathy, which mediates the volunteer tourism experience. While volunteer tourism supporters situate the practice within broader global justice agendas, in an ironic sleight of hand, these goals are co-opted by the market in ways that rearticulate in a particularly neoliberal fashion. Indeed, "the ways in which international volunteering seems to both exemplify neoliberal ideas of individual autonomy, improvement and responsibility and at the same time allies itself to notions of collective global citizenship, solidarity, development and activism" (Baillie Smith and Laurie, 2011, p. 545).

Cosmopolitanism describes "an ethos, 'a habit of the mind,' a set of loyalties to humanity [as] a whole, to be inculcated through a distinctive educational program emphasizing the commonalities and responsibilities of global citizenship" (Harvey, 2000, p. 530). Beck points out how "'[C]osmopolitan' refers to the 'global player,' the 'imperial capitalist,' or 'middle-class intellectual without local roots,' and as such is a loaded concept" (Beck et al., 2003, p. 16). Clifford suggests that "the term cosmopolitanism, separated from its (European) universalist moorings, quickly becomes a traveling signifier, a term always in danger of breaking up into partial equivalences: exile, immigration, migrancy, diaspora, border crossing, pilgrimage, tourism" (Clifford, 1998, p. 363). Similarly, Robbins notes how:

The willingness to consider the well-being of people who do not belong to the same nation as you is not ... something that is mysteriously pre-given by the simple fact of belonging to the human species. Larger loyalties can either be there or not be there. They have to be built up laboriously out of imperfect historical materials—churches and mosques, commercial interests and immigrant diasporas, sentimentality about hungry children and technorapture over digitalized communication—that are already at hand. They do not stand outside of history like an ultimate court of appeal (Robbins, 1998, p. 6).

Yet, cosmopolitanism may be more accurately described in the plural form, as "cosmopolitanisms," to account for the range of historical experiences that the term connotes. Noting the limitations of a singular "cosmopolitanism," Robbins points out how:

The 'very old ideal of cosmopolitanism,' in Martha Nussbaum's words, referred to 'the person whose allegiance is to the worldwide community of human beings,' [yet,] according to this ideal, there could be only one cosmopolitanism, for there is only one 'worldwide community of human beings' (Robbins, 1998, p. 2).

"Counter cosmopolitanisms" (Harvey, 2000) or alternative cosmopolitanisms emerged in opposition to mainstream conceptualizations of cosmopolitanism. Examples include Hollinger and Cohen's cosmopolitanism as "rooted" (Robbins, 1998) as well as Asian (Ong, 1998, Schein, 1998) and African (Appiah, 1997, Appiah, 2006, Malcomson, 1998) cosmopolitanisms (Robbins, 1998). Cosmopolitanism, particularly as it articulates with humanitarian discourses, shapes the volunteer tourism experience. The experience is mediated by promotional materials that promise global citizenship. For example, one international volunteering guidebook explains:

Today ... one story dominates, and it is spreading around the world. It portrays us humans as narrow materialists, ego-encapsulated consumers, ultimately driven by our own selfishness to endlessly accumulate. We, all of us, must be willing to jump out of the water in order to see that this story is a shabby caricature of human nature. And when we do, we will also begin to see the truly diverse range that is human possibility ... Only then can we choose—hopefully—that which is truer, more and more life-serving. Leaving the knowns of our own culture—through proactive action such as volunteering overseas can give us the tools to be helpful at the level our planet now needs ("How to Live Your Dream of Volunteering Overseas," *An International Volunteering Guidebook*, Collins et al., 2002, p. xii).

Media rearticulate discourses of humanitarianism and construct an "imaginary of moral relationships" (Tester, 2010, p. viii). Tester argues that what he calls "common-sense humanitarianism" or the "hegemonic form of humanitarianism … becomes very dubious once an interpretative unpicking begins; it appears to rest on myths and, more insidiously, the vestiges of a distinctly imperial mindset, which established the West as the only right actor in the world" (Tester, 2010, p. ix). How well-intentioned volunteer tourists, global justice activists and commodity activism navigate within this global political order is still being worked out on the local, national and global stage.

Volunteers are usually well-educated, affluent and globally conscious individuals. When asked about the recent expansion of volunteer tourism, they often allude to the globalization of media and communication technologies that allow people in the West to learn about and participate in volunteer projects in developing countries. For example, Martin, a 20-year-old German volunteer explained that volunteer tourism has emerged: "[B]ecause globalization is going on and Thailand is not excluded from globalization … every country moves in a certain way. Everything gets globalized." Similarly, John, an 18-year-old volunteer from Ireland suggests how English is one way host community members can participate in global culture:

> I guess in this new age, the people have become open minded to new cultures and with that they've grown to realize that we function as one world, we all have to work as one actually we can't stand alone anymore and such and that by getting involved with other countries by helping we can understand each other, interact each other, function as a better world as a whole through volunteering and giving back. Yeah so, I mean by teaching people English, helping them in that way you get them involved in the world not just, so they are situated by themselves or from the rest of the world but they get involved, they get to see different part of the world and so they can better their lives or I guess better the way they live I mean English may not be a necessity as such but as things are going and with kids moving out it'll help them a lot with business and life they'll be available to make this business and have interaction with more people and have fun and its and there's, maybe they might want to travel eventually and share their culture with all the other people overseas in different countries and it's just kind of bringing the world together in a closer way.

Yet, this desire to help "the world" is not limited to Western volunteers. Indeed, many host community members and Thai NGO practitioners similarly recognized the need for people to help the less fortunate. For example, Vadit-Vadakan, the Chairperson of the Center for Philanthropy and Civil Society (CPCS) of Thailand, explains how "NGOs should provide a counter-model to society in which ethics and human decency as well as values, compassion, sharing, and selflessness should be the founding principles for a different approach to life." "I believe," she continues, "that NGOs could raise the consciousness of the rich and the 'the haves' about the plight of the poor and the 'have-nots'" (Miller, 2010, p. 125). Similarly, Manit, a host community member and orphanage manager explains:

Everyone in this world, we should all help each other. We shouldn't just choose some people depending on the country and only help them develop and not be interested in other countries. That would not be fair because now that we are completely global, we should all help each other by communicating and exchanging ideas about social development, the environment or whatever.

When further asked if he thought others thought similarly he suggested:

They should think like this. Every country should think like this, it should be the goal of every country to be able to totally cooperate together. This is something that would be very good. Some people can help. But only some people. Other people, it depends on their education level and understanding. But not everyone thinks the same way as everyone else. But most people probably think in this same direction ... trying to help others who have less opportunities.

In volunteer tourism, cosmopolitanism emerges in varied ways. Lyons et al. suggests that "[C]osmopolitanism, and the global citizenship it infers, requires that an individual be able to negotiate a world full of diverse interests while developing a personal narrative that is inclusive of the 'other,' thus internalising a sense of global homogeneity and shared humanity" (Lyons et al., 2012, p. 364). While host community members recognize the need for moral action on the part of the haves on behalf of the have-nots, they also articulate this concern in ways that diverge from the volunteer tourists' experience of "giving-back," the commodification of which is described by many host community members as incomprehensible.

Unlike host community members, Western NGO practitioners usually have extensive experience in developing countries. Eric, the founder of Borderless Volunteers, was two years old when his family moved from Ireland to South Africa. He grew up in South Africa and joined the army at the age of 16. In the army, he lived in several different countries, and by 1984 he made Thailand his permanent home. He explains, "I'm probably British. My children are Thai-ish ... I am really a global citizen. My family and I cover almost every corner of the globe. I feel just as much Thai as I do Irish." Eric's story is not uncommon. Jen, a 28-year-old volunteer coordinator from Los Angeles explains how she had lived abroad for more than five years prior to coming to Thailand. She often spoke of her previous residence in Uganda where she worked for a development agency. She often reminisced about the food, the men and the night life that occupied her time there. One night at an Italian restaurant in town she noted matter of factly: "this may sound corny but I feel like a citizen of the world." In this way, the sense of cosmopolitan responsibility is met with the articulation of cosmopolitan identity formations. This is in part because global citizenship and cosmopolitanism are "processes rather than end points [that] reveal the contingent and multilayered ways subjectivities evolve and are performed through international volunteering" (Baillie Smith et al., 2012, p. 127). These cosmopolitan identity formations contribute to notions of "global citizenship." For example, it is commonly believed that "travel to other cultures—to learn about them—is a strong underpinning of the cosmopolitan sensibility and perhaps the best way for individuals to outwardly demonstrate their claims to global citizenship" (Lyons et al., 2012, p. 363).

Western humanitarian interventions have a long, sordid history in non-Western countries. The historical legacy of missionaries, colonialism, war and pillage are not easily forgotten, and today moral interventions are often met with skepticism by local people. NGO interventions emerge out of this legacy as the most prominent signifier of universal morality of our time. Commenting on this history, Hardt and Negri demonstrate how:

> The arsenal of legitimate force for imperial intervention is indeed already vast, and should include not only military intervention but also other forms such as moral intervention and juridical intervention. In fact, the Empire's powers of intervention might be best understood as beginning not directly with its weapons of lethal force but rather with its moral instruments. What we are calling moral intervention is practiced today by a variety of bodies, including the news media and religious organizations, but the most important may be some of the so-called non-governmental organizations (NGOs), which, precisely because they are not run directly by governments, are assumed to act on the basis of ethical or moral imperatives … such humanitarian NGOs are in effect (even if this runs counter to the intentions of its participants) some of the most powerful pacific weapons of the new world order—the charitable campaigns and the mendicant orders of Empire. These NGOs conduct 'just wars' without arms, without violence, without borders (Hardt and Negri, 2000, pp. 35–6).

NGOs that use volunteer tourism as a strategy from which to develop their own "moral-missions-without-borders" capitalize on tourists that have moral aspirations while on holiday. Heins argues that "to the extent that NGOs are symptomatic for a fundamental change, they signal the shift away from a politics based on national and class interest to a politics based on moral values and emotions. NGOs epitomize the rise of an 'other-regarding' ethic that is increasingly taking hold in Western societies, often cutting across the divide between governmental and nongovernmental forces" (Heins, 2008, p. 1). New tourism is especially associated with the expanding role of new social movements and associated with broader socio-economic shifts in Western societies (Babu, 2008, p. 189). For example, as Mowforth and Munt observe how "a pseudo-ethical and moral infrastructure underpins the growth of Third World tourism (Lea 1993), with new middle-class tourists (or travelers) contrasting their morally justifiable means of travel with the morally reprehensible practices of tourists" (Mowforth and Munt, 2009, p. 141). Similarly, Vrasti explains how "[B]eing 'at home in the world' is no longer the mark of the cosmopolitan aristocracy, like in the days of the nineteenth-century Grand Tour, but a requirement for all workers who wish to enter the ranks of the middle class" (Vrasti, 2012, p. 130). Indeed, volunteer tourists often distinguish themselves from mainstream tourists through their moral superiority (Butcher, 2010).

New Social Movements, Global Justice and Volunteer Tourism

Unprecedented global economic, social and environmental inequalities have given rise to the global justice movement which may constitute the most substantial threat to market globalism.[1] Global justice politics are based on issues of globalization and their implications for global society and the environment (Steger, 2009a, Huntington, 1996, Huntington, 1993, Escobar, 2004, Escobar, 1995, Alvarez et al., 1998). Steger (2009) explains how "at the center of the justice-globalist critique of the dominant paradigm lies the unshakable conviction that the liberalization and global integration of markets leads to greater social inequalities, environmental destruction, the escalation of global conflicts and violence, the weakening of participatory forms of democracy, the proliferation of self-interest and consumerisms, and the further marginalization of the powerless around the world" (p. 128). Consequently, the global justice movement is a significant challenger to the hegemony of neoliberal capitalism. Several transnational organizations have used global justice networks to resist market globalism on the local and national level. For example the Zapatistas were effective in gaining international support for resisting the free trade policies of the Mexican government through online communities. The leader of the movement, Subcommandante Marcos wrote: "[W]e will make our collective network of all our particular struggles and resistances. An intercontinental network of resistance against neoliberalism, an intercontinental network for humanity" (quoted in Steger, 2009a, p. 102). The First Intercontinental Meeting for Humanity and Against Neoliberalism in Chiapas was the outcome of their efforts where more than 4,000 people from 30 countries participated (Steger, 2009a, p. 102). The meeting was evidence that "globalization from below" was possible and proved to be a victory for global justice activists. Yet, these programs as well—as new social and global justice movements such as the anti-globalization, sustainability, fair trade and anti-free trade movements—have been progressively co-opted by the market (Hart, 2007, Wearing, 2001, Wearing, 2002, Wearing, 2003). Neoliberal policies, which have "swept the continent in recent years appear in some cases to have weakened popular movements and unsettled existing languages of protest placing movements at the mercy of other articulating agents, from conservative parties and narcotraffic fundamentalist churches and transnational consumerism"

---

1   Market globalism is described as "the dominant ideology of our time. Over the last three decades, it has been codified and disseminated by global power elites ... Serving as the chief advocates of market globalism, these individuals saturate the public discourse with idealized images of a consumerist, free-market world" Steger, M. 2009b. *Globalization: A Short Introduction*, New York, Oxford University Press.

(Alvarez et al., 1998, pp. 21–2). The uneasy relationship between global justice movements and neoliberal globalization are still being battled out within the international marketplace where:

> Programs such as FOSIS operate by creating new client categories among the poor and by introducing new individualizing and atomizing discourses such as those of 'personal development,' 'capacity building for self-management,' 'self-help,' 'active citizenship,' and the like. These discourses pretend more than the self-management of poverty. In seemingly Foucaultian fashion … they appear to introduce new forms of self subjectification, identity formation, and discipline. It is thus that participants in these programs come to see themselves increasingly in the individuating and economizing terms of the market (Alvarez et al., 1998, p. 22).

Recent global political events, the threat of "terrorism" and an increased understanding of global environmental degradation have contributed to the tendency for Westerners to find security in finding problems that they feel they can do something about. Uncertain economic times have also set the stage for growing dissent, especially among over educated and under employed youth. Indeed:

> [N]o matter how adaptable, flexible and calculating we are, we can still end up as debt-driven, job-seeking individuals who can barely make ends meet (Southwood 2011: 4). The message of 'We Are the 99%' (http://wearethe99percent.tumblr. com/) campaign blog, which features thousands of testimonies from the people who made all the 'correct' calculations about their future and still ended up without a job, a home, or health insurance. What more and more people are coming to realize after the 2008 economic crisis is that the homo economicus discourse touted by neoliberalism as an infallible recipe for success has in fact little bearing on actual economic performance. Its primary goal is to enlist our compliance with a system designed to benefit only a small number of winners (Vrasti, 2012, p. 135).

In line with this critique, Eric has sought to take matters into his own hands by creating a responsible tourism alliance. Like similar alliances, Eric's responsible tourism alliance moralizes the tourism market in Thailand through environmentally and economically sustainable tourism practices. While Eric has many reasons for creating this alliance, he suggests that he is primarily motivated by the need to create a more moral tourism industry because he has a responsibility to the next generation. He notes how this need is especially urgent in Thailand, where a high percentage of the GDP comes from tourism, yet much of this income does not benefit local communities (Foreign Office, 2006, Lacher and Nepal, 2010). Like Eric's responsible tourism alliance, tourism organizations around the world are linking up with global justice activists in unprecedented ways. For example, "the formation of the Tourism Interventions Group, with its collaboration with the global justice movement meeting under the auspices of the World Social Forum, shows that justice tourism aims for a fundamental transformation of the contemporary global order" (Higgins-Desbiolles, 2008, p. 345).

Global Inequality and Justice

Local, national, and transnational organizations work to bring attention to the widening gap between the rich and poor where "of the top one hundred economic entities in the world, fifty-two are corporations and only forty-eight are countries. Moreover, the gross annual sales of such huge TNCs as General Motors exceed the gross domestic product of countries such as Norway, South Africa, and Saudi Arabia" (Steger, 2009a, p. 120). The World Social Forum (WSF) has had a particularly vocal reaction to neoliberal ideologies and policies of market globalism. The WSF is in the business of building an alternative modernity as it "was born with the desire to be a meeting point of social movements opposed to neoliberal globalization and express an alternative to the guidelines of the World Economic Forum in Davos, which brought together annually businessmen and political leaders" (Vivas, 2010). The Executive Director of the Brazilian Institute for Social and Economic Analysis and cofounder of the WSF Candido Gryzbowski explains that creating a counter hegemonic discourse to rearticulate global consciousness about inequality and injustice is a major goal of the movement (Steger, 2009, p. 125).

The global justice movement builds on new social movements with an intensified focus on transnational networks and global issues. It emphasizes several "anti" platforms, such as anti-free trade and anti-globalization (Mowforth and Munt, 2009). Ferguson notes how:

> Over the last couple of decades, what we call "the Left" has come to be organized, in large part, around a project of resisting and refusing harmful new developments in the world. This is understandable, since so many new developments have indeed been highly objectionable. But it has left us with a politics largely defined by negation and disdain, and centered on what I will call 'the antis.' Anti-globalization, anti-neoliberalism, anti-privatization, anti-imperialism, anti-Bush, perhaps even anti-capitalism—but always "anti," not "pro." This is good enough, perhaps, if one's political goal is simply to denounce "the system" and to decry its current tendencies. And indeed, some seem satisfied with such a politics (Ferguson, 2010, p. 166).

Volunteer tourism participants are, in many ways, taking the "antis" to task by suggesting new ways of coping within the current socio-political system. For example, volunteers regularly claim that the expansion of volunteer tourism is at least in part due to a growing consciousness about global issues. Michelle, a 20-year-old volunteer from Holland explains how volunteer tourism emerges from an "increased awareness of poverty, especially with the Millennium

Development Goals, climate change, carbon credit systems and carbon off sets that's becoming quite big with traveling." Similarly, Jenny, a 23-year-old American volunteer explains:

> I guess in this new age, the people have become open minded to new cultures and with that, they've grown to realize that we function as one world, we all have to work as one actually we can't stand alone anymore, by getting involved with other countries by helping we can understand each other, interact with each other, function as a better world as a whole through volunteering and giving back ... I guess they feel we might feel the need to help them grow as people not to just guide them all the way along but give them skills they need to guide themselves towards a better country and a better world.

And Melissa, a 23-year-old Australian volunteer notes:

> Once I go back I can spread the word and start, maybe start a small organization. I know just by me thinking about it and telling friends that I'm going to do something. My friends also seemed interested and at least it kind of opens their mind to the possibility that next time they travel maybe they can do a voluntary project as well.

While volunteer tourism certainly will not solve structural inequality, climate change, or chronic poverty, it is worth considering its social movement recruitment potential. As the authors of one international volunteer guide suggests, people are becoming increasingly aware of the disparities between them through the media and the ease of travel for citizens of wealthy countries and that there is an emerging "willingness to act" among young people (Ausenda and McCloskey, 2006, p. 6). Indeed, they argue that "in the last few years, a 'political' movement has emerged" and that:

> It is a movement common to many ideologies: the political left, environmentalism, and various religious beliefs. This is the 'anti-global' movement characterized (with some exceptions) by a strong, inspirational solidarity [and] it is not by chance that in the last few years, part of this desire to act has been directed towards developing countries (Ausenda and McCloskey, 2006, p. 6).

The guide calls for its readers to join in this broadening social movement: "this guide is a tool for those people (even without previous volunteer experience in poor countries) that no longer just want to be spectators" (Ausenda and McCloskey, 2006, p. 6). Through guides like this, popular humanitarianism increasingly occupies the spaces of popular culture where international volunteering has become the new fashion for the internationally mobile elite. Illustrating this trend, *Forbes Magazine* describes:

John Wood, a former Microsoft executive, traveled to Nepal in 1998 with no intention to do philanthropic work. But an encounter with a school district resource officer who decried the area's lack of educational resources changed Wood's mind. The next year, he formed Room to Read, a nonprofit that has built schools and libraries in Southeast Asia and South Africa (Ruiz, 2008).

TIME Magazine similarly reports how a former flight attendant became involved in volunteer work and local empowerment through volunteer tourism:

> On one of her first group trips to El Salvador in 2001, explains Nancy Rivard, who founded Airline Ambassadors to expand on relief work she began as a flight attendant for American Airlines, volunteers helped 150 families acquire land and rebuild homes devastated by earthquakes. They were scheduled to open a vocational-training center near those homes during the last week of July and stock it with sewing machines carried to hilly El Salvador in volunteers' suitcases. "We're creating a way to empower local people," Rivard says (Fitzpatrick, 2007).

John and Nancy's experiences are implicated in and contribute to the broader discourse of popular humanitarianism in the West where participants identify as globally conscious world citizens (Lyons et al., 2012). Called to duty through their experiences in developing countries, these stories motivate potential volunteers who seek cross-cultural experiences as well as to broaden their participation in the global justice agendas.

Cross-Cultural Cosmopolitans

Cross-cultural learning is marketed as a core aspect of the volunteer tourism experience. Indeed, volunteer tourism websites invariably refer to the opportunity to broaden one's horizons through cross-cultural experiences and the NGOs on which this research is based are no exception. Volunteers often comment on how they have gained a new perspective on the world and a newfound appreciation for other cultures. Tom, a 22-year-old volunteer from Canada explains, "Well, I definitely see the world differently now. It is pretty amazing to be exposed to a new culture and really get to know it. Get to know the authentic Thailand, not the touristic Thailand. I feel like I really know Thai culture now. I can even speak a little Thai." Similarly, Jan, a 24-year-old volunteer from the US notes, "I appreciate the opportunity to learn a new way of life. They don't have many material things, but they are happy. They appreciate what they have. That is part of their culture. I think I have become less materialistic because of my experience too. In many ways, I think they have it better here. They have each other and they are happy." Comments like Tom and Jan's are regularly made by volunteers who have come to, as Jan further notes, "learn from the Thais, learn the Thai way of life."

However, despite their newfound appreciation for other cultures, there is also the possibility that "[D]eclaring their tolerance and appreciation for local culture and people is a way for volunteers to profess their solidarity with people in radical position of inequality and counteract painful feelings of boredom and uselessness. In the absence of a political pedagogy, however, the economic and environmental exploitation that banishes ... to the backwater of modernity is overlooked in favour of a misguided appreciation for the 'poor-but-happy' lifestyle of local people" (Vrasti, 2012, p. 123). I concur with Vrasti that volunteers do have a misguided appreciation for the "poor-but-happy" lifestyle and the desire to make friendships and learn from the other does seem to assuage the uncomfortable inequality of the encounter (Crossley, 2012). Yet, it is also worth reflecting on the role of these kinds of experiences in our shared historical times. Hearn, for example, asks, "[W]hat ... does it mean to 'do activism' in a sociocultural context increasingly defined by neoliberal ideas about self-reliance, entrepreneurial individualism, and economic responsibility" (Hearn, 2012, p. 2)? Indeed, how do host community members' related desires for cross-cultural experiences reflect on the cultural politics of volunteer tourism?

While many host community members shied away from the volunteers, the most outgoing individuals sought out regular interaction with the volunteers. In some situations, cross-cultural experiences occurred between the host community members themselves. Anchali, a Thai woman at the women's shelter in Chiang Mai explained how the shelter was a cosmopolitan village where volunteer tourists and host community members come with various cultural experiences: "people exchange culture here. Especially at Orchard Home, there are lots of tribal people. So we exchange culture, Hmong culture, I learn how Hmong culture is. It's like that." While most host community members have never left Thailand, they take pleasure from the cultural differences of the international volunteers as well as other host community members. In a unique blend of what Beck refers to as cosmopolization, volunteer tourism from the host community members' perspectives reflects new forms of cosmopolitanism in an increasingly transnationalized world (Beck et al., 2003, p. 16). These cosmopolitanisms have important implications for the current and potential role of volunteer tourism within global justice agendas.

Peace Through Tourism

Since the end of WWII, tourism has been acknowledged as a potential conduit for world peace. The 1980 Manila Declaration on world tourism institutionalized a "peace through tourism" campaign where tourism is noted as a "vital force for peace and international understanding" (Higgins-Desbiolles 2003, pp. 35–6). This bill was further supported by the 1985 WTO proclamation that suggested how tourism can contribute to mutual understanding and enhance international cooperation (ibid.). This code was later followed by the Charter for Sustainable tourism that suggests how "… tourism affords the opportunity to travel and to know other cultures, and that the development of tourism can help promote closer ties and peace among peoples, creating a conscience that is respectful of diversity of cultures and lifestyles" (ibid.). In 1999 "The Global Code of Ethics for Tourism presented to the WTO's General Assembly meeting in Santiago, Chile asserted that 'through the direct spontaneous and non-mediatized contacts it engenders between men and women of different cultures of friendship and understanding among the people of the world'" (Higgins-Desbiolles 2003, p. 36). There are several institutions and non-profit organizations that foreground their support of peace through tourism initiatives. For example, "such diverse transnational organizations as the United Nations, the World Bank, and the World Travel Organization have on various occasions alluded to tourism as mechanism for world peace" (Chambers, 2009, p. 48). Advocates of alternative tourism are especially vocal about tourism's potential role in the realization of world peace (D'Amore, 1988a, D'Amore, 1988b, Var et al., 1989, Higgins-Desbiolles, 2003, Higgins-Desbiolles, 2005, Higgins-Desbiolles, 2008). The emerging proposition of peace through alternative tourism is evidenced in the growth of "responsible" and "ethical" travel guidebooks such as the Rough Guide to Ethical Travel and the Lonely Planet series, popular web sources as well as UNESCO's Chair in Cultural Tourism for Peace and Development (Schein, 1998).

The International Peace through Tourism (IIPT) non-profit organization is one such example. Louis D'Amore founded IIPT in 1986 "based on a vision of the world's largest industry, travel and tourism—becoming the world's first global peace industry; and the belief that every traveler is potentially an 'Ambassador for Peace'" (International Institute for Peace Through Tourism, 2007). IIPT offers various "World Peace Tours." For example, the organization describes the Tanzania World Peace Tour and declares that:

> For many visitors, a safari to Africa is the trip of a lifetime but as with anything truly special it hinges on the connection you make, and with the people of Tanzania; that connection will remain in your memory forever. Their hospitality is bountiful and based on the concept that to experience peace you must extend peace to others. A thought that is evident as you travel throughout the countryside and further reinforced by the children's smile (International Institute for Peace Through Tourism, 2007).

These sentiments are similarly called upon in volunteer tourism where the child's smile is a core symbol of the experience. Indeed, it is widely assumed by volunteer tourism organizations that through intimate encounters with the host culture, the volunteer tourist is envisaged as part of the peace-building process. Organizations and events such as those offered by the IIPT and, more recently, volunteer tourism are testimony to the growing confidence of tourism's ability to promote peace, encourage environmental sustainability and help reduce global poverty.

Taking a macro view of tourism as a conduit for world peace, Higgens-Desbiolles explores international documents, codes and missions by both governmental and non-governmental organizations (such as the World Tourism Organization and the United Nations) and the rhetoric surrounding tourism's potential to promote global peace. She finds that its advocates promote the notion that "tourism can contribute to knowledge of other places, empathy with other peoples and tolerance that stems from seeing the place of one's own society in the world" and that "the premise that tourism fosters peace and tolerance is one of the mainstays of important international documents and codes" (Higgins-Desbiolles, 2003, p. 35). Volunteer tourism advocates are similarly quick to point out the indirect, potential peace-building benefits of volunteer tourism. For example, a *TIME Magazine* article reports how: "'Americans don't have the best reputation in the world right now,' says Doug Cutchins, director of social commitment at Grinnell College and co-author of *Volunteer Vacations: Short-Term Adventures That Will Benefit You and Others*. 'For Americans to get out and represent a different side of America ... I think that has a tremendously positive benefit.'" (Fitzpatrick, 2007). Volunteer tourists tend to agree that volunteer tourism can contribute to improved economic relations. John, an 18-year-old volunteer from Ireland states:

> Well I guess about 20 years ago there weren't as many foreigners. So with governments and the people as well, the people were more skeptical about foreigners ... Just thinking of most tourists and the government, they probably don't know about such opportunities like volunteer tourism ... I guess they can't even imagine that you could just not—just be a tourist. They're volunteers who are coming here to experience a new country but also contribute and get involved and interact with the people themselves. I guess they'd never thought of that yet because they don't know about it and there's such a gap between the countries.

John further notes how volunteer tourism can contribute to a more reciprocal form of globalization and better international relations:

> Like there may be tensions between countries or some countries might not want foreigners to come into their country because of globalization or the Western world taking over the Eastern world. But by actually getting involved, like the Western world getting involved in the eastern world instead of just bringing in products and westernizing them, by actually getting involved with people and knowing their culture, respecting their culture and uplifting them in a way, it can help improve relation and the governments can see that this is happening and see that it's actually to benefit of the country itself. Then they might ensure future programs such as this to help better their country and get other countries, other international countries involved.

Mellissa, a 24-year-old volunteer from Australia similarly notes:

I think kind of bridging the gap between the Western world and the developing world. Also fixing some of the myths about what the developing world's like because I know lots of people think that it's just so different and that you can't understand how it works but I think coming here and seeing how things do work kind of allows you to see that sometimes it's better here than in the West.

These sentiments are corroborated in online forums where one tourism blogger suggests:

As peace increasingly has become a focus of my travel, I have been exploring ways to use my photography and travel anecdotes to promote greater understanding of unfamiliar and controversial places. Part of that involves a dedication to giving a fuller picture of cultures and dispelling stereotypes. With pervasive negative impressions of the Middle East, it may be surprising to know that in traveling to over 50 countries, the Middle East is where I have experienced the most hospitality. This hospitality has seemed genuine as it frequently has been initiated by strangers. My photos attempt to show some of that hospitality and broaden the range of images of people from the Middle East beyond stereotypes of 'terrorist' and 'victim' (Greene, 2007).

While there is a widespread belief that tourism can contribute to world peace, it is also acknowledged that travel does not always contribute to greater intercultural understanding. This may be particularly true when volunteer tourists and host community members come from highly disparate social, cultural and economic backgrounds (Chambers 2003, p. 48). Anchali, a host community member at a women's shelter explains: "If the whole world was peaceful and was happy, it would be very good. But how can it happen? I don't know. If the whole world lived together like family, and looked after each other, it would be good!" Volunteer tourism's potential for cross-cultural consciousness raising and peace building has encouraged its advocates to consider its social movement possibilities.

Is Volunteer Tourism a Social Movement?

Current struggles over the meaning of social activism and social movement participation are reflected in volunteer tourism where there is a clear alliance with both new social movement ideals as well as commodity activism (Hearn, 2012, p. 1). In this respect, Sturken asks, "[W]hat do new modes of consumerism tell us about the different kinds of subjectivities emerging in the context of neoliberal societies? What do social activism and social change become in such contexts?" (Sturken, 2012, pp. ix–x). Since the 1980s new social movements' focus on identity politics has departed from previous collective struggles over resources. Identity is central to these new movements and this emphasis contributes to new forms of social engagement where indigenous, women's, gay, human rights and ecological groups have become core aspects of participation (Alvarez et al., 1998).

The ways in which broader political economic processes are implicated in local cultural articulations and social structure illustrate how social movements play out on the ground (Dolinhow, 2005). The student uprisings of 1966 were a key event in the expansion of new social movements as these events "express[ed] political frustrations of a new educated middle class or brain workers—ICT (Information and Communications Technology) specialists or the caring professions (doctors, lecturers, social workers) generated by post-industrialism and the welfare state" (Kaldor, 2003, p. 84). Distinguished from traditional social movements, a primary concern among new social movement activists is human rights rather than the effects of industrial society (although these interests intersect in various ways). Kaldor explains that "among the principle innovations of the new movements, in contrast with the workers' movement, are a critical ideology in relation to modernism and progress; decentralized and participatory organisational structures; defense of interpersonal solidarity against the great bureaucracies; and the reclamation of autonomous spaces rather than material advantages" (Kaldor, 2003, pp. 84–5).

Volunteers and NGO practitioners participate in volunteer tourism with various visions for their involvement, yet the links that chain them together are an engagement with global justice agendas. For example, in regards to new social movements, Bebbington notes how "there does need to be a significant overlap among these visions in order to sustain the movement and give it coherence" (Bebbington, 2007, p. 801). Participation in new social movements can range from donating money and time to social causes to active engagement and recruitment in a major organization, and both external and internal forms of participation should be considered (McGehee, 2002). Since at least the mid-nineteenth century, tourism has been used as a medium through which its participants seek to accomplish economic, political and environmental goals motivated by social movements[2] (Higgins-Desbiolles, 2005, Higgins-Desbiolles, 2008). Attempts to access the political through the tourism market are part of a much broader transition in contemporary society where "cultural notions of liberal democratic subjectivity transform into capitalist citizenship, and rituals of consumption increasingly stand in for other modes of democratic engagement with profound consequences for what counts as 'civic resistance.' And, as participation within public spheres is increasingly shaped and secured by one's capacities to consume these transitions exact their heaviest price from marginalized constituencies—women, nonwhites, and the poor" (Hearn, 2012, p. 9).

Volunteer tourism illustrates new social movement participation in a particularly neoliberalized fashion. Social movements are important sites where the status quo is opened up for debate. In volunteer tourism, debates about the appropriate response to global economic inequality are addressed. By treating

---

2   Recent attention by anthropologists to the potential role of tourism in the global justice and other related movements is evidenced by the 2010 American Anthropological Association Meeting agenda where these panels such as Contemplating New Movements in Tourism, Neoliberal Transformations, and Mobilities of Development take up these issues.

social movements as the discursive (re)articulation of social, political and economic life, power relations that mediate our experience are denaturalized and opened up for inspection. For example, they open up space to debate how civil society is to engage with chronic poverty or systemic violence against the poor. Thus, social movement activists seek to "contend meanings of core ideas that underlie policy debates, challenge dominant notions about what counts as legitimate knowledge in the process of forming policy, and argue that alternative actors and alternative sources of knowledge ought also to influence policy-making processes (cf. Alvarez et al., 1998; Dagnino, 2007). Here, social movements are best understood as the vectors of particular discourses and forms of questioning the world" (Bebbington, 2007, p. 800), and "... emerge to contest social relationships and dynamics of capital accumulation that are implicated in the creation and reproduction of poverty ..." and often seek to expose economic, social and political discriminatory policies and practices (Bebbington, 2007, p. 796). Post-structural analyses are important to understanding social movements as they "insist that culture—meanings, ideas, practices—constitute one of the most important terrains in which social movements operate, and which they seek to change" (Bebbington 2007, p. 800). Additionally, social movements play a critical role in defining the limits and scope of political action.

Consciousness raising is a core aspect of social movement participation. Volunteer tourists are often keen supporters of social activism and are often willing to buy into environmental conservation, cultural exchange and poverty reduction as key "commodities" (McGehee and Santos, 2005a). For example, Tancy, a Cross-Cultural Solutions, Guatemala volunteer writes:

> Before I went to Guatemala, I was already quite actively involved in Fairtrade and responsible consumerism and I will continue to be. However, having read the reasons why CCS opposes donations to the individual program placements and seen the work of CARE in empowering by giving loans rather than donations, it has made me re-think quite seriously about the effects of charity, and how I want to give my money to sustainable projects only from now on.[3]

Volunteer tourism, as an alternative form of consumption, is becoming an increasingly important option for individuals who seek to contribute to and to improve upon their participation in global justice and environmental issues.

The Moral Economy of Volunteer Tourism

The moral economy is "an economy that may rely on markets and money but that is governed or at least constrained by local community values and expectations" (Wilson, 2004, p. 12). Scott's original use of the term "moral economy" was

---

3   http://www.crossculturalsolutions.org/volunteervoices.asp, December 14, 2008.

in the context of peasant societies where community relations—sometimes
at the expense of potential profit—are integral to economic decisions. Today,
communities are perceived in regional, national, international and global terms.
The re-spatialization of the community has profound implications for moral
economies. As noted above, cosmopolitan empathy builds on the ideals of
world peace that mediate earlier versions of alternative tourism. Cosmopolitan
empathy is a corollary of the cultural logic and economic policies of neoliberal
global capitalism that have given rise to alternative, responsible and ethical
consumption markets. Within cosmopolitan empathy, "we find the resistance
strategies of historic social movements co-opted into tactics of 'brand aid' and
'shopping for a change' campaigns led, with little hint of irony, by corporations,
corporate philanthropies, and media celebrities" (Hearn, 2012, p. 2). Like other
forms of moral consumption, volunteer tourists unwittingly contribute to the
expansion of the cultural logic and economic policies of neoliberalism—the very
logic and policies they seek to contest. This is because "[V]olunteer tourism
expresses a genuine desire for community, mutual aid and cosmopolitan sociality
that neoliberal government does not know how to accommodate, other than by
packaging it as a luxury commodity with feel-good value" (Vrasti, 2012, p. 119).
The expansion of moral economies is well represented by the food, fashion and
technology industry where examples proliferate. Indeed, Hearn observes how:

> [B]uying Product RED items—ranging from Gap T-shirts to Apple iPods to
> Dell computers—means one supports the Global Fund to help eliminate AIDS
> in Africa. Consuming a "Caring Cup" of coffee at the Coffee Bean and Tea
> Leaf indicates a commitment to free trade and humane labor practices. Driving
> a Toyota Prius, likewise, points to the consumer's vow to help resolve the global
> oil crisis as well as fight global warming. Purchasing Dove Beauty products
> enables one to participate in the Dove Real Beauty campaign, which encourages
> consumers to "co-produce" nationwide workshops to help girls and young
> women tackle problems of low-self-esteem, many of which are created by the
> beauty industry itself, within which Dove has been a significant player. Using
> their star capital and the force of their celebrity, public figures such as Angelina
> Jolie, Brad Pitt, and Kanye West launch social activist programs ranging from
> UN-sponsored humanitarian actions to protesting the global trade in blood
> diamonds to rebuilding low-income neighbourhoods in hurricane-ravaged New
> Orleans. All of which is to say that within contemporary culture it is utterly
> unsurprising to participate in social activism by buying something (Hearn, 2012,
> p. 1).

Like related moral consumer items, volunteer tourism recreates resistance as a
sign value that is ready made for the market. Within this market, human relations
are easily objectified while commodity fetishism takes on a humanized form
(Hearn, 2012, p. 13). Touristic consumption has become a significant mode of
political action where the "sustainable lifestyle movement" Habermas (1981)

refers to represents a new politics that is centered on the "antis" (Mowforth and Munt, 2009, p. 28). Describing the growing popularity of volunteer tourism, for example, Jen, a 22-year-old Dutch volunteer comments: "Why not. Let's go be a volunteer somewhere. I think the internet. I searched for volunteering in Thailand and there were 20 different organizations you can choose from. I think it's becoming more popular now. Now we can do a lot more. It's not like missions, that is more about your religion, now you can just go anywhere and you know there are so many outlets to do it."

The individualistic, seemingly unique desire to volunteer abroad is part of an emerging habitus among Western consumers. Habitus describes the internalization of the structural configurations of society and our seemingly natural participation within them (Bourdieu, 1984). Despite the perceptively spontaneous nature of our attitudes, perceptions and behavior, these "personal" characteristics are socially conditioned through categories such as class, gender, race, ethnicity and so on. Individualism is a key aspect of alternative tourism and tends to be seen as a uniquely human attribute unconditioned by society. Yet, individualism is regularly critiqued by volunteers who are enticed by the communitarianism of host community members. Volunteer tourists regularly search:

> for communion with others to counteract the hyperindividualism and quotidian nihilism of modern existence. In both instances we find the 'surplus knowledge, surplus creativity, surplus sociality and surplus relationality' (Haiven 2011) autonomist Marxists warned us cognitive capitalism would product but not know how to contain. But whereas the latter is a for-profit instrument that reduces our longing for community and self-determination to economic cooperation to stage a dramatic exit from capitalism (Vrasti, 2012, p. 136).

Yet, it is through the desire for community belonging and identity that volunteer tourists simultaneously distinguish themselves from others. The growth of individualistic touristic experiences is associated with the growth of the new petite bourgeoisie. For example:

> Hutnyk (1996) observes backpackers in Kolkata (India) where a 'popular alternative critique of travel' emerges from their reflections, and manifests itself in: a) The search for 'authentic' experiences; b) dismay at the effects of tourism; and c) condemnation of other tourists and sometimes themselves. The correlates of these three moments are a) claims to the 'once-in-a-lifetime' experience; b) nostalgia for the days when such and such-a-place was not so well known; and c) 'of course I'm doing it differently' stories (Hutnyk cited in Mowforth and Munt, 2009).

What Hutnyk's observation illustrates is that individualism mediates the new petite bourgeois experience. This class fraction is uniquely positioned as low on economic capital, yet high on cultural capital. Volunteer tourists tend to prefer "responsible travel" experiences that they perceive to be "just off the beaten track." Glynn, a 26-year-old English volunteer, notes that "Some people see [volunteer tourism] as more of a tourist experience. I think it is responsible traveling." It is because people want to participate in "responsible travel" that alternative, responsible, ethical and niche tourism markets are increasingly successful within previously mainstream tourism destinations. This trend is perhaps most conspicuous in volunteer tourism where there is a clear linkage between responsibility and recreation. Commenting on this linkage, Vrasti asks: "[W]hat is it about the present moment that requires individuals, especially young adults, to organize their lives, even their space time, around imperatives of cosmopolitan sensibilities and personal responsibility" (Vrasti, 2012, p. 2)? It is to this question that I turn to in the following chapter.

Chapter 5

The Cultural Politics of Sentimentality in Volunteer Tourism

> When sentimentality meets politics, it uses personal stories to tell of structural effects, but in so doing it risks thwarting its very attempt to perform rhetorically a scene of pain that must be soothed politically.
>
> (Lauren Berlant, 2004, p. 641)

As Carol and I enter the decaying temple school cafeteria, I notice several of the novice monks' eyes follow us as we locate an empty seat among the sea of orange-colored robes. It has only been a few months since the international volunteers started teaching English at the all-boys temple school. Many of the novices seem bewildered by the Western females who have become increasingly present in their classrooms and cafeteria. As we sit down at an empty table, I asked Carol how her volunteer experience has been going. Carol is a 66-year-old volunteer from Canada who has been volunteering in Chiang Mai for three weeks at a home for single mothers where she manages the day care. Because of Carol, the mothers are able to take time away from their young children to learn English from Ellen, 23, and Jake, 24—a vibrant Ivy League educated young couple from New England. Carol takes a few bites of her pad thai as she begins to share with me her experience of volunteering at the shelter. At first she was frustrated—she admits—because she did not know what to do or where to start. She had not been provided with supplies, and because the babies did not wear diapers she had to constantly mop urine from the floor. Despite these difficulties, by the end of her experience she had fallen in love with the women and children. Carol recalls her affectionate goodbye ceremony: "… all the mothers got dressed up with their babies on their laps. They were all sitting around adjoining rooms, and even the ones that had trouble speaking English in my class got up and thanked me, and they gave me cards, 'I love you, I love you, come back, thank you for helping us, thank you for helping our children, we love you,' and this totally overwhelmed me."

NGO practitioners also describe their motivations for participating in volunteer tourism in sentimental terms. This type of passion seems to drive much of the NGO industry today. It is likely that many of the coordinators who dedicate their lives to Others were once intrepid travelers who were moved to take action against poverty along the backpacker circuit in Southeast Asia. Helen, a 28-year-old NGO practitioner from Scotland lamented: "I was a bit disappointed because I didn't get any cuddles today. Usually I get some cuddles." I met Helen upon jumping into the back of a pick-up truck after a long day of English camp at a rural elementary school 20 km outside of Chiang Mai City. Helen looked forward to such sentimental exchanges each day and as an NGO practitioner, she felt slightly let-down when they did not occur. A few weeks later over a bowl of noodle soup, Helen commented how the most memorable aspect of her experience is the bonds she creates with the children at the schools.

Host community members also foreground sentimental aspects when describing their most memorable experiences. However, these descriptions emerge from a decidedly different context and therefore take on new meanings. While sitting on the steps of the school—a small room on four bamboo stilts—Po, an 18-year-old Hmong resident at the single mother's home, describes the most memorable aspects of her experience: "[F]riendship. It's like we live with them. They smile at us and talk with us and it is good. They welcome us ... it makes us feel good. I don't feel nervous. They think we are somebody" (also cited in Conran, 2011). The volunteer tourism experience for most participants is defined by moments like these. Indeed, "many friendships are ... made between the visitors and visited, but the relationships between visitors and hosts give rise to a range of other outcomes" (2009, p. 260).

Although volunteers and host community members both felt that volunteer tourism involved a rewarding sentimental exchange, these shared perceptions emerge from different historical and geo-political contexts. Sentimentality—specifically intimacy, love and compassion—are dominant themes in participants' accounts of the volunteer tourism experience. However, in pointing to the shared experience of these affects, I do not want to suggest that they are in any way universal, as these sentiments have widely variant meanings and expressions in different linguistic, historical and geographic contexts. Thai people, for example, interpret intimacy, love and compassion in sometimes radically different ways than North Americans or Europeans. Furthermore, these sentiments are not always fully captured by language itself. For instance, Europeans' conceptions of love do not directly translate into North American English. Speaking of the peculiarities of translation in ethnographic fieldwork, Clifford notes how "[P]articipant observation obliges its practitioners to experience, at a bodily as well as intellectual level, the vicissitudes of translation. It requires arduous language learning, some degree of direct involvement and conversation, and often a derangement of personal and cultural expectations" (Clifford, 1988, p. 119). To control for the fact that these terms are not ahistorical, but rather take on different meanings and nuances in different contexts, I rely upon speakers' own definitions and use of these terms to avoid imputing outside systems of meaning.

By turning questions of structural inequality into questions of individual morality (Conran, 2011), the inequality on which the experience is based and obfuscates the political essence of the human made suffering that volunteer tourism seeks to ameliorate (Butler, 2002, Ahmed, 2004, Berlant, 1998, Berlant, 2000, Berlant, 2004). This theoretical stance is informed by Ahmed (2004, pp. 20–21), who shows how the political is veiled by the cloak of the sentimental through her examination of television advertisements that ask viewers to donate money to landmine victims in Cambodia. She suggests that by constructing the landmines as the cause of pain is to miss the point—landmines are the effect of human avarice. In a similar vein, Vrasti asks: "How do individuals become emotionally invested in neoliberal ideology?" (Vrasti, 2011, p. 1). Sentimentality in volunteer tourism is a phenomenon that is microcosmic of sentimentality in capitalist modernity: constructing the issue of sentimentality in volunteer tourism in terms of individuals and individual communities alone fails to fully capture the how sentimentality structures and is structured by political, economic and social inequality. Thus, volunteer tourism uniquely illustrates the role of sentimentality in capitalist modernity. Illouz describes this intersection of emotions and the economy as "emotional capitalism" by which she means, "a culture in which emotional and economic discourses and practices mutually shape each other, thus producing … a broad, sweeping movement in which affect is made an essential aspect of economic behaviour and in which emotional life—especially that of the middle classes—follows the logic of economic relations and exchange" (Illouz, 2007, p. 5).

Feminist and queer scholars have shown how emotions are psychological states as well as cultural practices (Lutz, 1986b, Lutz, 1986a, Malcomson, 1998, Keese, 2011, Ahmed, 2004, Woodward, 2004, Garber, 2004, Berlant, 2004, Davidson and Milligan, 2004, Knudsen and Waade, 2010, Ahmed, 2006). In this way, affective relations are intimately entangled with economic relations in both political and cultural ways where "[F]ar from being pre-social or pre-cultural, emotions are cultural meanings and social relationships that are inseparably compressed together" and "deeply internalized and unreflexive aspects of action, but not because they do not contain enough culture and society in them, but rather because they have too much" (Illouz, 2007, pp. 2–3). Hence, while volunteer tourism participants' sentiments of intimacy, love, and compassion may indeed be sincere, they are also cultural as well as political. The perception that "critique seeks to befoul its object—is especially acute in response to writing on what we might call the humanizing emotions: compassion, sentimentality, empathy, love, and so on" (Berlant, 2004, p. 5). Yet, this is not my intention. Rather, I highlight the ways that emotion and culture intersect with economic systems of distribution. In this way, "affect becomes a primary technology for consolidating the job of consumerism, the hatred for gendered and racialized corporalities, communal attachments to fascist and fundamentalist milieus, the comforting effects of identity and diversity politics and personal rewards of exploitative and unsustainable forms of labour" (Vrasti, 2011, p. 7). The commodification of the encounter as well as its corollary politics are ensconced by the focus on sentimentality—which Solomon describes as the core of humanity (Solomon, 2004). This double pursuit of authenticity—through the seemingly unmediated and sentimental encounter—strategically positions volunteer tourism as an authentic experience. Yet this is only through the concealment of the commerce of the relationship which is buried deep within the encounter.

Historicizing the Sentimental in Volunteer Tourism

From the modern European colonial period through to the contemporary
neoliberal "voluntary turn," sentimentality has been used as an obscuring device
against systemic inequality, structural discrimination and the cultural politics of
the volunteer tourism encounter (Woodward, 2004, Garber, 2004, Berlant, 2008,
Berlant, 2000, Ahmed, 2004, Ahmed, 2006). Sentimentality has been intimately
linked with popular humanitarianism (Tester, 2010, p. vii). A significant reworking
of the cultural phenomenon took place under the colonial era, producing what
Stoler refers to as "sentimental colonialism" (Stoler, 2002, p. 7). Stoler points
out how "[C]olonial states, not unlike metropolitan ones, had a strong motivation
for their abiding interest in affective politics" (Stoler, 2002, p. 19). Analyses of
how sentimentality works as an apparatus of the colonial state emerged with the
philosophy of affect, including the works of Locke and Hume (Stoler, 2002, p. 19).
These authors, Stoler suggests, exemplify "how much the politics of compassion
was not an oppositional assault on empire, but fundamental to it" (Stoler, 2002,
p. 19). Moreover, popular sentimentality reflects the complexity of relationships
during the colonial period (Hafen, 1997, Bhabha, 1984). It is noted how "the
colonial 'gaze' (*le regard*, in French) was to be at once broad, reflexive, and
intimate" (Stoler, 2002, p. 1). Sentimentality tended to emerge within periods of
crisis and ambivalence about the colonial project and was used to both justify
and condemn it (Pratt, 1992, Huhndorf, 2001, Torgovnick, 1997, Spurr, 1993,
Bhabha, 1985, Cooper and Stoler, 1997). Indeed, "[D]omains of the intimate
figured … prominently in the perception and policies of those who ruled"
(Stoler, 2002, p. 7).

Despite the centrality of sentimentality to the colonial project, Stoler (2002,
p. 12) notes how in the context of archival, historical research, we are "[U]nused
to pushing the affective up against the political, we leave sentiments to literature,
dismiss references to them as the emotive fluff rather than the real stuff of official
archives." Recently scholars have begun to examine how sentimentality mediates
the colonial encounter. Wexler (2004), for example, shows how during the
Victorian Period (1837–1901) the sentimental novel contributed to the feminization
and "sentimentalization" of American culture. This feminization, she suggests,
"encouraged the idea that appropriate notice of the painful social dislocations of
nineteenth-century capital and urban industrial expansion could be given symbolic
expression in literary rather than theological works" (Wexler, 2000, p. 94). The
effect of this relocation of the site of expression for the dissatisfaction of the social
world from public to the private world of the sentimental novel "was not, as the
writers of these works often alleged, to foreground and correct social inequalities
but rather to provide an emergent middle-class readership with permission for a
kind of aesthetic and emotional contemplation that was underwritten precisely
by its refusal to actively 'interfere' in civil life" (Wexler, 2000, pp. 94–5). While
often feminized and associated with irrationality, sentimentality was central to
the colonial project (Stoler, 2002, Wexler, 2000, Huhndorf, 2001). Moreover, the

imperial project of sentimentalism worked to ameliorate the ambivalence of the colonial period by reframing the encounter as a benevolent act of compassion (Wexler, 2000, p. 101). While white middle-class women were its primary readership, the sentimental novel was not oriented towards readers who were "seriously committed 'to an ethic of love' ... Rather, it aimed at the subjection of people of different classes and different races, who were compelled to play not the leading roles but the human scenery before which the melodrama of middle-class redemption could be enacted" (Wexler, 2000, p. 101). Despite the feminine virtue and innocence that the sentimental novel provokes, the novel's major role was maintaining a complacent middle class during the colonial period.

While the sentimental novel provided its white, female, middle-class readership solace from the offence of colonialism, it rarely inspired the radical political upheaval that its writers promoted. Wexler observes how sentimental fiction was, "the myth that the avowed reform goals—widespread instruction in domesticity and vigorous pursuit of social reform based explicitly and insistently on affective values—were ever really intended to restore vitality of the peoples that domestic expansion had originally appropriated" (Wexler, 2000, p. 105). The focus on sentimentality during the modern European colonial period worked to overshadow the cultural politics of the colonial project. Following Wilson (2004, p. 11), "my approach is premised on the often-overshadowed notion that economic systems are not separate from intimate life, as orthodox conceptions of the economy suggest, but are inextricable from social relations and identities" (Wilson, 2004, p. 11). In Thailand, capitalism and consumer culture penetrates all aspects of society. The intimate realms of everyday life increasingly intersect with capitalist logic. Sentimentality is of cardinal significance to modern global capitalism as a conduit through which individuals find solace for their dissatisfactions, for example, through "intimate economies," or the intersection of social life and economic systems of production and consumption (Wilson, 2004). In this way, the depoliticizing effects of neoliberalism in late modernity are, at least in part, a legacy of sentimental colonialism during the colonial period.

Intimacy

In the introduction to the edited volume *Intimacy*, Berlant (2000) asks the reader to consider how attachments make people public and go on to produce "transpersonal identities and subjectivities." In response to her own question, Berlant calls upon intimacy, which she suggests, is a question of scale that links the individual to the collective. Berlant explains how intimacy:

> ... is to communicate with the sparest of signs and gestures, and at its root intimacy has the quality of eloquence and brevity. But intimacy also involves an aspiration for a narrative about something shared, a story about both oneself and others that will turn out in a particular way (Berlant, 2000, p. 1).

Intimacy also includes "features of people's daily lives that have come to seem noneconomic, particularly social identities (e.g., woman) and relationships (e.g., kinship)" (Wilson, 2004, pp. 9–10). The aesthetics of intimacy and attachment create a narrative of continuity and security within our often fragmented and unpredictable lives (Berlant, 2000, Stoler, 2006). Intimacy is used here to "capture the deeply felt orientations and entrenched practices that make up what people consider to be their personal or private lives and their individual selves" (Wilson, 2004, pp. 9, 11). In the context of volunteer tourism, intimate experiences with host community members allow volunteers to create a narrative about themselves as they identify with their other.

More than three decades ago, MacCannell (1973, p. 33) suggested that the division "of society into front and back center[s] on popular ideas of the relationship of truth to intimacy. In our society, intimacy and closeness are accorded much importance: they are seen as the core of social solidarity, and they are also thought by some to be more 'real' and morally superior to rational and economic factors that affect social relationships. Being 'one of them,' or at one with 'them,' mean, in part, being permitted to share back regions with 'them.'" (MacCannell, 1973, pp. 591–2). MacCannell argues that through Western travel narratives tourists seek out pre-capitalist, authentic others through which they refashion their self/other identity (MacCannell, 1992). In volunteer tourism, the desire for "backstage" experiences is often realized. Indeed, among volunteer tourists, intimate interaction is almost invariably described as the motivating factor for participation. John, a 17-year-old volunteer from South Africa, for example, explains:

> Like traveling you are just kind of watching it like window shopping in a way. But by volunteering … you get to, like I am doing, go to the schools, see the children, see the villages, see the rural life and also meet the people and get involved with the people … you actually get to participate in the children's lives.

He goes on to state:

> I would just say just by traveling you only see, it's a mask of the country, you only see what kind of things they want you to see. All the tourist attractions and it's nice and pretty but you actually don't get to know the people and how the people work and the culture itself. By volunteering you get to know the children you teach, you get to know the follow up generation of the country and also the rural people, the actual in this case the Thai people who they are, how they go about their daily lives without all this globalization which is affecting so them so heavily. You get to know them when they are just being themselves. And that's the real experience, that's the real nice part.

Like John, most volunteers suggested that the most memorable aspect of their experience was the relationship they established with host community members. For example, Lea, a 21-year-old Norwegian volunteer stated: "I think for me it has been holding the kids hands and, like one of them grabbed my arm and it is just things like that that makes it worth it." Amy, an American volunteer of the same age similarly states: "I think mine is kindness. I love coming to school every day because they all sing together, everyone looks at me and says 'Good morning teacher' and they all smile at me and giggle, maybe a way to say thank you or I don't know what. You can tell that they appreciate it."

Similarly, Marla, a 22-year-old Dutch volunteer, comments on how the kids really like her which makes her feel good:

> ... if the kids are really laughing and having fun and you see that they really like you and they are happy to see you that's really great ... if you're here in the morning, we come here and all the kids run to the fence to greet us and give us a high fives ...

Commenting on the most memorable aspect of her experience, Cindy, a 19-year-old volunteer from Holland explains:

> Most memorable, well, I guess in the morning we come and in the afternoon when we leave, they all come to us and give us high fives and dance and they don't want us to leave before we do that. And there is one time, a little boy cried because we left and he didn't want to leave. So I guess, yeah, the kids, I'm going to miss them.

Ann, a 20-year-old Norwegian volunteer also notes how at first she was nervous about how the encounter would work out, but eventually she was able to connect with the children:

> At first, I was really, really nervous about going to a bunch of Thai kids and what should I do with them and I am just so amazed about the connection I felt I made with the children, that's the really amazing thing that in only two months you could make such a connection and with not being able to talk to them.

Many volunteers further commented that through these sorts of encounters they had begun to feel "at home" in Thailand. Alexandra, a 23-year-old girl from the US states: "[B]eing here for two months. It's kind of like having a new home. To experience the culture here and just to communicate with the people, just being with them."

The intimate encounter with local people is what distinguishes volunteer tourism from other types of travel. Carol from Canada explains how she and her husband came to Thailand to "get to know the people." It is not her intention, she declares, to stay in a fancy hotel because that "is not how you meet people ... this is why this volunteering is so amazing. You really get to meet people and get in touch with real Thai culture. You don't get to do that in a hotel. It is not the same culture." Remembering her most memorable experience, Carol recalls:

I was very touched when I saw them Saturday, because when I went with them to the park, I said to Sam, you have to get the camera out. Unfortunately, he didn't have it out at the welcome. They ran to me, a few of them and a couple of little kids and even the moms ... I thought ... I've been there for a week ... big deal, so they'll see me, they'll say hello, big deal. They were so happy, the hugs I got ... Yeah, I was very overwhelmed ...

John, a 17-year-old volunteer from Ireland similarly explains how his previous trip to Thailand as a tourist was different to his current experience as a volunteer because this time he had close interaction with Thai culture and people:

I've come here before but that was just for about two weeks and I mean I didn't get the whole view of Thailand as I'd like to. I just saw many of the cities and the tourist attractions like the night market and the stuff like that but actually now that I am getting involved in this program, I am actually getting to know the Thai people whereas before I'd just say hello and just think what their daily life was like, but here I can actually see what their daily lives consist of, see what they do, see how they live, see what they do for a living. Now like I know how a village can interact to support each other. Like before I didn't know there was such a thing as a village headman or stuff like that but now I am actually finding out more about the Thai culture and how it works. And it's much, its good because you get into the nitty gritty of that because you have whole new view on this.

These highly sought after intimate experiences are valued because they allow participants to construct narratives about their friends or even new "family"[1] from afar.

NGO practitioners facilitate these types of highly desired intimate exchanges that volunteer tourists have come to expect. Of course, this relationship is mediated by capital, yet this fact is cleverly overshadowed by the promise of authentic interactions with local people. The "search for authenticity" is intimately related to a desire to experience a more traditional and seemingly authentic "host and guest" relationship that exists outside the hospitality industry. In an effort towards maintaining the uniqueness of volunteer tourism, the intimacy of the encounter is brought to the foreground, while the commercial nature of the experience is almost always hidden from the volunteers' point of view so tourists are able to feel more like "guests" rather than customers. Tourists come to believe that the staff are more like "friendly helpers" (Bruner, 1995), and NGO practitioners "place high priority on the quality of interactions between tourists and host communities and recognize that this interaction must move beyond superficiality" (Wearing, 2001). These priorities are consistent with the decommodification agenda that underpins

---

1   Several volunteers suggested that they feel like the host community members were like their new family.

alternative tourism" (Lyons and Wearing, 2008, p. 7). For example, Eric, an NGO practitioner from South Africa and longtime Thai resident suggests that volunteer tourism is a more meaningful experience because its participants are able to meet locals at the "grassroots level:"

> I think the first thing, is if you set out to travel around the world and you want to meet new people and cultures etc., you're not really going to do it as tourist. So you're not going to fulfill the objective of your search. You will forever be just a tourist. It's very difficult to get in and to meet people at a grass roots level. Volunteering can do that where tourism can't.

Olga, a 52-year-old NGO practitioner and lay missionary from the Philippines emphasized the importance of intimate relations between host community members and the volunteers. She observes:

> What I learn from the foreigners who come, they learn more about the culture when they are with the simple rural folk, they say this because they have more interaction with them. That is some of the feedback I got from them in their evaluation. Feeling their heartbeat, is what was said by one volunteer; the heartbeat of Thailand. They saw and felt the heartbeat of Thailand in the simple rural living.

One volunteer similarly notes how Ted, an NGO practitioner was aware of the volunteers' desires for intimate interaction: "Ted [the NGO practitioner] is always asking our group why we arc here and we say to give something back instead of just traveling. We all seem to have the same motives and to experience the culture, be closer to the local people, I think Ted knows that." Notably, most of the NGO practitioners were previously volunteers themselves. An examination of volunteer tourism websites quickly reveals the value placed on the intimate experience. As a consequence of this recognition, volunteer tourism organizations tend to highlight close encounters in their advertising campaigns. For example, BV notes how: "During the evenings, you will have the opportunity to spend time with the villagers who are eager to engage with volunteers" and volunteers "Work along-side villagers" (Borderless Volunteers, 2009).

Intimacy also permeates host community members' articulation of their experiences. According to my informants, there were many opportunities to experience meaningful exchanges with the volunteers. An analysis of these exchanges draws attention to the embodied nature of the encounter. It is notable that most participants cannot communicate verbally as none of the volunteers could speak Thai and host community members rarely spoke conversational English. Interestingly, while language was almost always a barrier to more complex forms of communication, it was often suggested that it could be circumvented through other forms of communication. Po suggests: "[W]e don't have to talk with each other. We can just smile at each other. Some people cannot speak Thai so if they can't speak Thai then we speak only a little bit. It is fun."

Similarly, several of the women at Orchard Home explained that since the volunteers cannot speak Thai they have to rely on other mediums for communication. When I asked Pim, a 19-year-old host community member about this, she responded: "Like what Noi said, we use hand language for words we don't know in English." I further asked: Do you have any other methods besides using hand language? Pim responded: "Smiling." She continues, "Smiling is the only other thing. We don't know what else to say" (also cited in Conran, 2011). Prang, another woman at Orchard Home remarked: "We try to speak to them [in English]. We try to think of the word. We try to speak but we cannot speak. If we speak incorrectly or correctly, it doesn't matter as long as we try to get them to understand." Noi from Orchard Home explains:

> The foreigners that come here have a high IQ so they can understand us. When we speak, they can understand it, really! They get the point of what we are saying no matter if they cannot understand exactly what we say. They can watch our body language and then they can understand what we are saying.

Noi further elaborated:

> Sometimes we ask them, "are you tired?" We don't know how to ask things in English. We are like [she puts her hands together and tilts her head to rest it on them] and use our body language to show them what we are saying. They don't mind. We can ask, "are you thirsty?" [she motions drinking from a cup] They can understand this very easily.

Yula, a 22-year-old volunteer from Norway explains how she didn't need to be able to talk with the host community members to communicate with them: "Even if I can't talk to them, I have an opportunity to communicate with them, working next to them I can see how they are." Hence, while none of the volunteers could speak Thai, it was frequently explained to me by the volunteers and host community members that communication was still possible through body language and "hand talking." These types of interactions are more involved than in an encounter between same language speakers. Just as volunteers and NGO practitioners perceive the close interaction with local people to be signs of the authenticity of their experience, local people similarly perceive the authenticity of this engagement and suggest that close interaction between the volunteers and themselves allows the volunteers to get to know the "real" Thailand. One elementary school teacher that hosts volunteers at her school in Mae On, commented that she thought that unlike tourists, volunteers at her school were able to get to know "real Chiang Mai people" (as discussed in Chapter 6). Manop, the orphanage worker explained how he felt that the difference between tourists and volunteers was that volunteers are able to make more of a connection with the local people:

> From the perspective of getting to know something about our customs and traditions, I think that the volunteers get to see a lot more. Because the tourists they come only for sightseeing and that is it. They come and see that this is like this and that is like that and that is it. But if they are a volunteer they have direct access and more connection to the local people.

He suggests that while the main goal of having the international volunteers was for the children at the orphanage to learn English, getting to know the foreigners on a more interpersonal level was also an important aspect of both the children and their own experience with the international volunteers.

While host community members seem to have an interest in volunteers, this interest is decidedly different in part because it is mediated by decades of postcolonial relations of power with the West. These postcolonial relations have contributed to the cultural and social capital that is often attributed to having "Western" friends. In the context of his experience growing up in Nepal with Peace Corps volunteers, Shrestha recalls:

> We sought ways to be close to Westerners, for we viewed them as the messiahs of development. Since the PC policy presented the best opportunity to be close to whites, we hailed it. PCVs were usually friendly and accessible unlike most high-flying diplomatic types and so-called development advisers. PCVs lived and socialized with local people, and rarely demonstrated the religious zeal of the missionaries. We constantly hung around the PCVs, and fantasized about going to America with them. We neither knew, nor cared about the motives and hidden agenda of the Truman/Kennedy plan. The degrading specter of colonialism appeared to have vanished like a shadow. The vituperative language of colonial hegemony and racial superiority had been replaced by a new language with a neutral tone. A euphemistic lexicon of American partnership and collaboration for development emerged. It proved to be a potent seductive force in the modern diplomacy of domination (Shrestha, 2002, pp. 273–4).

In this way, like in the volunteer tourism experience, the desire to make friends overshadowed the implications of the development agendas that they represented.

Love

An effect of the volunteer tourism encounter, "love" was frequently used to describe the volunteer tourism experience. Indeed, it is widely noted by Thais how many *Farang* return to Chiang Mai after "falling in love" with the city. One tourist blog headline reads, "Falling in love … with Chiang Mai" (Safina, 2009). The blogger continues, "I promised to myself that I would be back! Yes! That was the effect that Chiang Mai had on me" (Safina, 2009). A local Chiang Mai newsletter similarly comments "from now on, I'm not surprised that many people coming here are falling in love with the diverse city like Chiang Mai" (Open Chiang Mai, 2010). Tourists regularly fall in love with Chiang Mai and volunteer tourists are no exception. Several volunteers felt so strongly about their experience with Thai people that they tattooed themselves in Thai script. For example, a 22-year-old American woman tattooed "one love" in Thai on her arm. She stated, "I also got a tattoo, this means 'one love' in Thai. I like Thailand a lot." When asked why she decided to tattoo herself in Thai, she explained that her experience in Thailand opened her eyes to the world and she felt a strong attachment to Thai people (Conran, 2011). When I asked Carol about her volunteer tourism experience, she pulled out a copy of "Chiang Mai City Life," a local English language magazine. She explained how the article nicely captures her experience:

> There was an article in the new magazine, Chiang Mai City Life … There's an article that you have to read and it just … there's a quotation that I wrote down to bring home because it typifies what Chiang Mai does for people.

The quotation Carol refers to states:

> This country, [referring to the northern part of what is now Thailand] if not the Promised Land, is yet one which grows dearer to the heart the more one knows it, and makes the stranger feel that, if he must be exiled from his own native shores, he could not find a land of greater charm and sympathy in which to spend his days (Reginald Le May's "An Asian Arcady" (1926), quoted by Roy Hudson in *City Life Magazine*, November 11, 2008).

This sentimental portrait of northern Thailand is emphasized by international volunteers who "fall in love" with Chiang Mai. For example, Helen, a volunteer from Hong Kong writes on the Chiang Mai Friends reviews:

> [Chiang Mai Friends] has definitely made my trip marvelous and unforgettable. Living in Chiang Mai for 2 weeks as a volunteer, I had the precious opportunity to experience Thai life almost as a local. People here always wear a big warm smile, and the city would just melt everyone's heart. I would highly recommend volunteers to come teaching English to Monks. The satisfactory feeling that comes afterwards is truly rewarding! (Riina, 2009).

Similarly, lamenting her departure from Thailand another 22-year-old American woman commented to me how much love she felt in the country: "learning about the Thai culture and it's a land of smiles, I will miss that. When I reach America, I am going to hate it, everyone walks with their heads down, they don't look at each other, lots of love, there is so much love here. I want to bring that back with me" (also cited in Conran, 2011). Alex, an American volunteer who volunteered at the temple school and the single mothers' home explains:

'The Land of Smiles' is the perfect phrase coined for Thailand. Love radiates from this country through the smiles and warm greetings from the local people. Whether it was during my trip in Pai, the Chiang Mai Friends home, or at either of my volunteer projects, I feel that I made many unexpected friendships!

Host community members often suggest that the volunteers choose to volunteer in their communities because they have "good hearts" and were full of love. Yet, the meaning of "love" in Thai does not perfectly translate to English. In one sense, love is associated with all feelings, which have a prefix, *jai* and literally translates to "heart" while *rak* which literally translates to love, takes on different socio-linguistic connotations than love in English. While the meanings of these comments in Thai do not translate directly into English, they broadly refer to the mutual concept of affection and goodwill towards others. For example, Noi, a 38-year-old host community member and mother of two at Orchard Home notes why she thinks the volunteers come:

> They want to help, they want to help under privileged people without opportunities in the foundation. These people cannot go outside the foundation, there is nothing. So, the volunteers from America come to help. Now they come to teach English and to help with whatever like handicrafts for example. They want to come help like this, they are helpers … Americans, I think they come for touring right? And then they finish touring and see there is a foundation and want to help because they are good people. They want to help the world and the world society; that is in their hearts. It is like that.

Anchali, an NGO practitioner at Orchard Home similarly notes how, like the tourists, she observes a difference between tourists and travelers:

> The volunteers come because they want to help. But the tourists, they come because they want to sightsee. But the volunteers, they have good intentions and are strong and they want to help the children and the women here more than they want to sightsee.

She further notes how:

> Some volunteers went sightseeing already, but they got bored and so maybe that is when they decided that they wanted to help out. Some people go somewhere and get to know the place with a guide and the guide takes them here. Maybe they are bored and so then they come here to work. Some people have travelled a lot and so then they come to do good deeds.

Similarly, Ajaan Nui, a teacher at a rural elementary school explains that the volunteers seem to have a "heart" for teaching:

The important thing that we receive from the foreign volunteers is that they come to do research. They really want to help us. This impresses us. They also bring along some of the media. I mean, they have the heart to come out and help us as well as the children.

Additionally, when I asked Manop, an orphanage manager why he thought the volunteers came to his orphanage, he suggested: "I understand that they have a good heart for teaching the children. They want to let the children get to know English." While host community members expressed affection for the volunteers, it is unclear whether or to what extent it was an expression of emotional or affective labor (Hardt and Negri, 2000, Hochschild, 1979, Hochschild, 1983). In volunteer tourism the product that the volunteers consume is the interactions with host community members. If these interactions are not positively received by the host community members, like all markets, the volunteer-consumer can take their business elsewhere. Additionally, the host community members are already marginalized communities and may feel pressure to accept all forms of assistance.

The role of love in volunteer tourism parallels the Peace Corps experience. Hoffman explains how "a fundamental tension within the Peace Corps and its counterparts abroad" is that:

> volunteers recognized that 'love' was not sufficient to change the harsh conditions
> of poverty, yet only an emotional willingness to share in that suffering persuaded
> many volunteers to keep getting up for work every day. And in some cases, the
> resistance of cultures to change meant that 'love'—moral support—was all that
> volunteers fundamentally could give (Hoffman, 1998, pp. 9–10).

Yet, as the second director of the Peace Corps, Jack Vaughn, notes: "'The Peace Corps is about love,' ... But love operate[s] within political limits" (Hoffman, 1998, p. 9). Volunteer tourism operates within similar political limits.

Compassion

While intimacy and love are effects of the volunteer tourism experience, according to most participants, compassion is at least in part the cause. As scholars of compassion suggest, compassion cannot take place anywhere with anyone at any time. Rather, only some places, some people, at particular times are legitimated as objects of compassion, while others are not (Berlant, 2004, Ahmed, 2004). Rather than being a simple emotion, compassion is a highly mediated, political and complex experience (Berlant, 2004). This complexity is at least in part based on its etymology, which at its root, is based on inequality. Garber observes how "the problem with compassion begins with its etymology and history" (Garber, 2004, p. 20). Until the seventeenth century compassion meant to suffer together or "fellow feeling" but by the end of the century, it was increasingly used to refer to feelings towards "'a person in distress by one who is free from it, who is, in this respect, his superior.' When the first sense fell out of use, which it did fairly quickly, the remaining sense hovered between charity and condescension" (Garber, 2004, p. 20).

The term compassion is increasingly used in alternative movements such as the BC Compassion Club Society[2] which provides marijuana to patients with chronic illness, the book, "Compassionate Souls" which describes how to raise children as vegetarians and *Love! Valour! Compassion!*, a play about eight homosexual men (Garber, 2004, p. 25). Compassion is also used as a discursive frame for alternative consumption such as ethically and fairly traded goods and services, or "compassionate consumption." Alternatively, neoconservatives have appropriated the emotion as a central theme in their campaign for compassionate conservatism (Berlant, 2004). Thus "... compassion seems to waver politically between two forms of inequality: the benevolence of those who have (the power of the rich) and the entitlement of those who need (the power of the poor)" (Garber, 2004, p. 26).

Volger explains how "of the many species of tenderness directed toward others' troubles, compassion falls squarely in the range of affective orientations with a built-in clean-hands clause. This is, I would suggest, an important distinguishing mark of compassionate receptivity to others' misfortune" (Vogler, 2004, p. 30). Volunteer tourism is a compassionate form of touristic consumption which depends on compassionate consumers. Volunteers often perceive their actions as compassionate. Speculating on host community member's perceptions, John notes:

> I guess because they are people themselves and ... as the human race we have to show that we care and love other people. I mean even though they are a whole lot different—nearly a world apart—they're still people ... Yeah, I guess compassion.

Volunteers' descriptions of compassion are often coupled with "giving back" to society. As one NGO practitioner points out, being a volunteer tourist is: "[L]ike being a traveler and yet being able to give something to the place where they are going. Giving something back, like okay, they enjoy the culture the place and etc. But they also give something." Ann, a 19-year-old Norwegian volunteer suggests how giving back is an unselfish act:

> I noticed the girls in the house, all of us are not very selfish. I noticed that people who are selfish don't want to volunteer, you see all their motives and you see ... volunteering is to give back. You are not here to get what you want, so I think

---

2 "The BC Compassion Club is a collectively-run non-profit natural health centre providing safe, high-quality medicinal cannabis and the services of a full wellness centre. Since 1997, we have served over 5,000 members with serious or terminal illnesses" (http://www.thecompassionclub.org/ April 2, 2010).

someone who thinks they are privileged and gives that back to someone. It has been such a learning experience, all these monks and everything.

Yet most volunteers were conscious of the fact that they also benefited from the volunteer experience and thus it was not exclusively altruistic. Many volunteers talked about how they gained work experience as well as felt good about their efforts. For example, Andrea commented: "[W]hen I work for the single mother's home, it feels great that I made those kids laugh, that's the important thing."

Host community members perceive the volunteers' motives for participation to be one of compassion. As Don, an 18-year-old Thai host community member suggests, international volunteers come to their single mother's home because they sympathize with their situation and feel compassionate enough to take action: "I think that they usually read the brochure, which causes them to sympathize with the single mothers. Then they think that it is not enough to just sympathize with us so they choose to come to [Our] Home. They choose [Our] Home because the brochure makes them think, 'I want to help the women and support them because they are in a very difficult situation.'" When I asked Preecha, a Thai orphanage manager why he thought the volunteers came to his orphanage, he suggested that it was "Because [Traveling Teachers] surely saw that we were without volunteers and we were just starting, so we didn't have anything. That's probably why they wanted to come help us here."

These descriptions of compassion illustrate how "compassion is only identifiable as morality when it is the basis of distinctive forms of social action on the part of the actors who together constitute the audience" (Tester, 2001, p. viii). For example, when asked about the most memorable aspect of her experience with the international volunteers, Anchali, a host community member, turned NGO practitioner at Orchard Home explains:

> I think that the thing I remember the most is that they make a special effort to come help even though they are not paid for their work. They have the heart to come help Thai people. There aren't many people that would come help like this. If Thai people were not paid they would not do this work.

Like all sentiments, compassion emerges over a longer history of encounters between both near and distant strangers (Ahmed, 2004). Host community members are aware of the structural inequalities on which the compassionate encounter is based. For example, Tom, the *tuk-tuk* driver comments about the volunteers privileged position from which they are able to enact their compassion:

> They come from the basis that they have a secure job and surplus of money already and so they have enough surplus so I can help others. Suppose that you didn't have any money, then you couldn't help anyone. And your family too. First everything else must be okay before you can help others.

The objects of compassion in volunteer tourism in developing countries raise critical questions about the cultural politics of compassion as well as the political economy of popular humanitarianism. Our feelings about who is and is not worth "saving" are mediated by images of starving children, the poor and the marginalized, which are now regularly depicted in both local and international media and play a core role in extending the humanitarian gaze (as discussed in Chapter 1) (Tester, 2001, Boltanski, 1999, Ahmed, 2004). Ahmed explains how "to be moved by the suffering of some others (the 'deserving' poor, the innocent child, the injured hero), is also to be elevated into a place that remains untouched by other others (whose suffering cannot be converted into my sympathy or admiration). So it is not a coincidence that it is a child's suffering that touches the nation" (Ahmed, 2004, p. 192). From this perspective, it is unsurprising that the most common objects of compassion in volunteer tourism are children.

The role of children in volunteer tourism may be related to the perpetual "search for authenticity," which is in part a search for an unmediated experience beyond the realm of capitalist modernity. Manzo suggests that "the iconography of childhood expresses institutional ideas and the key humanitarian values of humanity, neutrality and impartiality, and solidarity" as well as legitimizes the idea of development (Manzo, 2008, p. 632). This may be in part because children appear to be unmediated by history, colonialism or capitalism (Goss, 2010). By nature, children are less constrained by cultural norms—allowing the volunteer to feel authentic intimacy, love and compassion for the child. Indeed, the child will not make the volunteer feel guilty for the inequality of the encounter as she allows the volunteer to feel intimate with the host community. Sentimentality over children in developing countries is a powerful semiotic operator within popular humanitarianism that intersects with postcolonial empathy in complex and often contradictory ways.

Empathy and the Postcolonial Complex

On my way to lunch one day at the local temple school Bridgette, a 27-year-old Australian volunteer explained that volunteering was not easy because of the emotionality of the experience: "[I]t takes a lot out of me. When I am done for the day I am drained and need a nap because I give everything I have to the kids. I love them. I really love them." This emotionalization of the experience is part of the broader discourse of neoliberal governmentality that is situated within what Illouz (2007) refers to as "emotional capitalism." In this context, the neoliberal professional is expected to develop a particular type of emotional response to the suffering of distant strangers as part of a range of flexible, cultural competencies. Vrasti argues that "[T]he only way for capitalism to perpetuate its rule is to acquire the social goal it was accused of never having. Yet neither approach takes seriously enough the power of neoliberal ideology to put forth the credible affective structures and the ability of individuals to derive genuine pleasure from them" (Vrasti, 2011, p. 1). Neoliberal subjectivity is supported and justified by myriad institutions and narratives that are socially organized and that facilitate new geographies of care (Rabbitts, 2012, Milligan et al., 2007, Lawson, 2007, Conradson, 2003). These relationships are perhaps most conspicuous in spaces of tourist consumption where the producer (host community member requiring "care") and consumer (volunteer tourist providing "care") directly encounter each other. Pedwell argues that within neoliberal governmentality, there is "an obligation to be a caring and empathetic individual not only because it is 'the right thing to do' but also because empathy, as an emotional competency, has become part and parcel of being a self-managing and self-enterprising individual within a neoliberal order" (Pedwell, 2012b, p. 286). The emotionalization of the volunteer tourism experience is widely noted by volunteers who frequently comment on the intensity of the experience for self-transformation (Crossley, 2012).

The ambivalence of the postcolonial period materializes within host-guest encounters among middle and upper class travelers from former colonial empires in Thailand. The focus on "Third World children" as the primary benefactors of volunteer tourism is one—albeit contradictory—way in which the industry seeks to overcome this ambivalence. NGOs' use of images of children creates a dynamic tension between humanitarian principles and colonial practices where "associations of childhood with universal human rights are relatively recent tropes of innocence, dependence and protection have a far longer lineage in colonial ideology (including the child-centrism of missionary iconography) and development theory" (Manzo, 2008, p. 636). "Going native" has similarly become a strategy for Westerners in the Third World—including anthropologists—to attempt to overcome their postcolonial guilt (Douglas, 2009, Cohen, 1988). Indeed, going native is a familiar Euro-American pastime (Huhndorf, 2001), where individualism and identification with the other in volunteer tourism attempt to circumvent postcolonial critique (Mowforth and Munt, 2009, p. 130). In the context of American anxieties about Native Americans, Huhndorf explains how "[I]n its various forms, going native articulates and attempts to resolve widespread ambivalence about modernity as well as anxieties about the terrible violence marking the nation's origins" (Huhndorf, 2001, p. 2). This tendency towards "going native" is central to the postcolonial complex. The "significance of going native extends well beyond the relations between European Americans and Native Americans. Often, these representations and events not only articulate and attempt to resolve anxieties about history and modernity, they reflect upon other power relations within the broader society" (Huhndorf, 2001, p. 9).

In Third World tourism, these anxieties are magnified by the uneasy relationship between citizens of former colonizing and colonized states. While Thailand was never a formal colony, it is widely considered an economic colony of the US, Japan and other allies who encouraged the adoption of widespread neoliberal structural adjustment programs, which have fractured the country (Hewison, 2003, Hewison, 2000, Hewison, 2005, Rigg, 1991, Wilson, 2004: see also Chapter 3, Costa, 2001). Wilson observes how "[T]hese asymmetrical relations can be considered imperialist or neocolonialist, and Thailand shares aspects of the postcolonial condition with the rest of Southeast Asia" (Wilson, 2004, p. 16). Volunteers and NGO practitioners in Thailand respond and attempt to overcome these postcolonial anxieties through directly addressing some of the implications of colonialism (e.g. widespread poverty, environmental degradation). This form of tourism allows the traveler to assuage her own postcolonial guilt and engage in a sense of imperialist nostalgia (Rosaldo, 1989) through intimate interactions with the local communities. Volunteers describe local host communities as "authentically Thai," and suggest that host community members embody the natural and spiritual essence of Thailand; an essence perceived to be eroding by an ensuing Western contamination. In a related context, Huhndorf observes that Native peoples are often perceived as "idealized versions of themselves, as the embodiments of virtues lost in the Western world" (Huhndorf, 2001, p. 2). Torgovnick similarly argues how "the primitive is the sign and symbol of desires the West has sought to repress—desires for direct correspondences between bodies and things, direct correspondences between experience and language, direct correspondences between individual beings and the collective life force" (Torgovnick, 1997, p. 8). Yet, as Huhndorf further asserts, while these representations glorify the Other, they "also reaffirm the racialized, progressivist ethos about industrial capitalism" (Huhndorf, 2001, p. 14).

Western travelers' tales about intimate interactions and "going native" in developing countries re-create discourses of Third World authenticity (Mowforth and Munt, 2009). Thus, they "are a modern (or perhaps postmodern) continuation of the stories of colonial encounters and a useful way to demonstrate how discourse is used to represent or recreate a reality and impose meaning, in much the same way as the fantastic tales retold by colonialist in the nineteenth century" (Mowforth and Munt, 2009, p. 138). Through the articulation and normalization of the "First World giver"–"Third World" receiver discourse, the volunteer tourism encounter recreates colonial relations of power (Simpson, 2004). Ultimately, like so many well-meaning projects of international development, volunteer tourism seems to follow suit. In this vein, Ahmed notes how, in the context of Western-led development:

> The West gives to others only insofar as it is forgotten what the West has already taken in its very capacity to give in the first place, [for example,] feelings of pain and suffering which are in part effects of socio-economic relations of violence and poverty, are assumed to be alleviated by the very generosity that is enabled by such socio-economic relations. So the West takes, then gives, and in the movement of giving repeats as well as conceals the taking (Ahmed, 2004, p. 22).

In volunteer tourism, those in the position to give often overlook what has already been taken in order for them to give. Or when the inequality of the encounter is acknowledged, it is assumed that volunteering can forgive the debt owed to those who have suffered on their behalf. These aspects of the encounter normalize the relationship between volunteers, NGO practitioners and host community members in volunteer tourism. It is to this relationship that I focus on in the following chapter where I examine how volunteer tourism participants' interests converge and diverge at the nexus of authenticity, intimacy and cross-cultural volunteer tourism experiences.

Chapter 6

Converging Interests? Cross-Cultural Authenticity in Volunteer Tourism

Pom, a 26-year-old wife and mother who lives in Mae Nam Village explains: "If they interact with the community members and the community members can learn things and get a profit, then [volunteer tourism] is okay—it is good. But if they aren't bringing anything to the community then [volunteer tourism] is not good. If [the volunteers] come here they should benefit the community." Pom recently moved from Sukhothai to Mae Nam Village in the Mae On District of Chiang Mai. She lives with her husband Arthit, 28, and her three-year-old son. We are sitting in the guest eco-lodge where she works five days a week. Pom cleans the lodge and cooks for the volunteers and staff for around 3,000 baht (USD $100) per month.[1] When there are volunteers at the lodge, Pom is usually the first host community member to meet them. I met Pom in 2006 when she wanted to become a trekking guide. It was expected that volunteers would help expand the hiking trail system that ecotourists were to pay 200 baht to enter. Six years later this goal has yet to be realized. However, there is still hope that they will someday arrive *en masse* as has been promised by BV, the NGO that leases Mae Nam Village's land where the lodge is located. While there are seldom tourists of any kind in Mae Nam Village, there are a growing number of Euro-American staff who speak English and have been hired to build trails and market the lodge to international clientele. Pom learns English informally from staff that frequent the lodge. English-speaking Thai guides from outside the village are being trained as trekking guides and Pom makes their food and cleans their rooms.

Pom's experience illustrates how despite the good intentions of the NGO operators, host community members' interests and expectations can be marginalized in pursuit of others' goals. Many of the volunteers' and host community members' interests converge and diverge in ways that are symptomatic of broader systemic inequalities and opportunities that both groups work within—and, indeed, often against. The interests of the volunteers and host community members emerge at the nexus of an expanding consciousness of economic inequality and an emerging cosmopolitan morality within developing countries (Goodman, 2005, Goodman, 2004, Tester, 2001, Tester, 2010). Mowforth and Munt explain:

> Tourism is widely touted as a beneficial cultural exchange for all parties
> involved, as having contributed to the general well-being of peoples around the

---

1   The average income for Mae Nam Village is $7,000 baht (USD $232) per month.

world, as having stimulated economic development and as 'promoting better understanding between races, religions and human beings worldwide' (UNWTO 1999). With such descriptors one might be forgiven for believing that the relationships between tourists and local people in the visited destination areas are always rosy (2009, p. 260).

Despite widespread praise among academics and popular media for volunteer tourism as a "win-win" development strategy, critics charge the industry with a re-articulation of colonial encounters and a superfluous feel good experience (MacKinnon, 2009, Guttentag, 2009). As a *TIME Magazine* correspondent asks: "[A]re volunteer vacations ... merely overpriced guilt trips with an impact as fleeting as the feel-good factor? Or do they offer individuals a real chance to change the world, one summer jaunt at a time?" (Fitzpatrick, 2007). Answers to questions like these are still being debated among academics, the popular media, NGOs and other volunteer tourism participants who seek to determine the "real value" of volunteer tourism for its participants (Sin, 2009). As the Lonely Planet's volunteer tourism guide, *Volunteer: Making a Difference Around the World* notes, "there's the problem that not all volunteering is good volunteering" (Hindle, 2007, p. 9). Concurring with academic critiques of the industry, they warn that "[T]here are plenty of volunteer organizations that are not meeting or responding to the local needs, not working in proper partnership with host communities and certainly not working towards sustainable solutions" (Hindle, 2007, p. 9). Additionally, academic critiques of volunteer tourism point out that it may be inappropriate to assume that sending volunteers to the Third World will necessarily benefit the host communities (Raymond, 2008, p. 50). Rather, "[I]t is increasingly being suggested that volunteer tourism does not always represent a mutually beneficial form of tourism and that while volunteer tourists may experience a range of benefits, in many cases, the organizations that host such volunteers gain far less" (Raymond, 2008, p. 49). MacKinnon from a Malawi NGO comments how "[S]ome dismiss volunteer tourism as 'a morally seductive adaptation of modern mass tourism' ... Many volunteer projects serve the egos of the tourists more effectively than they serve the locals. Even the idea that it creates a pool of people committed to ending global poverty is questionable. At least as many come home with their optimism in tatters" (MacKinnon, 2009). I explore volunteer tourism as a "cross-cultural" encounter in this chapter to examine the corollary converging and diverging interests of host community members and volunteers to illustrate how questions of authenticity, (self-)development and cross-cultural exchange emerge within the complex cultural politics of volunteer tourism.

Cross-Cultural Authenticity

Despite the new contexts in which volunteer tourism emerges, the traditional Western tourists' "search for authenticity" in seemingly pre-modern or pre-capitalist peoples and places (MacCannell, 1973, MacCannell, 1976, Culler, 1981, MacCannell, 1992) has not lost its power. Rather, it is re-framed as the authentic cross-cultural encounter. This narrative of "pre-modern" authenticity is ironically developed within the development project in volunteer tourism (see Chapter 3). Western development discourse is frequently disrupted by the volunteers' interest in host communities' "culture" which is sometimes perceived to be "better" than the "Western way." While the overarching themes in volunteers' expressions of their interests include the long-standing "search for authenticity" and "development," these themes are interrupted by the reality of their experiences. Volunteers' and host community members' interests are intimately linked with the desire to participate in an emerging global modernity which can seemingly be realized within the cross-cultural experience that volunteer tourism facilitates. Volunteers' concern with meeting local people and having a rare glimpse into the "real" Thailand permits them to broaden their perspectives, challenge themselves, and reaffirm their self-proclaimed identity as a global citizen. International friendships are a sign of cosmopolitan modernity that allow volunteers to enact their globally conscious identity. While host community members' interests vary because of the different circumstances under which they become involved in volunteer tourism, there is a complementary interest in cross-cultural experiences and making friends from afar.

Volunteers' and host community members' interests converge in myriad and sometimes unpredictable ways. The underlying goals for the volunteers and host community members are built around various modes of participation in an emerging and increasingly global conversation within contact zones of popular humanitarianism (see Chapter 1). These conversations perpetuate an international discourse of cross-cultural understanding between "hosts" and "guests." While the volunteer tourism encounter is recognized as a uniquely intense space of cross-cultural exchange, what participants learn about each other as a result of the encounter is rarely explored (Beaver et al., 2006, Collins et al., 2002, Jackiewicz, 2004, Hindle, 2007, Singh and Singh, 2004, Raymond and Hall, 2008). Vrasti argues that while "[T]hese stressful and exasperating encounters [teach] volunteers how to cope with cultural anxieties and nervous conditions, mediate cross-cultural conflicts and communicate more effectively" they do "not encourage them to critically reflect upon their racial privilege or pursue deeper relations with the local population. In effect, racial tensions [are] better at producing the flexible and employable citizen-workers required in a multicultural society and a multinational economy than at unsettling the white privilege this subjectivity rests upon" (Vrasti, 2012, p. 124). Volunteer tourism is illustrative of this emerging global forum where participants from disparate socio-economic backgrounds encounter each other on an unequal basis and perpetuate familiar stereotypes of culturally different Others. The implications of this encounter have yet to be fully worked out for what they represent in our shared historical times.

The Search for Authenticity

Authenticity has been a central concern in the Anthropology of Tourism for over four decades. In its persistence, volunteer tourism has been re-framed as an authentic cross-cultural encounter. However, volunteers seek out an "authentic" experience in developing countries *vis-a-vis* development projects. In other words, they seek out seemingly underdeveloped communities with the intention of helping to develop them—but they do so with awareness that "developing too much" would adulterate the "authenticity" of the experience (see Chapter 3). Volunteers negotiate this irony by expressing their desire to "help" with caution; and poignantly describe their worry that host community members will become too Westernized. Host community members echo the dominant "development" discourse and seek ways to become further incorporated into the global capitalist economy. In this respect volunteers and host community members approach volunteer tourism from variant perspectives: volunteers engage in a "search for authenticity" in a seemingly pre-capitalist existence, while host community members overwhelmingly seek further incorporation into global capitalism. These apparently divergent interests converge around their concurrent affirmation in development. Yet, a counter-narrative punctuates this dominant development discourse. As their experience progresses volunteers like Jenny, a 25-year-old American, begin to question development and suggest how "maybe they [host community members] are better off than we are." On the other hand, Thai host community members suggest that perhaps they do not need "cars and big buildings" as much as they once thought, because they "have culture and nature." While the interests of volunteers and host community members seem to converge around different, yet mutual interests in a cross-cultural encounter, the volunteers' interests are primarily mediated by their "search for authenticity," while the host community members' interest seems to be mediated by their interest in "development." Yet, within the intimate spaces of the volunteer tourism encounter "authenticity" and "development" are reconstituted through (inter) personal cross-cultural experience, which lends itself to alternative and sometimes counter-narratives of the development project.

Glynn, a 26-year-old English volunteer illustrates how the broader "search for authenticity" is a core aspect of a meaningful experience that cannot be found in the West:

> I think there are some things in the West people are looking for that they can't get.
> A lot of people who travel and come back did so because it's nice and amazing.
> I certainly felt something. When you are traveling, the positive experiences of volunteering have definitely made me more open to more people.

This search for authenticity tends to intersect with the decommodification of experience and renouncing of materialistic lifestyles. Volunteers, for example, frequently describe an interest in "non-consumerist" consumption. Approximately 80 percent of the volunteers in this research suggested that they did not pay attention to brands or did not buy brand named items. This observation illustrates how "the Other of modernity—which corresponds to particular tourist objects and experiences—is defined by an absence of design—of calculation or of interested self-awareness. It must therefore exist outside the circuit of commodity relations and exchange values (although it is only accessible through this circuit, one form of the basic contradiction of the tourist experience)" (Frow, 1991, p. 129). Broad and Spencer note that the growth of the new middle classes has been met by an "emphasis on 'lifestyle,' which includes the places people choose to live, the activities they engage in and also the holiday choices they make" (2008, p. 216).

Indeed, many volunteers expressed their newfound "appreciation of the little things" or how they have become "less materialistic" as a result of the volunteer tourism experience. Jen, a 24-year-old volunteer from New Zealand, for example, notes:

> There is so much more to life. You have so many comforts at home ... I realized there is so much more that I don't need, but the relationship with people, the little moments, they are so much more important than other things. These things matter. I mean I won't go back home and see my computer and say, oh I don't need it. It's just the attachments you have, they are so many things at home that I don't really need. It's like a cycle. I don't know how to explain.

Ann, a 26-year-old volunteer from Germany similarly explains:

> It makes me realize what a materialistic life I've been leading. I mean, not a hundred percent because I've always done volunteer work and looked after the underdog and older people, sick people, relatives who don't have children who need help. I'm just that kind of a person, right. It made me realize how fortunate I really have been and I am and what I hope to bring back is to realize that these are meaningless things that are just things and to carry on like the last years of my life maybe just accepting where I am, the changes, you know we've gone through a lot of changes ... this kind of helped us make that transition because we realized how fortunate we really have been.

Corroborating these claims, Cross-Cultural Solutions, the largest volunteer tourism organization in the US, notes how the experiences they offer are similarly life changing. Kathleen, a Cross-Cultural Solutions Costa Rica volunteer writes:

> Cross-Cultural Solutions was the most amazing experience I have ever had! I have never felt so good inside as I did in the short two weeks I worked in San Carlos ... I will never take for granted the little things in life ever again (Cross Cultural Solutions, 2008).

Similarly, Jillian, a Cross-Cultural Solutions Brazil volunteer comments:

I would just like to commend the entire Cross-Cultural Solutions organization. The work I did in Brazil was the first time in my life that I had accomplished something that I was truly proud of; and the most humbling part of it all, was that the only thing I really had to do in order to make a difference was show up every day. Just by being with the kids, I may have made their lives a little better. To what extent that's true may be something that I'll never get to hear, but every day since I've been back I think about them and how they all made me realize how lucky I am to have so much here in the States. And I guess they'll never know either just how much better they made my life just by being in it (Cross Cultural Solutions, 2008).

Johntine, a Cross-Cultural Solutions Costa Rica volunteer further comments:

I think that trips like this one really help to put life in perspective. My "problems" just didn't really seem like problems anymore. I really hope I never lose the sense of how blessed I am, and how important it is to go outside of your comfort zone and take trips like this one that teach you how to appreciate life (Cross Cultural Solutions, 2008).

What these comments indicate is that volunteer tourism encourages volunteers to reflect on their own materialistic and "lucky" lifestyles thus depoliticizing the inequality of the encounter and indeed inequality more generally. This newfound reflexivity for one's privileged position within the global capitalist economy helps to perpetuate notions of inequality that are based on what Simpson, following Quincy, refers to as "lotto logic." Simpson notes how rather than focusing on others, gap year volunteers overwhelmingly focus on their own self-development and …

… ascribe some form of 'lotto logic' (Quincy, 2002) to the disparities that they observe. 'Lotto logic' is allowed to replace discussions on inequality and oppression. Gross material differences can then be explained through a fatalistic faith in the 'luck of the draw,' rather than in structures and systems in which we all participate, and which are, ultimately, open to change. Learning that living conditions and life are products of a randomized process of luck, sets particular parameters for social justice, wherein wealth and poverty are not part of the same process, but attributed independently of one another (Simpson, 2004, p. 689).

Cross-cultural experiences in volunteer tourism have the potential to both justify and overshadow or interrogate broader structural inequalities that the experience is based on.

They Have "Hi" and We Have "Sawadee"

One day while picking lettuce in the community garden at Orchard Home, Prang explained to me how "The foreigners bring new things and new information. They want to come and teach. They have 'hi' and we have 'sawadee.' So it is fun. We can talk and exchange cultures and learn new things." Prang's interest in cross-cultural experiences extends to other host community members in my research who echo the volunteers' desire to "get to know Thai culture" through their interest in getting to know "Farang culture." Anu from Orchard Home similarly asserts: "We exchange ideas and culture and that helps us gain a broader perspective." In most cases, communication was highly superficial and primarily realized through body language. Indeed, when I asked Pom about her experience with the volunteers in Mae Nam Village, she noted "We don't interact with the tourists. We don't talk with the tourists. We don't have much to do with them." This is despite the fact that the volunteers stay in the lodge where Pom works during the week. Yet, this did not mean they do not want more interaction. Indeed, while conducting this research, several host community members became emotional over my interest in their perspectives and ways of life. I often left homes with fruit, woven baskets and requests to return soon. Yet, in other host communities, more intense interactions between the volunteers and host community members led to makeshift communication techniques. Nong from Orchard Home, for example, refers to "hand talking." It was noted in several instances that body language and "hand talking" sufficed as effective modes of communication (Conran, 2011). Noi, from Orchard Home explains how the most memorable aspect of her experience with the volunteers are "greetings and smiling, taking care, saying hello, these things are good memories." Despite lack of linguistic communication between the volunteers and host community members, interactions and relationships are a core aspect of the encounter.

   Volunteers often talk about the interactions with host community members as a primary example of how they partake in cross-cultural experiences. For example, optimistically commenting his volunteer tourism experience, John, 18, from Ireland explains:

> I get to experience the cultures of different people. For example, Satomi, she is from Japan and we get to experience Japanese culture. We exchange how all different nationalities work, we learn about different cultures and get to work with the variety of people: it's like a little U.N. here in Chiang Mai.

This suggestion that Chiang Mai is like a little UN is reflective of the cosmopolitan atmosphere the volunteer tourism facilitates. This atmosphere is positively experienced by most participants who enjoy the cosmopolitan virtues of meeting people from diverse geographical and cultural backgrounds and consider themselves global citizens. The different kinds of experiences that volunteers have compared to their backpacking counterparts are what they suggest set them apart from "tourists." For example, Marla, 26, from Holland explains how volunteering is better than "just" being a tourist: "Because you see, you have more contact with the people. You help people and you get to know them and they get to know you." Ann, a 19-year-old volunteer from Holland similarly notes how she taught Thai people something about Holland while she "learned a lot about Thai culture and also about Buddhism." Satomi notes how working with the local people allows her to learn more about Thai culture: "Working with people is different from just spending time or talking to them. It's also, I can see culture working with them and I know about Thai culture now." These kinds of comments are echoed throughout the volunteer tourism experience where getting to know Thai culture is a primary objective and this culture is seemingly absorbed through proximity rather than linguistic communication.

While volunteers often spent the first few weeks getting used to Thailand, by the end of their volunteer experience they appreciate and even prefer Thai cultural norms. Conversing about this scenario, Sanne, 22 and Marshan, 21 explain:

> Sanne: Yeah, it's a whole other way of living life because in Thailand you kind of live life on the streets and live in the moment, but in Denmark, you can just isolate yourself. Drive to work, and go back home.

> Marshan: Yeah. We look straight past each other to use a bathroom, you have to use your own bathroom and it has to be silent all the way to the bathroom. That's really hard sometimes because we are not really used to this [sharing bathrooms]. In Denmark, you close your doors and people knock before they come in.

Volunteers' interest in the cross-cultural experience is often articulated as:

> wanting to get to know "real" Thai culture. Volunteers' efforts to understand Thai culture are generally appreciated by host community members. For example, the volunteers' inclusion in Buddhist festivals and their adoption of Buddhist practices (for example, wearing Buddha images) ... support claims in the literature that tourists can be subjected to the demonstration effect, and that rather than being negatively commodified, the local's culture and beliefs can be promoted in a positive manner (Broad and Spencer, 2008, p. 223).

Like the goals of the Peace Corps, the goals of volunteer tourism are developed around mutual understanding (see Chapter 2). NGOs, the primary facilitators of volunteer tourism in developing countries, prioritize the quality of interactions between the tourists and community members (Wearing, 2001). Cross-Cultural Solutions illustrates this aspect of their experience in its selected memoirs from former volunteers. For example, a volunteer in Morocco writes:

What was most memorable for me was not the teaching specifically, but instead the general interaction with the inmates and how fun it was trying to overcome the language barrier using the few Arabic and French words I knew—there were many rounds of Charades! I felt like most of the students were really eager to learn. Those who were not so interested in English were just as eager to get to know me and the other volunteers (Cross cultural solutions.org).

Similarly, the Lonely Planet's volunteer guide, *Volunteer: Making a Difference around the World* asks:

Are you looking for a more meaningful experience? Do you want to give back to the communities you visit, make a genuine connection with locals, meet like-minded travelers and build your skills? International volunteering opens up all these opportunities (Hindle, 2007, back cover).

NGO practitioners are often keen to facilitate friendships between the volunteers and host community members. Tasanee, a BV NGO practitioner became close friends with Satomi, the 22-year-old volunteer from Japan. They stayed in regular contact after Satomi returned to Japan and Satomi came back to Thailand the following year to visit Tasanee. Describing the most important aspects of volunteer tourism, Satomi notes: "You'll get to make many local friends." She explained how this was an important aspect of her experience and that she will "definitely" stay in contact with them—and she did. It is these kinds of extended, personal relationships that are the memorable aspect of Satomi's experience. Today these kinds of long-lasting connections are more frequent in part because of social media sites such as Facebook and Twitter. For example, Satomi's ongoing relationship with Tasanee was at least in part facilitated by Facebook. Satomi explains the most memorable and meaningful part of her experience: "when I felt like I built a real friendship with people who are here and when I felt like I could trust them. I felt very happy ... I realized that I could trust them when I was able to talk to them about personal things and the things you wouldn't talk to people you don't really know, you don't trust." Satomi is referring here not to a host community member, but Kat, a Thai trekking guide whom she became close friends with and months later returned to visit in Chiang Mai.

Host community members often have an interest in the insights of the volunteers' cultural values and beliefs. Dang from Orchard home explained: "Before coming here I had never talked with *Farang*. I only saw them pass by." After daily encounters with *Farang* volunteers, Dang quickly became the most outgoing woman at Orchard Home in her interactions with the volunteers. Among other Thai women at the shelter, for example, many women were interested to learn more about the volunteers' life experiences. Host community members often describe the volunteers as "developed" and "strong." Most of the volunteers were young women who traveled to Thailand alone or with friends. This was seen as evidence of their "development" and empowerment as individuals from the

West. Many of the women at Orchard Home believed that they benefited from the volunteers as role models. Po explains:

> The women see the value of the international volunteers. The international volunteers make a special effort to come here to teach them. They want to know why the volunteers come to help them. They want to know how they can develop themselves. Like you, they come to help them. You want them to be able to develop themselves. You want them to learn and be able to go on with life. When they leave Orchard Home, they are going to have to support themselves. They want to be able to take care of themselves and not have someone else taking care of their children.

Anchali similarly explained:

> I like helping the women and learning about the women and how their husbands were. I want to know how men are. I want to know about their experiences with their husbands ... In the future when I meet men I can decide how they are. I can learn from the experiences of some of the women that the women have told me.

Pom explained that she benefited from the volunteers by "Interacting with foreigners ... now I feel I can talk to them. Like at the market, when we went together I was not afraid."

Host community members also simultaneously felt that the volunteers did not understand Thai culture. For example, Anchali explains:

> About the volunteers, I have seen that some people don't really understand Thai culture. Thai people don't touch people's heads right you know? But some *Farang* come and touch people's heads. And they sit in an impolite way. They keep their feet up in a way that Thai people think is impolite. If they come to Thailand they should act polite. They should learn about the culture.

Anchali's comments are interesting in part because CMF, the sending NGO, spends considerable time explaining Thai cultural norms to the volunteers during their two-day orientation. Nonetheless, volunteers continued to overlook Thai cultural norms in the interactions, contributing to an uncomfortable encounter with some of the volunteers.

Converging Interests?

When I asked Alex, a 22-year-old volunteer from the US why she thought the host community members were motivated to participate in volunteer tourism, she explained: "Because they need us!" Ann, a 19-year-old volunteer from Holland similarly explained: "I mean I really wouldn't know why you would not need volunteers. People are going to come and give for nothing." Additionally, volunteers often suggest that host community members benefit from experiencing generous people and learning about people and cultures beyond Thailand. For example, Sara, 26, from the US comments:

> It's good for them to see that people want to give. I explained to them that I was a volunteer and I wasn't getting paid and that I had to pay to come here and I think that gives them a sense of care that people care especially for the orphans. Also to let them know that there is more than just Thailand. Because most of them don't know outsiders or anything about them. They don't understand other countries; they don't understand any of it ... Yes they get to have foreigners come in and pay so and I guess it's good for the kids to get to know about other countries and cultures so they're not just exposed to their own culture and maybe the neighboring countries. People come from across the world and maybe later in life they'll remember this.

Yet, the ways volunteer tourists' and host community members' interests converge and diverge are not always so obvious or simple. The encounter is often mediated by cultural confusion, naiveté and at times arrogance that punctuate easy narratives of people who "need" and people who "give." Participants navigate their and their counterparts' interests in sometimes predictable and at other times surprising ways.

Sustainable Volunteer Tourism?

Mowforth and Munt note that, "an increasing number of reports tell of work projects that construct unwanted buildings, take jobs which would otherwise be taken by locals, promote projects which are opposed by some segments of the populations, plant saplings which will not be tended, and leave 'white elephants' which cannot be sustained or maintained by local communities involved" (Mowforth and Munt, 2009, p. 127). During my fieldwork it was not uncommon for volunteers to develop programs or construct projects that were completed by past volunteers or that were demolished soon after the volunteers' departure. BV volunteers, for example, built bathrooms at an elementary school near Mae Nam Village. When I returned to Chiang Mai the following year I found that they had been demolished to put up another building. This example demonstrates a conflict between the logistical goals of the host community and interests of participants.

Sustainability discourses are a point of divergence between host community members, NGO operators and the volunteers. These differences were made explicit in Mae Nam Village where BV works within northern environmentalist discourses, while host community members engage with local discourses of sustainability. For example, part of the BV mission is to enhance environmental awareness for the community in order to develop the ecotourism business.

With the objectives of BV and its volunteers in mind, I asked Pom if she benefited from learning about the forest in Mae Nam Village. She explained, "I haven't seen that. We only benefit from the money that comes in." Yet, BV's discourse is passed down to its volunteers who also tend to see the benefits of biodiversity modeling, plant identification and other "environmental" projects which are meant to promote environmental sustainability in the village. For example, John, the founder of BV notes:

> Overall … this generation of villagers will benefit from their knowledge of surrounding lands and the vegetation and animals benefits us and we can work together that way. And the kids, where as they might move away, may now want to stay here, learn this knowledge from the older people in the village and put it to use in these programs and also benefits them by giving them jobs.

John explains how the village is located in a well managed watershed forest. Additionally, he points out how local people have a symbiotic relationship with their forest, which is their primary livelihood resource. When I asked community members about BV's potential contribution to environmental sustainability of the land, they invariably answered that they already had extensive knowledge of the forest and that the volunteers could not teach them anything as they already had extensive knowledge of the land that they had been cultivating for more than 200 years.

Additionally, the sustainability of the social development projects was a point of frustration for host community members who complained about the irregular flow of volunteers to teach English. For example, Noi from Orchard Home describes her excitement about learning English from a volunteer from the US. Yet, this excitement quickly turned to disappointment when the volunteer left after one month:

> When this one volunteer came, I can't remember her name. But they couldn't speak Thai. Shoot, I can't remember her name. But she could teach us and it was very impressive. At first I thought "I'm not sure if she could teach us English or not." I was so anxious. She couldn't speak any Thai! Would I understand? She was able to teach us to understand. She tried really hard. Maybe she prepared herself very well. Normally we … For example like you say "what does this say?" You can ask in Thai. But this person, they could not communicate. 'I can't speak Thai so you must speak English with me,' This was impressive. But just when we were about to speak English she left. That person, they came only one month. We were able to speak English and have a conversation with her and we didn't use any Thai at all!

While Noi explained how she and her classmates made significant progress in their English language proficiency, she believes that without uninterrupted lessons, this progress is only short lived:

> We don't have the opportunity to continuously study. If the volunteers don't continue to come, then maybe we skip a month. It is like that. So sometimes they don't come for a month and so we stop. If we had the chance to continuously study then maybe we could do it. But we study in intervals, it's not continuous. If we don't speak English very much then we forget. Normally we should speak all the time. We must practice and study often. We should study every day. If we did that we could speak. But, when there aren't any volunteers I just go work in the garden.

The volunteers' English lessons were often poorly managed. For example it is typical for volunteers to go to schools to teach English without knowing what the last group of volunteers taught. Thus, it becomes common for volunteers to repeat the similar names, colors and animals lesson.

"Making a Difference"

"Making a difference" is almost invariably uttered by volunteer tourists who identify "giving back" as a primary motivation. Indeed, "[P]hrases like 'giving back to the community' and 'making a difference in the world' that litter the brochure discourse are meant to tickle the post-materialist and anti-modernist sensibilities of the Western ethical consumer looking to demonstrate their superior social capital by 'traveling with a purpose'" (Vrasti, 2012, p. 2). Glynn, a 26-year-old English volunteer suggests that he wants to do something meaningful and make a positive impact in the lives of others. Describing his job in England, Glynn states:

> [My job] wasn't as satisfying as I wanted it to be because I always felt like there is something missing. I wanted to do something more. I felt like this would be an opportunity to do something positive or constructive rather than mundane work on the computer. Yeah, something meaningful I guess.

Mellissa, a 24-year-old volunteer from England who is a development studies major explains that for her, volunteering is about moving beyond academia and actually being part of development—making a real impact:

> I always wanted to volunteer; I've always been interested in development, in aid organizations and making the world a better place. And that's what I'm studying, so for me it's interesting not only volunteering but actually to put some theories that I've learnt into practice … I think you take a bigger piece of where you were with you when you go home, because you made an impact.

Alex, a 22-year-old volunteer from the US notes how she was motivated to participate in volunteer tourism because she knew she made an impact: "If I come back in a couple of years to this school they will still know who I am, probably. Knowing I will make and leave an impact motivates me." Ann, a 19-year-old volunteer from Holland also notes how she is motivated to participate in volunteer tourism because she will make an impact on the local people and be able to take that with her: "I think you take a bigger piece where you were with you when you go home, because you made an impact."

Volunteers become increasingly confident throughout the volunteer tourism experience. Explaining how he benefited from his experience, John, an 18-year-old volunteer from Ireland notes: "I feel better about myself and I am giving to them but anyway they're giving back to me too. So it's really cool." Similarly, Satomi commented that through volunteer tourism she gets "to see a different world than tourism, and it's very rewarding that what you are doing is not only for yourself and it's useful for some other people." Similarly, Domenico, a 54-year-old, Canadian school teacher explains:

> There is something in it for me. It's not just helping others, it's helping me. Doing something worthwhile. Even care givers, they have self-interest. It's good to me. It makes me look good in front of others. Other people generally look at me with some kind of admiration and respect I get. And we all need that. It makes me feel good.

When I asked John, an 18-year-old volunteer from Ireland what five words he would use to describe his experience, he stated that it was amazing, enlightening, strengthening, exhilarating, and exciting. When I probed what he meant by his answer, he stated:

> I guess I'd say I am happy that I feel better about myself and it has been like eye opening for me too … More confidence … I feel like I am definitely more confident about myself and it's definitely helped me to become a better person even in the short time and I am looking forward to next few months of becoming an even better person, yeah.

When I asked him what he meant by "a better person," he stated:

> We'll like—I'm a bit nervous—confidence has always been a big issue to me. I've gotten better over the years but especially teaching these kids to sing. We are a whole culture apart and language apart, but they're actually willing to get involved and be themselves around me. So I can be myself around these people who barely understand what I am saying or the culture I am from. We're still connecting on some level and that's just, let's just say it put a bit more of confidence in me.

Glynn similarly explains:

> I think it is especially beneficial for young kids. I think you have to be stupid and play games and run around. You get to have fun and I think it boost your confidence a lot, you know. Makes you more relaxed. It is a new experience. Before I started volunteering I hated doing presentations at work. After teaching, and just standing in front of people, it starts to become mundane and in the end, it becomes easy.

Volunteers often suggest that they notice differences in themselves and had "developed" as individuals as a result of their experience. For example, Alex, a 22-year-old volunteer from the US explains:

> Like I won't just lie down on a couch. I mean living in this house and stuff, I have been doing so much, and the few hours that I lie around feels weird to me, like at home, I am a little bit more lazy. Like, I eat something and leave the dishes in the sink for a few hours. And I realize how much more time there is in a day here, and I want to use every minute of it to do something. Well just like when I get home I will use my time better rather than waste it like before.

These experiences of "self-development" through volunteer tourism are corroborated by recent studies which identify this phenomenon as a major benefit of the experience (Raymond and Michael Hall, 2008, Zahra, 2007). Additionally, volunteering abroad is often seen as a rite of passage to young adulthood (Coghlan and Noakes, 2012, Butcher, 2010, Dowling, 2003). Elizabeth, a volunteer from the US explains how she didn't know what she wanted to do after college. While she had considered joining the Peace Corps, she decided that she didn't want to commit two years, so volunteering abroad was the next best option:

> I wanted to go to the Peace Corps after college, but then I did not want to make that kind of a commitment because you have to sign up for 2 years I think. So I was graduating in December in 8 months and I didn't know what to do with 8 months before I graduated and I wanted to give back and go somewhere … so I always wanted to come to Thailand and I wanted to experience Buddhism give back to wherever I was going, I don't know but it makes your vacation more meaningful. I mean it so feels like I am on a vacation now even though I am working, you know. I will totally do it again as I am having such an amazing time.

Similarly, Caroline, the 68-year-old volunteer from Canada describes how she and her husband, Steve were moving to Vancouver from Montreal upon their return. This was a major life change and they believed that doing something like "volunteering in the Third World" would be a good transitional experience. In this way, volunteers enter a liminal existence in which they have new experiences, act in unordinary ways, and ultimately find themselves in order just in time to begin a new chapter in their lives.

Education through Interaction

Self-development is often spoken of in terms of career development, an often unforeseen benefit of the volunteers' experience. Many volunteers suggest that because of their volunteer experience, they decided to go into professional teaching or non-profit work. Moreover, while some volunteers recently graduated high school, others were in college or considering graduate school. For example, Melissa a 26-year-old volunteer from England notes that she will use her experience in her graduate studies in international development: "I know definitely I'll be able to use experiences that I may have had here in my study." She elaborates:

> Yeah to see because I know they're trying to bridge the *Farang* people and the Thai people because there are lots of refugees across the border and that results from the State and the State is giving funds to schools, the orphanage for the Burmese or Myanmar people, so that would be interesting and I'm going to be studying forced migration and human rights and international law so that hopefully will put into contact some of the learning in the future. And I know there are lots of international organizations that work out there like the rescue committee units and others as well. Hopefully I will!

Sanne, a 23-year-old Finnish volunteer who seeks to become an elementary school teacher also explains:

> Well I've only been here a week so I've learned a bit about how to interact with kids, preschool aged kids … I've learnt from the other volunteers that you need to be a bit silly and a bit funny to kind of get their attention, that's been really good.

Similarly, Julie, 24, comments that before coming to Thailand she had doubts in her ability to successfully teach the children, but after her experience she has become interested in becoming a volunteer coordinator:

> I had doubts that I wouldn't be able to handle this. I had a lot of anxiety before I came, I now have this belief in myself, I feel like I can do, not anything, but I believe more in myself. Another one is it got me interested in working as a volunteer as a job, I would like to be a volunteer coordinator. I would love to live in a different country and I would like to do what Ted does, open a house somewhere and do like that. It inspired me to do something. Maybe have it as a side job. I don't know. It got me wanting to get into a volunteer career type.

Additionally, "'traveling' has emerged as an important informal qualification, with the number and range of stamps in a passport acting, so to speak, as a professional certificate; a record of achievement and experience. Not only is travel a professional prerequisite for employment in parts of the tourism industry, but it is also an important attribute in many new professions, such as international development work; it has become a rite of passage into certain occupations" (Mowforth and Munt, 2009, p. 132). Often described as "curriculum vitae builders," for volunteers that "can afford it, the experience represents an institutionally accepted and professionally valuable asset" (Vrasti, 2012, p. 124). Volunteers' interests depart from the host community members' interest in more tangible forms of social and economic development such as material wealth and English.

The value of learning English was frequently expressed by host community members. Pom, for example, explains that the most valuable aspect of her experience with the volunteers was with Lori, an American volunteer who taught her English. She explained that many people from the village joined her lessons and that everyone was interested in learning English, particularly because they wanted to speak with the *Farang*. Similarly, Preecha, a 44-year-old Thai NGO practitioner of an orphanage that serves "Hill Tribe" children explains why he wants volunteers to come to his orphanage:

> [B]ecause I wanted the children to learn English because if the foreigners come, it is their language, so when the children learn to speak English (with them), they can speak clearly. There aren't any Thai people that can teach them to speak clearly ... because if they know English they can get a higher level of education and this is beneficial for the children. They can do email or websites or anything and this is good.

English lessons are highly valued by host community members in part because private courses are expensive and quality English teachers are reportedly limited. Moreover, host community members note how English language education can open up many employment opportunities, especially in the tourism sector. When I asked Pom about the benefits she gains from the volunteers, she explained: "Gaining knowledge ... I learn English from them ... Because I don't have any other opportunity to study so they come to teach us and I get to absorb some English from talking with them ... I would like to speak well and be a trekking guide." Women from Orchard Home were also motivated by opportunities to learn English. Noi from Orchard Home explains:

> English is something that I can't learn outside here. It is very expensive to study English. The women here at Orchard Home, they don't know any English. Since I have come here, I have gotten to know about English. I can speak a little bit, but just some things. I can listen and understand but I cannot answer. The most important thing is learning English because if we were outside of Orchard Home we wouldn't have opportunities to learn English because it is so expensive. The

women here at Orchard Home come and some of them don't know any English at all. Since coming to Orchard Home, I have become familiar with English. Before coming here I did not think about speaking English. But now, I feel that I can speak a little bit. It may be a little bit but I can speak. Sometimes I listen and I understand what people are saying but I cannot answer them. And sometimes I listen and I know what they are saying and when I answer them I don't know what to say. I can only speak a little bit.

Host community members involved with Traveling Teachers—which are primarily school children and teachers—are almost exclusively involved with the volunteers to learn English. For example, one teacher at a rural school explains her motivation for participating in volunteer tourism:

Volunteers from Traveling Teachers came to help our school. Ours is a small school for the underprivileged children. There's no native English-speaking teacher to teach this language. The volunteers come in to help with conversational and written English. This is beneficial to these underprivileged children.

Preecha, a 44-year-old Thai NGO practitioner at an orphanage for "Hill Tribe" children notes how the children benefit from the volunteers: "The children will learn English much better and have the opportunity to speak English much more; they would develop much better English skills."

"We have Nature and Culture"

The motivations of volunteers are not always clear to host community members. For example, when I asked Pom how she thought the volunteers benefited, she explained: "I don't know. I never asked them why they want to come here or what they get out of it." Despite this tendency, when host community members did suggest how the volunteers benefited, they often explained that the volunteers benefited from Thai "culture and nature." Pom explained that if she came to Orchard Home as a volunteer, she would benefit by the opportunity to "get to know about Thai people that I didn't know about before … They help the mothers here learn and get to know things and they help the women gain stability." Similarly, as Manop, a 35-year-old orphanage worker suggests:

The benefits for them, maybe … I don't know what benefits each group that comes hopes to gain. But I think that for most of the people that come, they get to communicate with Thai people. They get to know about Thai customs and traditions and the differences of Thai people for each area and they get to know how other countries are and how their country is and how their own country can develop.

Anchali explained:

> They want to help and want to learn about Thai culture … They learn Thai culture. Some people come to teach culture and about life skills. Some people come to learn about the story of the women here, what their lives are like. About having a boyfriend, and getting pregnant and leaving their husbands … I don't know about anything else.

In a related vein, Po from Orchard Home explains: "They come to learn about the lives of the women here at Orchard Home … Mostly they [the volunteers] come here because of the culture, yeah?" This was a common response among host community members who often suggested that Western volunteers were attracted to Thailand because of the "culture." Echoing this claim, Ajaan Nui at a rural school just outside of Chiang Mai notes: "From my observation, they would like to learn about culture, way of life, and offer their love to the children, they have a heart for the children." Pom suggests that volunteers come to Thailand: "Probably because Thailand is interesting … Probably Thai people have a good disposition and they speak nicely. Their character is good." These references to Thai culture as the primary motivating factor for the thousands of volunteer tourists who come to Thailand each year is not unfounded. It reflects how a unified Thai culture is embedded in the discursive constructions of the Thai state, Thainess and modernity in Thailand (see Chapter 3) (Costa, 2001, Thongchai, 1994).

At Mae Nam Village and Orchard Home, nature was almost always identified as a motivating factor for volunteers who are believed to live in "electric cities." When I asked Pom what was interesting about Mae Nam Village, she noted: "There is a waterfall and pristine forest." Similarly, Noi from Orchard Home notes that the volunteers probably come for "nature." She explains:

> Maybe the *Farang* are attracted to nature. *Farang* that come here love nature! They don't like to live in places that have things like traffic jams very much. They love nature. So, when they look at the website they see that Orchard Home is in harmony with nature and the international volunteers, maybe they see that. They open the website and become interested and see that the place here is very comfortable for living. I think that this is why they come here. I think they must have seen the website and I think they can see that this is how our home is. Our home is surrounded by nature.

In this way, host community members seem to have internalized the volunteers' desire to seek out "culture" and "nature" as important signifiers of an authentic Thailand.

"Real Chiang Mai People"

Most volunteers explained that they volunteered in Thailand rather than their home countries because they wanted to "do something different" than "just" being a tourist. For example, Carol, a 68-year-old volunteer from Canada explained that her 43-year-old daughter and 26-year-old niece gave her and her husband Sam the idea to volunteer in the Third World. They suggested that it would be good for them to do something "different":

> It's interesting that in my daughter's generation … my daughter's 43 and my niece who's 26, and a lot of her friends, more so my niece than my daughter's friends … my daughter would have wanted to go but you know, she has two children. She's like dying to get up here with her family, move somewhere for a year and do some volunteer work in a Third World country or something. She's actually the one who gave me and Sam this idea … She turned around to us one day … and said, "Why don't you guys do something in a Third World country or do some volunteer work. You have so much to offer and it would be so good for you to get away and just do something a little different for yourselves." We went home. We looked at each other and we said, "It's brilliant, like if we don't do it now, we'll never do it. Why don't we try? Why don't we see if something's available?" The first website we got on to was Chiang Mai Friends and it's like our language and we thought about it and said, okay we'll take a course and there was one offered in Asia. We were very excited. We applied. We sent our resumes and a week later, we got a response.

Marsha, a 20-year-old volunteer from Germany similarly notes:

> I just want to do something very different from normal traveling and I wanted to do something good for other people so not only traveling or giving money to poor countries … Do something on my own. I think that is my motivation.

Mandy, a 20-year-old volunteer from Holland similarly states:

> Yeah, kind of just to help the people and to learn some more, to see different things … it's nice to have a totally different goal and just to … you learn so much more and I think it's a good experience and also, you can connect more with people if you know there are different things in the world and I don't know. It's just different … You see a lot of different things and you meet other people, you're helping people and you're learning so much more about the culture and like for instance when we go to eat, they have a little ritual and they say thank you and you would never know that if you wouldn't volunteer but it's also … you learn things about the culture and about the people … and you just see different things. You notice different things.

Mandy further explains that what is different about her experience is the opportunity to learn about "real" Thai people. John, an 18-year-old volunteer from Ireland notes how he had been to Thailand before as a tourist, but now he was able to see the "real Thailand:"

> Well, I am experiencing the different culture, I've come here before but that was just for about two weeks and I mean I didn't get the whole view of Thailand as I'd like to. I just saw many of the tourist attractions like the night market and stuff like that but actually now that I am getting involved in this program, I am actually getting to know the Thai people whereas before I would just say hello but here I can actually see what their daily lives consist of. See what they do, see how they live, and see what they do for a living. Now like I know how a village can interact to support each other like before I didn't know there was such a thing as a village headman or stuff like that but now I am actually finding out more about the Thai culture and how it works. And it's much better because you get into the nitty gritty of that because you have whole new view on this.

Being a volunteer was distinguished from being a tourist by opportunities "to really get to know the people beyond a superficial level." This is primarily accomplished through longer stays, accommodation "just off the beaten track" and most importantly "hanging with the locals."

An emerging aspect of the touristic value system is that the meanings of the "tourist" and the "traveler" are increasingly re-negotiated by more than just those on the move. Host community members increasingly engage in debates about what amounts to an "authentic" Thai experience. While tourists can be found in almost all corners of Thailand, the majority of Thais do not interact with them on a personal level unless they are directly involved in the tourism industry. According to the host community members that I spoke to, most had seen international tourists, but never had direct interaction. Because of this, some host community members were interested in getting to know the volunteers. Echoing the volunteers, host community members also often suggested that through direct interaction, the volunteers could get to know the "real" Thailand. Nid, a 36-year-old Thai teacher who hosts volunteers at her elementary school comments that unlike tourists, volunteers were able to get to know "real Chiang Mai people":

> It is very good to have volunteers that have something to do with tourism because Thailand or Chiang Mai is a very good tourist destination … Real Chiang Mai people look happy and cheerful, smile brightly and are very friendly. If the volunteers can get to know the locals for real, that would be very good.

Additionally, Po commented:

> The tourists come to take a look to see what Orchard Home is like. The volunteers come to help Orchard Home. They come and do activities with the women here

at Orchard Home. The tourists just come to see how Orchard Home is and that is it.

Another host community member similarly remarks:

> I think that they [the volunteers] are better than the people who come to sightsee and go back without helping, they are not, they should help and not only come for sightseeing. They should help and then go back. Otherwise, they can only say, 'I went to the beach.' But the volunteers, they can say that they travelled and 'we also helped other people. We helped people all over the world!'

The cultural capital sought after in volunteer tourism is often embedded in identity negotiations where there is an attempt to reconcile the semantics of volunteering with tourism. With the introduction of increasingly varied identity labels for volunteer tourism such as "international volunteering" and "volunteering abroad programs," the range of touristic identities has broadened. More than four decades ago MacCannell observed that "the term 'tourist' is increasingly used as a derisive label for someone who seems content with his obviously inauthentic experience" (MacCannell, 1973, p. 592). Today volunteers continue to prefer to refer to themselves as volunteers or at least travelers rather than tourists. The desire to be a traveler rather than a tourist is grounded in conceptions of the tourist as the ultimate signifier of the inauthenticity of the capitalist mediation of social relations (MacCannell, 1999). The distinction between the traveler and the tourist is symptomatic of the distinction between pre-capitalist authentic social relations and postindustrial alienation from community. The tourist is associated with superficiality and in-authenticity which falls within the same semiotic field of postindustrial consumerism. To be a traveler may be seen as in contradistinction to the tourist. Mowforth and Munt suggest that the "search for authenticity" in volunteer tourism is a strategy used by volunteers to stoke up on cultural capital through their experience with "authentic" natives as "travelers" rather than "tourists" (Bourdieu, 1984, Mowforth and Munt, 2009, Broad and Spencer, 2008).

Semantically, the traveler is associated with exploration, authenticity and pre-capitalist relations—beyond the realm of consumer driven relations (Culler, 1989). Martin, a 21-year-old German volunteer notes: "A lot of times I am treated like a tourist and this means people are trying to get some money from you ... I don't feel like a tourist. So I don't want to be a tourist in their eyes. For them, I want to be someone here to teach, not to be a tourist." When I asked him if it made a difference how Thai people saw him, he answered: "If they see me as a tourist, I'm a victim of blood sucking and if they see me as a volunteer or understand this, then I think there is another behavior. They would treat me another way." If they knew he was a volunteer and not a tourist, Martin believed that locals would treat him with more respect. Ann, a 23-year-old volunteer from Norway similarly notes, the main difference between volunteering and traveling abroad is that as a volunteer you: "Don't feel like tourists, you feel like you are part of the community. You feel like you live here, you feel like you have a home and pretty much have a job." Martin and Ann's comments echo Culler's observation that "part of what is involved in being a tourist is disliking tourists (both other tourists and the fact that one is oneself a tourist). Tourist can always find someone more touristy than themselves to sneer at" (Culler, 1989).

Volunteer tourists similarly sneer at other volunteers who are less authentically volunteering than themselves. For example, Anna explained to me the difference between real and implicitly "fake" volunteers:

> To be honest there are 2 kinds of people who volunteer. There is a girl in our [CMF] home and she is doing it because she can say she did volunteer work and she did it for 2 weeks and not for the right reasons. As far as the other real volunteers, it depends on what kind of projects they are doing … You have to be social in order to do it. I don't know it's hard to explain … I think you have to enjoy life a lot.

Glynn explains the difference between traveling and volunteering abroad:

> I think volunteering you get to experience the culture more. You are in the position that you have to be available in a certain length of time in a certain place which you don't have much freedom, but that is positive in some ways because like you really experience that place where you can travel a lot in it for more than 3 days. Then you would be saying okay I have seen it, now I'm moving on.

In a similar study of volunteer tourism in Cuba, Broad and Spencer explain that volunteers "did not like to be categorized as tourists and preferred to describe themselves as a traveler or a local, and as a result, would seek future tourism experiences that would provide similar opportunities to experience a different culture and see things that tourists do not normally get to see" (Broad and Spencer, 2008, p. 221). This type of identity formation is a core aspect of the volunteer tourism experience where both "hosts" and "guests" engage with others in ways that re-spatialize political, economic and cultural boundaries. Vrasti notes how "[I]dentity formation lies at the heart of our political engagement with transitional others. World politics needs to be recognized as a process of cultural interactions in which the identities of actors are not given prior to or apart from seemingly mundane exchanges like those produced through international tourism (Anand 2007: 13)" (Vrasti, 2012, pp. 22–3). In this way, volunteer tourism is a site for cross-cultural exchange where converging and diverging interests are negotiated within new identity formations that have the potential to contribute to the perpetuation of structural inequality or make space for new forms of social solidarity and indeed, social change—the topic of the concluding chapter.

Chapter 7

Conclusion—Re-mapping the Movement: Popular Humanitarianism and the Geopolitics of Hope in Volunteer Tourism

I am once again landing at Chiang Mai International Airport. The Bangkok Airways flight I am on has a special edition in-flight magazine on ethical and responsible tourism in mainland Southeast Asia in which Chiang Mai is highlighted as a "responsible tourism destination." The placement of Chiang Mai at the center of responsible tourism in the region does not surprise me. There is a long history of social and ecological movements in the North (Forsyth, 2001). The movement of activist oriented foreign residents is now a well-trodden path in Chiang Mai. Combined with locally based Thai Buddhist inspired movements, an atmosphere of social and environmental consciousness is apparent. As the plane is being taxied on the runway, I call my friend, Aum to tell her I have arrived. I met Aum in 2004 at the guesthouse that she managed and where I stayed while taking intensive Thai language courses at Payap University nearly a decade earlier. I am greeted at the gate by Aum, her English husband Adam, and their two-month-old baby girl, Alis. Adam drives us to their house behind Chiang Mai University. I drop my backpack in their house, and we quickly head to Mr Mechanic, a motorcycle rental shop where I rent a red 150cc Honda Dream motorcycle. As we drive to the shop I feel nostalgic for the pad thai and fried rice stands, the moat that surrounds the city and is always there to help you find your way, the sea of bright orange robes that canvass the city, the golden temples that glitter in the sunlight, the mingling of *Farang* and Thais at the local restaurants and bars around Thapae Gate, the vividly colored fruit stands with mounds of mangosteen, and the bite-sized pineapple and papaya in conveniently placed clear plastic bags. Over the past decade I have lived in Chiang Mai for more than two years. Within that time I have seen Chiang Mai grow and change in innumerable ways. I am never surprised to find new guesthouses, handicraft shops, hotels, bars and restaurants around the city.

As I collect the keys to my motorcycle, I am impatient to visit my friends and colleagues. I begin driving to Bo Sang towards Orchard Home, and I notice that several tour companies now offer volunteer tours. I also notice BV's large advertisement outside of the Night Bazaar. The volunteer tourism industry seems to be growing in Chiang Mai—as I expected it would. When I arrive at Orchard Home I am shocked to see a giant yellow building. I later learn that it is the new home for Mic and Leslie and their two girls. They have also expanded their gardens and now have two rice fields well under way. I am impressed by the rate at which they have developed these projects. I learn that most of the women that were there last year have also moved away. Pim, an 18-year-old woman with one young son is now married and has a second child on the way. We used to sell smoothies, homemade candles and used clothing at the Walking Street and Sam Kamphaeng Markets together. To my delight Arthit, a 38-year-old woman and mother of two is still living at Orchard Home. Arthit is the most senior woman, thus she commands much respect from the others. Po is also still around. She is now a college student studying to become a math teacher. Mic and Leslie continue to expand Orchard Home to accommodate more women. They want Orchard Home to be self-sustainable and hope to have some of the women who now live there manage the home when they leave in three or maybe five years.

As I pull into Orchard Home I go to Arthit's room and yell her name hoping she will recognize my voice. She does! Arthit runs out of her room and screams, "Mary!" She tells me about what she has been working on, how she is still learning to speak English and how a lot of the women that I had known have returned to their families or started new ones. She also tells me that there have been numerous volunteers from various organizations. They are now learning to make cards and other crafts that they hope to sell at the market—although they have not been to the market in a while. I am pleased to hear that things are going well. Arthit jokingly complains that the only problem is that there are not any male volunteers and asks me why I did not bring any with me. Anchali tells me that she has moved into Matt and Elaine's old house with her son and some of the other staff. She is excited to have her own place. I am delighted to be back—even if only for a short time. Over the next couple of weeks I returned to Orchard Home several times to visit Matt, Elaine, Arthit and the other women. I also visited the other communities where I conducted my research including Mae Nam Village where tourists and volunteers continue to be a relatively rare sight. Most of the people in Mae Nam Village who used to work at the eco-lodge now build homes for Bangkok residents who are buying land to build vacation homes at an impressive rate. I arrive at the head man and head woman's house by motorcycle. Mae Luang, the head woman is home. She screams with excitement when she sees me. I am also excited to see her. We have been out of touch because cell phones do not work in this area. I learn that Arthit now builds houses, while Pom still works at the ecolodge, despite the fact that there are rarely any guests. However, as Eric the founder of BV explained to me every year, the volunteers are coming.

My return trips to Chiang Mai and the communities on which this book is based have afforded me a longitudinal perspective on volunteer tourism as well as refine my thoughts on the intersection of tourism and development in volunteer tourism. While there are many points of critique—many of which are presented in this book—that can and probably should be launched against this industry, critique alone would fail to fully capture the nature of the experience. Like the participants I interviewed, I also believe that the most motivating and beneficial aspects of my fieldwork experience are the people that I met and the friendships that I made. This is very much like most social researchers that I know. Anthropologists in particular have the peculiar habit of making friends or even finding surrogate families from afar. When the opportunity arises—which may be one week to several months later—they often ask questions about meaning, motivations, and beliefs. It is indeed important to remember that the "translation of the research experience into a textual corpus separate from its discursive occasions of production has important consequences for ethnographic authority" (Clifford, 1988, p. 131). This authority feels unnatural, especially while in the "field" where the anthropologist often occupies the most vulnerable position within the community. But, when our time or funding has run out and we return to our universities to translate our experiences into articles or book publications, hugs are exchanged and tears flow—because despite the structural inequalities that often mediate our relationships—embodied experience is more immediate than the theories that warn us of the politics of the encounter.

From Critical Theory to Critical Action

Tom, the *tuk-tuk* driver who takes volunteers to Orchard Home observes that "It is like if there is only one stick, it can easily be broken, but if there are a bunch of sticks, they will not easily break …" Like Tom, social justice activists highlight how through collective action we the public—are strong. Critique is useful in describing its object's optimisms and exclusions (Berlant, 2004, p. 5)—yet, it can do more. Swain observes that "[C]ritical Tourism Studies had emerged to engage inequalities (Tribe 2005), but our emancipatory solutions remain elusive" (Swain, 2009, pp. 506–7). Indeed, tourism scholars are speaking up in these conversations, where they ask: "can new forms of tourism become a significant force in global development?" (Mowforth and Munt, 2009, p. xii). Its supporters suggest that it can, arguing that volunteer tourism is a "win-win" strategy which contributes to social and economic development, international goodwill and broadens its participants' perspectives. On the other hand, its critics suggest that it is a superficial endeavor that lacks the means to make material, political or economic changes in host communities. Hence, "it is unclear to what extent particular development vehicles, such as tourism, are effective as means of addressing these problems and challenges" (Tefler and Sharpley, 2008, p. 8). Yet despite the uncertain long-term benefits of the tourism industry, it is important to not lose sight of its immediate implications for host communities. It is noted that tourism "cannot be understood as just a means of having some enjoyment and a break from the routine of every day, an entirely innocent affair with some unfortunate incidental impacts. Rather a deeper understanding of tourism is needed to appreciate fully its content and expression as well as its potential impact" (Mowforth and Munt, 2009, p. 1).

While volunteer tourism alone will obviously not solve the issue of global inequality, its potential to become a platform for contributing to broader social justice agendas should not be overlooked (Hutnyk, 1996, Pezzullo, 2007, McGehee and Santos, 2005b, McGehee and Norman, 2001). Indeed, "[I]t is not enough just to raise questions about the moral propriety of First World youth taking holidays among the people of the Third World; it is not enough to encourage discussion of such contradictions in cafes along the banana-pancake trail. Nor is it sufficient to reflect critically upon the politics of charity, while working—because something must be done" (Hutnyk, 1996, p. 222). Various responsible, ethical, and activist oriented tourism organizations are now promoting tourism as a strategy towards cross cultural understanding, gaining international support for local issues and the cultivation of global consciousness. For example, Spencer argues that "[S]olidarity through tourism, in whatever form this emerges, can be considered an important tool for development agencies, social movements, and NGOs in terms of new and explicit ways of promulgating issues of rights, social justice and good governance. In this way, solidarity connects directly with rights-based development" (Smith, 1997, p. 195). Volunteer tourism may be one strand in this broader tourism mediated social justice movement. For example, in the context of development tourism in Cuba, Spencer illustrates that if a tour can "encourage or intensify solidarity with Cuba or social movement participation in some form then the results could be used to promote rights based tourism as a means of encouraging organized social action and rights based development" (Smith, 1997, p. 197). We need to complicate our criticisms of market-mediated activism and consider that while "the exploitative possibilities of tourism remain important to consider, tourism also suggests opportunities for embodied engagement, counter experiences of everyday life, education, interpretation, and advocacy" (Pezzullo, 2007, pp. 50–51). For example, local communities that seek to utilize volunteer tourism as a strategy for economic development and as a platform from which to gain support for local issues may find that their agendas are in many ways compatible with those of tourists. Thus, such communities may find the touristic space a profitable site of engagement (compare Westerhausen and Macbeth, 2003, McGehee and Santos, 2005b, Higgins-Desbiolles, 2003, Higgins-Desbiolles, 2005, Hutnyk, 1996). In this way, simplistic dualisms between commodity orientations and social activism are insufficient for capturing the contemporary ways that the market articulates with social resistance in neoliberal times (Hearn, 2012).

Yet, as I have argued in the preceding pages, it is also crucial to recognize how the sentimental response to structural inequality is insufficient. This critique is not easy to swallow and it will not surprise me if it is not welcomed by all readers. This is no doubt in part because as Berlant explains:

> It makes sense that people object when analysis of the intimate emotions makes those desires for attachment seem equally like instruments of suffering. In the liberal society that sanctions individuality as sovereign, we like our positive emotions to feel well intentioned and we like our good intentions to constitute the meaning of our acts. We do not like to hear that our good intentions can sometimes be said to be aggressive, although anyone versed in, say, the history of love or imperialism knows volumes about the ways in which genuinely

good intentions have involved forms of ordinary terror (think about missionary education) and control (think of state military, carceral, and police practices). We do not like to be held responsible for consequences we did not mean to enact (Berlant, 2004, pp. 5–6).

Yet, this is not to suggest that emotional or affective responses are immaterial. Many have argued for the centrality of the affective for the political (Pedwell, 2012b, Pedwell, 2012a, Ahmed, 2004, Vogler, 2004, Woodward, 2004, Tester, 2001). Spencer, for example, argues in the context of Global Exchange and Oxfam Tours that intellectual and affective exchanges are crucial sites of solidarity building— a core goal among participants. Indeed, in volunteer tourism sentimentality is a core aspect of the experience for most participants including volunteers, NGO practitioners, and host community members. While the affective and sentimental exchange is meaningful, I argue that it also inadvertently reframes structural inequality as a question of individual morality. By reframing the experience in this way, the inequality on which the encounter is based is depoliticized in a neoliberal sleight of hand where dissent is accommodated by the market through the materialization of commoditized concern.

This conclusion takes the analysis of volunteer tourism one step further by asking, if volunteer tourism ultimately supports the expansion of neoliberalism that we know to be exacerbating global inequality at unprecedented levels, then what do we do about the millions of people around the world or are involved in or support NGOs and other organizations upholding this developmental model? Should we dismiss volunteer tourism as a superficial experience that will only attract those who cannot see how they are supporting the expansion of neoliberal policies and practices that have contributed to the poverty and global inequality they seek to alleviate? Can they not see how giving hugs to children in orphanages and impoverished schools will not help ameliorate chronic poverty and systemic violence against the poor? As scholars it is easy to be dismissive about these types of experiences because "we" seem to know where it is all leading, but being snarky never solved anything! And Western volunteers will continue to go to the Third World with or without anthropology!

Volunteer Tourism and New Social Movements

The abbreviated spectrum between good and evil, as Hoffman explains, "makes the use of words like idealism, altruism, and humanitarianism problematic, because they are so laden with unrealistically positive connotations" (Hoffman, 1998, p. 7). These kinds of binary articulations preclude more diverse kinds of social action that intersect with consumerism, technology and private enterprise (Mukherjee and Banet-Weiser, 2012). Indeed, one of the core characteristics of globalization is the widespread ability to connect a broad network of transnational social movements or groups of people who seek to unsettle and challenge the status quo. Unsettling of the status quo now takes place in multifarious ways that are not fully captured by traditional definitions of social movements. Steger points out how, "[T]he best way of challenging the established framework of globalism is to build a broad international support network that includes workers, environmentalists, consumer advocates, and human-rights activists" (Steger, 2009a, p. 109). Social movements seek to rearticulate the dominant power relations in society which maintain the existing state of affairs. Many of these movements are based on the increasingly palpable economic, social, political and environmental disparities within and between nations and "have responded to the failure of development and the social exclusion exacerbated by globalization through attempts to reframe development as a question of rights" (Smith, 1997, p. 50). Tourism is rarely identified as an impetus for social movements and "[V]ery little research has been conducted focusing on how tourism, especially alternative tourism, impacts the social movement participation of guests rather than hosts" (McGehee, 2002, p. 172). Yet, volunteer tourism in particular has been identified as a potential catalyst for social movement participation (McGehee, 2002, McGehee and Santos, 2005a).

Alternative tourists generally and volunteer tourists in particular are often well versed in environmental debates and seek to participate in experiences in line with their own middle-class ecological values. Mowforth and Munt observe the:

> ... apparent relationships between the growth of the new middle classes and a concern with 'otherness' which includes an interest in minority cultures, religion, ethnicity and, arguably most significant, a concern with environment and ecology. Notably, the 10–12 percent of all tourism that is attributed to new tourism activities is similar in proportion to that of the First World populations interested and concerned with these other issues (WTO/OMT, 1995: 28) (Mowforth and Munt, 2009, p. 142).

The leap from "life changing" experiences to social movement participation is not automatic. As Hutnyk explains, "[P]art of what is required now ... is a tourists' vigilance, and organizational forms which will attend to a social and political transformatory project adequate to combat the system. This always requires vigilance—of our Eurocentric representations, of the gaze and of our inscriptive zeal—and also of our complicities in the hegemonic production and circulation of this code" (Hutnyk, 1996, p. 223). What Hutnyk is suggesting is that what is left open is an active intervention in the Third World tourism imaginary "that would not simply replicate the market directives of capital. This is the rumour which must be spread; word needs to get around" (1996, p. 223). I similarly observed that rather than being unaware of the legacies of colonization, from which volunteer tourism emerges, volunteers often recognize and seek to overcome their own postcolonial positionality. MacCannell notes how "our collective guilt and denial of responsibility for the destruction of savagery and pleasure can be found infused in every distinctively modern cultural form" (MacCannell, 1999, p. 25). Volunteer tourism may be one strategy that tourists use to overcome this postcolonial guilt through the facilitation of dialogue between its participants:

> ... provides opportunities for connection between those being toured and those on the tour itself. Spontaneous conversations such as this one are constitutive of the tour's value. They illustrate the possibility for moments of solidarity among those facing common struggles as well as the ways in which a ... tour is multisensory, embodied experience for those touring (Pezzullo, 2007, p. 95).

Following their volunteer tourism experience in Cuba, many volunteers "expressed a strong sentiment for supporting the country in the face of the US imposed economic trade embargo, by travelling to and supporting development efforts in Cuba by establishing networks with local organisations" (Broad and Spencer, 2008, p. 222). Volunteer tourists may be an apt audience from which to gain political and economic support for local issues. This is illustrated in part by the interest in public service that frequently emerges following the volunteer experience. For example, one 26-year-old British volunteer comments:

> If everyone did this, if we come from a different place and do this, it can open everyone's eyes to diversity and you can bring the diversity with you or the culture and if we all experience something like this we all can benefit. The world can be a better place. You can humble yourself.

Similarly, another 22-year-old German volunteer suggests:

> By experiencing a different culture and a different way of life you can better yourself and also take it back to your own country and teach other people, get involved in other organizations ... By actually getting involved you kind of explore for yourself, get your own opinion and take it back to others, so they might be able to get a different perspective.

As its supporters illustrate, volunteer tourism can be life changing and as "industry veterans well know, make-a-difference sojourns often attract repeat customers. 'It's life changing' says Helen Jenkel, 68, of her 2005 caravan with Relief Riders International through India's Rajasthan Desert. On the 15-day trip, which included a night in a 257-year-old fort, the retiree from Chappaqua, N.Y., helped set up medical camps and distribute books to schools and goats to poor families. She found the experience so inspiring that she's going back in October" (Fitzpatrick, 2007). Life changing experiences are critical conjunctures at which people become involved in social movement participation (Haenfler et al., 2012, McFarlane, 2009, Edelman, 2001). Alex, a 22-year-old American volunteer, explains that by volunteering at the temple schools she has noticed personal change:

> Change in myself. Change for the better. These boys who don't have parents or can't see them and going to this school to get some education. I feel like I want to change that. Children who get poor education, I want to change that. Maybe someday I will come back and make a change for better schools.

Similarly, Ann, a 19-year-old Dutch girl comments that through her volunteer tourism experience she has developed a newfound confidence and desire to participate in volunteer work:

> I had doubts that I wouldn't be able to handle this. I had a lot of anxiety before I came, I now have this belief in myself, I feel like I can do, not anything, but I believe more in myself. Another one is it got me interested in working as a volunteer as a job, I would like to be a volunteer coordinator. I would love to live in a different country and I would like to do what Ted does, open a house somewhere and do like that. It inspired me to do something. Maybe have it as a side job. I don't know. It got me wanting to get into a volunteer career type.

The benefits of mutual understanding between cultures were self-evident to most participants. Manop, the orphanage worker suggests how the volunteer tourism encounter can encourage cross-cultural understanding. He explains that through volunteer tourism, people can:

> ... communicate with each other and know what was going on. They are able to do things and understand each other. They are able to discuss the international economy, society, politics and many other things. To put it simply, when we can talk to and understand each other and know what is going on, we can communicate with and understand each other.

Interactions in volunteer tourism do "provide many opportunities to exchange information about networks and to develop ties that might have never been developed had these individuals not participated in an expedition" (McGehee, 2002, p. 128). Volunteers often explained to me that their experience in Thailand has changed the way they envision "Third World countries." For example, when I asked Yurie, the 22-year-old Japanese volunteer about her volunteer tourism experience she explained: "[it] made me like Thai or Thailand more. I can trust them, trusting people. Because now I can tell that to my parents and I can tell them this is my experience and show them my interest, here people are nice you know." She identified this as an important benefit of volunteer tourism because, as she notes, "[S]ome people think people in developing countries are dangerous or primitive." Despite this, as Ted, the founder of TT notes, volunteer tourism can help alleviate "world problems ... solve misunderstandings about culture and society and being able to work on that ... from the world to get to know what's going on with another one and knowing from a young age ... really awesome and productive you know ... so then I was thinking release the stereotype ... kind of breakdown those stereotypes. Educating people about others about other groups of people, society and culture. So there aren't all these stereotype of these countries."

Consequently, while the goal of cross-cultural understanding is not sufficient for radical structural change, it is one aspect which can serve as a platform for consciousness-raising. McGehee argues that within volunteer tourism, "[T]he question becomes whether the unique motivations and attitudes of volunteer tourists, the catalytic potential of volunteer tourism organizations, and the agency of the host community can overcome the predominately western, capitalist environment in which they are often situated, an environment which depends upon production and consumption, supply and demand and the perpetuation of inequality" (McGehee, 2012, p. 87). Hutnyk argues:

> [T]here are reasons to consider a political activism among travelers and 'Third Worldist' Western youth (those into alternative travel, for example) which would seek to extend an awareness of an internationalist responsibility to fight for a redistributive justice that was more than mere charity. This would be informed by recognition of the exploitative structure of capitalist relations; an analysis of how that value is appropriated from workers in excess of that needed to reproduce life can be redistributed at system-wide advanced and equitable standards; and awareness of the political conditions, organizational forms, and specific tasks needed to achieve this (1996, pp. 222–3).

Through the expansion of global consciousness about the political-economic structural foundations of enduring global inequality, volunteer tourism *can* help bring about structural change.

Similar to consciousness-raising organizations, groups and movements, volunteer tourism has the transformatory potential to contribute to broader social justice agendas. Illustrating this potential, Glynn, a 24-year-old volunteer from England comments:

> The difference ... is that when you travel around and see the poverty or the underdevelopment, you kind of feel arrogant swinging around with your backpack and throwing money and sort of carry on ... it's more of wanting to put something positive there rather than walking happily and laying around there.

Broad and Spencer's study on volunteer tourism highlights how contact between the volunteers and host community members allows participants to create a sense of solidarity for social movements and gain political support for their causes. They illustrate how "exchange of knowledge and ideas is what underpins solidarity efforts and is the reason why Cuban people welcome the opportunity to meet people on study tours. It is an opportunity to develop international networks at grassroots level" (Broad and Spencer, 2008, p. 223). The Cuban experience is applicable to related forms of tourism outside its borders. For example, Global Exchange Reality Tours' website notes:

Our tours provide individuals the opportunity to understand issues beyond what is communicated by the mass media and gain a new vantage point from which to view and affect US foreign policy. Travelers are linked with activists and organizations from around the globe who are working toward positive change. We also hope to prompt participants to examine related issues in their own communities (Global Exchange, 2007a).

Maureen, a Global Exchange Reality Tourism Northern Ireland (1997) volunteer similarly writes:

I've just completed the two-week Global Exchange tour here in Ireland and on the whole very satisfied for having come. I felt the experience both realistic and valuable. I am more aware now how much the people of all parties in the North have suffered. It is my intention to become more active politically, both here and in the Bay Area, hopefully to increase awareness (Global Exchange, 2007b).

This type of emerging social consciousness is at the heart of the potential of volunteer tourism as a platform from which to develop structural changes. Jenny, a 26-year-old volunteer from Australia explains how the benefits of volunteer tourism include "broadening one's world view, seeing how 80 percent of the world lives. I mean even here in Thailand I'd say that they're not, they don't have, I'm sure they do have extreme poverty, then I'm sure some of them are living on less than a dollar a day, so seeing that is beneficial." When I asked her if she would recommend volunteering abroad to others, she explained:

I already have, definitely yes. It's hard to get other people, I guess because I'm from a privileged country I'm from Australia, lots of people, although people travel, lots of people don't yet care enough to volunteer and travel. People that aren't studying the same thing that I am and are not from the same kind of organizations that I'm from, so getting in say my high school friends, we all went to a private all girls' Catholic high school. Yeah, so they're very kind of, I don't want to say selfish but I guess all self-centered but I guess that's what they are. They think, my friends a whole group of friends coming to Thailand in two weeks, so they'll have fun and drink and party and do that kind of stuff they don't really, I would definitely recommend it getting people to come, actually come.

Caroline from Canada similarly explained that she plans to tell her friends about volunteer tourism because they too could benefit:

It's such a fabulous experience. It really is and you're giving … you're giving something, I mean, we have life experiences. We're sharing with the world and how positive is that? It's so positive. I mean, I will play it up for sure, absolutely. I think it's fabulous. It's a great experience. I thank my daughter every day.

Every time I speak to her I say it like, "you're a genius. How you came up with this for Daddy and I like, you know!"

While host community members did not frequently refer to volunteer tourism as "life changing," many suggested that they have become increasingly aware of global inequality. This observation is an important one: all social movements are necessarily grounded in consciousness of a problem. The growing class consciousness of host community members is an essential first step in the expansion of social movement agendas, of which they are the anticipated benefactors. Host community members also effectively become aware of and presented with the possibility to participate in broader social justice movements.

The Geopolitics of Hope in Volunteer Tourism

Volunteer tourism is a twenty-first century materialization of popular humanitarianism where the geopolitics of hope are remapped in a commodity oriented fashion. The cultivation of hope through consumerism requires both a de-historicization as well as an apolitical structuring of uneven development economic inequality. Sparke argues that it is precisely our responsibility to highlight the strategic framing of social justice debates as he calls for the persistent questioning of "what is left out of the consolidation of any particular geographic account, vision, map or idea" (Sparke, 2007, p. 338). The geopolitics of hope in volunteer tourism is mediated by imaginative geographies of possibility as it articulates with the geoeconomics of probability (Sparke, 2007, Appadurai, 2013b). In other words, volunteer tourism contributes to an international discourse on the appropriate response to uneven development and economic inequality. This response is rearticulated in popular humanitarian practices, such as volunteer tourism, that extend the message of hope to the actual or metaphorical benefactors of aid. Pain and Smith note how "[I]n very oppressive situations, particularly the Global South, hope is always present as a radical response to fear that galvanizes social action" (Pain and Smith, 2012, p. 209). Indeed, social action in the form of popular humanitarianism is now commonplace in the Global North where discourses of hope are widespread on chocolate bar wrappers, organic food containers, coffee tins, t-shirts, water bottles, music downloads, jeans, and brochures for volunteer vacations. Yet, these discourses effectively leave out broader historical and structural configurations that are the underlying cause of chronic poverty and systemic violence against the poor. Thus, in volunteer tourism the geopolitics of hope is mapped onto sentimental geographies of care without structural support for more systemic, structural change. The kind of change that is required for volunteer tourism and other forms of popular humanitarianism to work include, among other reforms, the expansion of social services, debt forgiveness, and a more general redistribution of global wealth through trade policies and agreements. Thus, we should understand hope in volunteer tourism as "a practice, rather than simply an emotion or a cultural attitude, most centrally involves the practice of creating, or trying to create, lives worth living in the midst of suffering, even with no happy ending in sight" and "involves the struggle to forge new communities of care" (Mattingly, 2010, p. 6). Mattingly observes that hope is "an existential problem [that] takes cultural and structural root as it is shaped by poverty, racism, and bodily suffering" (Mattingly, 2010). Volunteer tourism is uncomfortably situated within a politics of hope about the future of the Global South.

While variable, host community members' stated interests in volunteer tourism tend to reflect a broader interest in social and economic development as it is commonly articulated by development and aid agencies. This is not surprising, given the government's focus on "developing Thailand step by step" in the provinces. I believe that it is necessary to remain optimistic despite "the difficulty of inducing structural transformation out of shifts in collective feeling" (Baudrillard, 1993, p. xii). Through this lens of hope as both an emotion and a *practice*, the ethnographic investigation of the nexus of tourism and development reveals novel insights into the hope as a social practice in humanitarian travel. Appadurai highlights a "tectonic struggle" between "the ethics of possibility and the ethics of probability:"

> those ways of thinking, feeling, and acting that increase the horizons of hope, that expand the field of the imagination, that produce greater equity in which I have called the a capacity to aspire, and that widen the field of informed, creative, and critical citizenship. This ethics is part and parcel of transnational civil society movements, progressive democratic organizations, and in general the politics of hope. By the ethics of probability, I mean those ways of thinking, feeling, and acting that flow out of what Ian Hacking called 'the avalanche of numbers,' or what Michael Foucault saw as the capillary dangers of modern regimes of diagnosis, counting, and accounting (Appadurai, 2013a, p. 295).

This observation is central to the politics of hope in volunteer tourism. Volunteer tourism is increasingly appropriated as a form of popular humanitarianism by NGOs and local governments alike. What role volunteer tourism can and should have in sustainable development is debated on the international stage. The concept of humanitarianism itself continues to be hotly contested among academics and aid workers. In the context of international development, Bebbington highlights how "[T]he question becomes not why are some people poor in society, but why some societies tolerate poverty as an outcome and for whom, and how this toleration becomes embedded within institutional norms and systems" (Bebbington, 2007, p. 806). In a similar vein, Dove (1993) writes how "Rainforest Crunch" cereal promotes a narrative of helping save the rainforest through purchasing cereal so local people can be taken out of poverty and will not need to continue cutting down the rainforest. The narrative is that the tropical forest dwellers cut down their forest because they are poor. But the question of why they are poor is not addressed. Thus, the structure is not only left intact, but supported. Ultimately, it asks us to ask ourselves: "how can we help?" or "what can we give?" when what we should be asking is "how are we harming?" or "what have we taken away?" (Dove, 1994). Volunteer tourism development is similarly implicated in the helping discourse. Instead of asking why volunteer tourism emerges at this specific time and place, we are sidetracked by questions of how we can make volunteer tourism work. This detracts from asking the bigger picture: How can we make the structure work? Resistance to band-aiding structural sores is increasingly argued in the public arena. For example, responding to a *People Magazine* article on Christina Aguilera's trip to Rwanda, Natacha Nsabimana, a writer on the blog Africa is a Country, responded:

> War and poverty are the result of larger structural inequalities, part of larger historical, political circumstances that no individual can resolve. And certainly not Hollywood style celebrities: Aguilera, Invisible Children's Jason Russell or even Bono. Enough of these white celebrities scrolling out of nowhere wanting to save African lives. Keep to your various professions thank you very much (Nsabimana, 2013).

Yet, supporters of these Band-Aids might suggest that doing "something" is better than doing "nothing"—a core justification of humanitarian and development practitioners, including celebrity ambassadors. Thus, like other related forms of development work, in volunteer tourism, "the problem is this: Given a shared practical orientation that treats the individual person as the fundamental unit for ethics, how ought one to respond to a man-made injustice that is neither any one person's fault nor the sort of thing that any one person can remedy" (Vogler, 2004, pp. 31–2). This neoliberal problematic is at the core of volunteer tourism, where there the scale of change is often limited by the Peace Corps Effect (see Chapter 2) where the focus is on the individual or the community.

During my research I was continuously struck by the central role of sentimentality in volunteer tourism. This persistent observation encouraged me to organize the main argument of this book around highlighting how sentimentality mediates the volunteer tourism-development encounter. The focus on sentimentality in volunteer tourism deflects attention from the structural inequality on which the encounter is based. In so doing, the question of structural inequality is replaced by a question of individual morality. This is not to suggest that participants have negative intentions. However, I insist that the reader does not conclude from this book that there is anything inherently wrong with sentimentality in volunteer tourism. Rather, as Berlant writes:

> Scholarly critique and investigation do not necessarily or even usually entail nullifying the value of an affirmative phrase or relation of affinity. It is more likely that a project of critique seeks not to destroy its object but to explain the dynamics of its optimism and exclusions. If we challenge the affirmative forms of culture, it is not to call affirmation wrong but to see how it has worked

that forms of progress also and at the same time support destructive practices of social antagonism. Social optimism has costs when its conventional images involve enforcing normative project of orderliness or truth. This kind of bargaining demands scrutiny, in that desires for progress in some places are so often accompanied by comfort with other social wrongs (Berlant, 2004, p. 5).

In a similar vein, Ferguson refers to an 'anti-politics machine' or the tendency to remove politics from development and poverty debates by naturalizing the discourses surrounding its origin and intentions (1994). As explained in Chapter 3, development discourse has a long history that emerges from particular historical conjunctures that have always been political. In this book, I have worked to denaturalize the seemingly apolitical "helping narrative" in volunteer tourism and expose the cultural politics of global inequality and chronic poverty on which the encounter is based. As Bebbington argues, "[I]f chronic poverty is to become a concept that helps politicize poverty debates, then we might, playing on Ferguson, also talk of the importance of a 'politics machine'—one that produces politicizing discourses on poverty and holds open the possibility of shifting the contours of popular and policy debates on its reduction" (Bebbington, 2007, p. 815). The last few decades have witnessed the emergence of responsible, moral and alternative tourism experiences. Yet, the capacity for small-scale, locally-based NGOs and other participants to contribute to poverty alleviation remains tenuous. Indeed, it is increasingly the case that middle income countries such as Thailand have the financial ability to pull the poorest sectors of their domestic population out of poverty. Thailand is an example of what Sumner refers to as a "poverty paradox" where "most of the world's extreme poor do not live in the world's poorest countries" and that by 2020 "most of world poverty may be in countries that do have the domestic financial resources to end at least extreme poverty" (Sumner, 2013, p. 357).

In Chapter 3 I argued that volunteer tourism perpetuates and maintains market fundamentalism or the cultural logic of neoliberalism. Yet, to criticize neoliberalism and its corollary cultural logic is to overlook the potential emancipatory forms of activism that co-exist with neoliberalism. Hearn, for example, reminds us how "there is no 'outside' to the logics of contemporary capitalism, that resistance to indulge the popular cultural refrain, has perhaps, become futile" and that "movement tactics and paradigms of collective organizing themselves reveal a kind of 'commodity creep' so that even radical imaginaries of social critique seem to falter under the seductive force of neoliberalism" (Hearn, 2012, p. 11). Summarizing the arguments of contemporary critical scholarship, Ferguson concludes: "[T]he powerless, it seems, are getting the short end of the stick." And yet, he explains that "this is not exactly a surprising finding, of course (isn't it precisely because they *are* on the losing end of things that we call them 'powerless' in the first place?). Yet this sort of work styles itself as 'critique,' and imagines itself to be very 'political'" (Ferguson, 2010, p. 166). Following Ferguson, I suggest that it is important to ask "what if politics is really not about expressing indignation or denouncing the powerful? What if it is, instead, about getting what you want? Then we progressives must ask: what do we want? This is a quite different question (and a far more difficult question) than: what are we against?" (Ferguson, 2010, pp. 166–7). What we want is structural change in the form of debt forgiveness, the expansion of social services, and a more general redistribution of global wealth through trade policies and agreements, humanitarian action may address the cause rather than the symptom of global economic inequality and chronic poverty. It is only through this type of political-economic reorganization that the goals of volunteer tourism advocates (and other NGOs) may be realized. As social justice activists have argued, what is needed is "a 'global Marshall Plan' that would create more political space for people around the world to determine what kind of social arrangements they want" (Steger, 2009a, pp. 129–30).

Examining the cultural politics of volunteer tourism and its emotional competency not only provides more useful analysis but also contributes to a more politically engaged volunteer tourism. By not addressing these issues we run the risk of not realizing our humanitarian goals and perpetuating the unfettered expansion of neoliberal global capitalism. Widespread sentimental solidarity for the plight of the Global South is not enough. Berlant questions why: "[W]e can feel bad about it; we can feel compassionately toward those who suffer: why isn't it enough to have meant well, or not to have meant badly?" (Berlant, 2004, pp. 5–6). Highlighting the geopolitics of hope in volunteer tourism experience can contribute to a more theoretically engaged tourism scholarship which goes beyond questions of impacts and motivations. If volunteer tourism is to achieve its broader goals of contributing to a more equal and just global civil society, its current focus on the individual and the sentimental must be broadened. This focus must also address the current policies and practices that ultimately sustain the political, economic and social inequalities on which volunteer tourism is based.

Bibliography

Adams, K.M. 1997. Ethnic Tourism and the Renegotiation of Tradition in Tana Toraja (Sulawesi, Indonesia). *Ethnology*, 36, 309–20.

Adams, W. 2008. *Green Development: Environment and Sustainability in the Third World*, New York: Routledge.

Ahmed, S. 2004. *The Cultural Politics of Emotion*, New York: Routledge.

Ahmed, S. 2006. *Queer Phenomenology: Orientations, Objects, Others*, Durham: Duke University Press.

Alvarez, S., Dagnino, E. and Escobar, A. 1998. Introduction: The Cultural and the Political in Latin American Social Movements. *In:* Alvarez, S., Dagnino, Evelina and Escobar, Arturo (eds) *Cultures of Politics, Politics of Cultures: Re-Visioning Latin American Social Movements*, Boulder: Westview Press.

Anderson, B. 1978. Studies of the Thai State: The State of Thai Studies. *In:* Ayal, E.B. (ed.) *The Study of Thailand: Analyses of Knowledge, Approaches and Prospects in Anthropology, Art History, Economics, History, Political Science*, Ohio University, Center for International Studies.

Anthropology, E.R.I.A. 2010. *Anthropological Field School: Summer 2011, The Islet of Gozo (Malta)* [Online]. Expeditions. Available: http://www.anthropol ogyfieldschool.org/info/documents/files/flyer.pdf [Accessed 12/26/10].

Appadurai, A. 2013a. *Essays on the Global Condition*, New York: Verso Books.

Appadurai, A. 2013b. *The Future as Cultural Fact: Essays on the Global Condition*, New York: Verso.

Appiah, K.A. 1997. Cosmopolitan Patriots. *Critical Inquiry*, 23, 617.

Appiah, K.A. 2006. *Cosmopolitanism: Ethics in a World of Strangers*, New York: W.W. Norton and Company.

Asad, T. 1986. The Concept of Cultural Translation in British Social Anthropology. *In:* Clifford, J. and George, M. (eds) *Writing Culture: The Poetics and Politics of Ethnography*, Berkeley: University of California Press.

Assani, A. 2010. *Cultural Imagery and Exchange Programs as Sources of US Soft Power in West Africa: Unfolding US Cultural Relations with West Africa from 1957--1991*. PhD, Michigan State University.

Ausenda, F. and Mccloskey, E. (eds) 2006. *World Volunteers: The World Guide to Humanitarian and Development Volunteering*, Milano, Italy: Green Volunteers Publications.

Baillie Smith, M. and Laurie, N. 2011. International volunteering and development: Global citizenship and neoliberal professionalisation today. *Transactions of the Institute of British Geographers*, 36, 545–59.

Baillie Smith, M., Laurie, N., Hopkins, P. and Olson, E. 2013. International volunteering, faith and subjectivity: Negotiating cosmopolitanism, citizenship and development. *Geoforum*, 45, 126–35.

Barnett, C., Cloke, P., Clarke, N. and Malpass, A. 2005. Consuming Ethics: Articulating the Subjects and Spaces of Ethical Consumption. *Antipode*, 37, 23–45.

Baudrillard, J. 1993. *The Transparency of Evil: Essays on Extreme Phenomena*, London: Verso.

Beaver, E., Tortoroli, M., Livitz, I. and McDonald, M. 2006. *Let's Go Thailand*, New York: Martin's Press.

Bebbington, A. 2007. Social Movements and the Politicization of Chronic Poverty. *Development and Change*, 38, 793–818.

Bebbington, A., Hickey, S. and Miltlin, D. (eds) 2008. *Can NGOs Make a Difference?: The Challenge of Development Alternatives*, New York: Zed Books.

Bebbington, A.J. and Bebbington, D.H. 2001. Development alternatives: practice, dilemmas and theory. *Area*, 33, 7–17.

Beck, U., Sznaider, N. and Winter, R. 2003. *Global America?: The Cultural Consequences of Globalization*, Liverpool: Liverpool University Press.

Becki. 2012. Why Volunteering is an Invaluable Part of Travel. *Backpackerbecki. com: A Solo Female Traveller's Tales, Rants on the Road, Reviews and General Wanderings* [Online]. Available: http://www.backpackerbecki.com/an-invaluable-part-of-travel-volunteering-backpacker-becki.html 2013.

Berger, J. 2008. *Ways of Seeing*, London: Penguin.

Berlant, L. 1998. Poor Eliza. *American Literature*, 70, 635–68.

Berlant, L. (ed.) 2000. *Intimacy*, Chicago: University of Chicago Press.

Berlant, L. (ed.) 2004. *Compassion: The Cultural Politics of an Emotion*, New York: Routledge.

Berlant, L. 2008. *The Female Complaint: The Unfinished Business of Sentimentality in American*, Durham: Duke University Press.

Berlant, L. 2011. *Cruel Optimism*, Durham: Duke University Press.

Bernard, R. 2011. *Research Methods in Anthropology*, Maryland: Alta Mira.

Bhabha, H. 1984. Of mimicry and man: the ambivalence of colonial discourse. *October*, 28, 125–33.

Bhabha, H.K. 1985. Signs taken for wonders: questions of ambivalence and authority under a tree outside Delhi, May 1817. *Critical Inquiry*, 12, 144–65.

Boltanski, L. 1999. *Distant Suffering: Morality, Media and Politics*, New York: Cambridge University Press.

Bourdieu, P. 1984. *Distinction: A Social Critique of the Judgement of Taste*, New York: President and Fellows of Harvard College and Routledge & Kegan Paul Ltd.

Broad, S. and Spencer, R. 2008. Shifting Paradigms: The Convergence of Tourism, Conservation and Development. *In:* Babu, S., Mishra, Sitikantha and Parida, Bivraj (eds) *Tourism Development Revisited:Concepts, Issues, and Paradigms*, Los Angeles: Sage.

Broomhill, R. 2007. *Corporate Socal Responsibility: Key Issues and Debates*, Don Dunstan Foundation.

Brown, S. and Lehto, X. 2005. Travelling with a Purpose: Understanding the Motives and Benefits of Volunteer Vacationers. *Department of Hospitality and Tourism Management*, 8, 479–96.

Brown, S. and Morrison, A.M. 2003. Expanding Volunteer Vacation Participation: An Exploratory Study on the Mini-Mission Concept. *Tourism Recreation Research*, 28, 73–82.

Brumbaugh, A.M. 2010. The impact of diversity seeking and volunteer orientation on desire for alternative spring break programs. *Journal of Travel & Tourism Marketing*, 27, 474–90.

Bruner, E. 1989. Of Cannibals, Tourists and Ethnographers. *Cultural Anthropology*, 4, 438–45.

Bruner, E. 1995. The Ethnographer/Tourist in Indonesia. *In:* Lafant, M.-F. (ed.) *International Tourism: Identity and Change*, London: Sage Publications.

Bruner, E. 2005. *Culture on Tour: Ethnographies of Travel*, Chicago: University of Chicago Press.

Bryant, R. and Goodman, M. 2004a. Consuming Narratives: The Political Ecology of "Alternative" Consumption. *Transactions of the Institute of British Geographers N.S.*, 29, 344–66.

Bull, S. 2010. "Devastated" Brad Pitt and Angelina Jolie lead celebrity support and pledge $1million to help Haiti, *Dailymail UK* [Online]. Available: http://www.dailymail.co.uk/tvshowbiz/article-1243072/Haiti-earthquake-Brad-Pitt-Angelina-Jolie-lead-celebrity-support-pledges.html.

Butcher, J. 2003. *The Moralization of Tourism: Sun, Sand and Saving the World?*, New York: Routledge.

Butcher, J. 2010. "Making a difference": volunteer tourism and development. *Tourism Recreation Research*, 35, 27–36.

Butler, J. 2002. Violence, Mouring, Politics. *Feminist Theory Address.* University College London.

Campbell, L. and Smith, C. 2006. What Makes Them Pay? Values of Volunteer Tourists Working for Sea Turtle Conservation. *Environmental Management*, 38, 89–98.

Carroll, A.B. 1999. Corporate social responsibility evolution of a definitional construct. *Business & Society*, 38, 268–95.

Chaitrong, W. 2012. Thailand reflects Asia's growing income inequality. *Business* [Online]. Available: http://www.nationmultimedia.com/business/Thailand-reflects-Asias-growing-income-inequality-30179912.html.

Chambers, E. 2009. *Native Tours: The Anthropology of Travel and Tourism*, Long Grove, Illinois: Waveland Press, Inc.

Chen, L.-J. and Chen, J.S. 2011. The motivations and expectations of international volunteer tourists: A case study of "Chinese Village Traditions." *Tourism Management*, 32, 435–42.

Clemmons, D. 2010. *The Socially Desirable Response: Is It VolunTourism's Bane, Too?!?* [Online]. Voluntourist.org. Available: http://www.voluntourism.org/news-feature253.htm [Accessed 10/10/2010].

Clifford, J. 1988. On Ethnographic Authority. *The Predicament of Culture: Twentieth-Century Ethnography, Literature, and Art*, Boston: Harvard Univeristy Press.

Clifford, J. 1989. Notes on Travel and Theory. *Inscriptions*, 5, 177–88.

Clifford, J. 1997. *Routes: Travel and Translation in the Late Twentieth Century*, Boston: Harvard University Press.

Clifford, J. 1998. Mixed Feelings. *In:* Cheah, P. and Bruce, R. (eds) *Cosmopolitics: Thinking and Feeling Beyond the Nation*, Minneapolis: Minnesota.

Clothier, J. 2010. Voluntourism: The Benefits and Pitfalls You Need to Know. *CNN: International* [Online].

Cochrane, J. (ed.) 2008. *Asian Tourism: Growth and Change*, Amsterdam: Elsevier.

Coghlan, A. and Noakes, S. 2012. Towards an understanding of the drivers of commercialization in the volunteer tourism sector. *Tourism Recreation Research*, 37, 123–31.

Cohen, E. 1986. Lovelorn Farangs: The Correspondence between Foreign Men and Thai Girls. *Anthropological Quarterly*, 59, 115–27.

Cohen, E. 1988. Authenticity and Commoditization in Tourism. *Annals of Tourism Research*, 15, 371–86.

Cohen, E. 2001. *Thai Tourism: Hill Tribes, Islands and Open-Ended Prostitution*, Bangkok: White Lotus Press.

Collins, J., Dezerega, S. and Heckscher, Z. 2002. *How to Live Your Dream of Volunteering Overseas*, New York: Penguin Books.

Comaroff, J. and Comaroff J. 2005. Millennial Capitalism and the Culture of Neoliberalism. *In:* Edelman, M. and Angelique, H. (eds) *The Anthropology of Development and Globalization*, New York: Blackwell Publishing.

Conradson, D. 2003. Geographies of care: spaces, practices, experiences. *Social & Cultural Geography*, 4, 451–4.

Conran, M. 2011. "They Really Love Me!": Intimacy in Volunteer Tourism. *Annals of Tourism Research*, 38, 1454–73.

Cooper, F. and Stoler, A.L. 1997. *Tensions of Empire: Colonial Cultures in a Bourgeois World*, University of California Press.

Corps, U.S.P. 2010. *Peace Corps: Mission* [Online]. Washington, D.C.: United States Government. Available: http://www.peacecorps.gov/index.cfm?shell=learn.whatispc.mission [Accessed 4/20/2010].

Costa, L.R. 2001. *Developing Identities: The Production of Gender, Culture and Modernity in a Northern Thai Non-Governmental Organization.* PhD, University of Hawaii.

Creswell, J. 2009. *Research Design: Qualitative, Quantitative and Mixed Methods Approaches*, New York: Sage Publications

Crossley, É. 2012. Poor but Happy: Volunteer Tourists' Encounters with Poverty. *Tourism Geographies*, 14, 235–53.

Crouch, D., Jackson, R. and Thomas, F. 2005. Introduction: The Media and the Tourist Imagination. *In:* Crouch, D., Jackson, R. and Thomas, F. (eds) *The Media and the Tourist Imagination*, New York: Routledge.

Crush, J. (ed.) 1995. *Power of Development*, New York: Routledge.

Culler, J. 1981. Semiotics of Tourism. *American Journal of Semiotics*, 1, 127–40.

D'amore, L. 1988a. Tourism—The World's Peace Industry. *Journal of Travel Research*, 27, 35–40.

D'amore, L.J. 1988b. Tourism—a vital force for peace. *Tourism Management*, 9, 151–4.

Daley, P. 2013. Rescuing African bodies: celebrities, consumerism and neoliberal humanitarianism. *Review of African Political Economy*, 40, 375–93.

Davidson, J. and Milligan, C. 2004. Embodying Emotion Sensing Space: Introducing Emotional Geographies. *Social & Cultural Geography*, 5, 523–32.

Deleuze, G. and Guattari, F. 1980. *A Thousand Plateaus*, London and New York: Continuum.

Desjarlais, R. and Jason Throop, C. 2011. Phenomenological Approaches in Anthropology. *Annual Review of Anthropology*, 40, 87–102.

Dirlik, A. 2004. Spectres of the Third World: Global Modernity and the End of the Three Worlds. *Third World Quarterly*, 25, 131–48.

Dolhinow, R. 2005. Caught in the Middle: The State, NGOs, and the Limits to Grassroots Organizing Along the US-Mexico Border. *Antipode*, 37, 558–80.

Dove, M. 1994. Marketing the Rainforest: "Green" Panacea or Red Herring. *Asia Pacific Issues*, 13, 1–8.

Dowling, R.K. 2003. Volunteer tourism: experiences that make a difference: Stephen Wearing; CABI Publishing, Wallingford, 2001. *Tourism Management*, 24, 116–18.

Dunford, M. 2007. *Make the Most of Your Time on Earth*, London: Rough Guides Limited.

Edelman, M. 2001. Social Movements: Changing Paradigms and Forms of Politics. *Annu. Rev. Anthropol.*, 30, 285–317.

Errington, F. and Gewertz, D. 1989. Tourism and Anthropology in a Postmodern World. *Oceania*, 60, 37–54.

Escobar, A. 1995. *Encountering Development: The Making and Unmaking of the Third World*, New Jersey: Princeton University Press.

Escobar, A. 2002. The Problematization of Poverty: The Tale of Three Worlds and Development. *In:* Susanne, S. and Jane H. (eds) *Development: A Cultural Studies Reader*, Oxford: Blackwell Publishing.

Escobar, A. 2004. Beyond the Third World: Imperial Globality, Global Coloniality and Anti-Globalization Social Movements. *Third World Quarterly*, 25, 207–30.

Escobar, A. 2005. Imagining a Post-Development Era. *In:* Edelman, M. and Angelique, H. (eds) *The Anthropology of Globalization and Development: From Political Economy to Contemporary Neoliberalism*, Oxford: Blackwell Publishing.

Estava, G. 2007. Development. *In:* Sach, W. (ed.) *The Development Dictionary.* 12 ed. New York: Zed Books.

Exchange, G. 2007a. *Global Exchange Reality Tours* [Online]. San Francisco, CA: Global Exchange. Available: http://globalexchange.org/tours/index.html [Accessed 12/10/2010].

Exchange, G. 2007b. *Past Participants Share Their Experience* [Online]. San Francisco: Global Exchange. Available: http://globalexchange.org/tours/ saying.html [Accessed 12/10/2010].

Fechter, A.-M. and Hindman, H. 2011. *Inside the Everyday Lives of Development Workers: The Challenges and Futures of Aidland,* Kumarian Press Sterling, VA.

Feng, Y. 2011. Myanmmar Continues Efforts in Developing Tourism. *Xinhua* [Online].

Ferguson, J. 1994. *The Anti-Politics Machine: "Development," Depoliticization, and Bureaucratic Power in Lesotho,* Minneapolis, Regents of the University of Minnesota.

Ferguson, J. 2002. The Constitution of the Object of "Development": Lesotho as a "Less Developed Country." *In:* Susanne, S. and Jane, H. (eds) *Development: A Cultural Studies Reader,* Oxford: Blackwell Publishing.

Ferguson, J. 2010. The Uses of Neoliberalism. *Antipode,* 41, 166–84.

Fitzpatrick, L. 2007. Vacationing like Brangelina. *Time Magazine* [Online]. Available: http://www.time.com/time/magazine/article/0,9171,1647457,00.html [Accessed 07/26/2007].

Foreign Office, The Government Public Relations Department. 2006. *10th National Economic and Social Development Plan* [Online]. Bangkok. Available: http:// thailand.prd.go.th/view_inside.php?id=1457.

Forsyth, T. 2001. Environmental Social Movements in Thailand: How Important is Class? *Asian Journal of Social Science,* 29, 35–51.

Foucault, M. 1970. *The Archaeology of Knowledge.* Trans. A.M. Sheridan Smith, New York: Pantheon, 972.

Freidberg, S. 2003. Cleaning Up Down South: Supermarkets, Ethical Trade and African Horticulture. *Social and Cultural Geography,* 4, 27–43.

Friedmann, J. 1992. *Empowerment: the Politics of Alternative Development,* New Jersey: Blackwell.

Friends, C.M. 2010. *Volunteer in Thailand with Friends for Asia: Elephant Camp* [Online]. Chiang Mai: Friends for Asia. Available: http://www.volunteerthai land.org/projects-internships/elephant-volunteer/ [Accessed 01/20/2011].

Galani-Moutafi, V. 2000. The self and the other: Traveler, ethnographer, tourist. *Annals of Tourism Research,* 27, 203–24.

Garber, M. 2004. Compassion. *In:* Berlant, L. (ed.) *Compassion: The Culture and Politics of an Emotion,* New York: Routledge.

Gibson, C. 2010. Geographies of tourism: (un)ethical encounters. *Progress in Human Geography,* 34, 521–7.

Gmelch, S.B. (ed.) 2010. *Tourists and Tourism: A Reader,* Long Grove, Illinois: Waveland Press Inc.

Good, B. 1994. *Medicine, Rationality, and Experience: An Anthropological Perspective*, Cambridge: Cambridge University Press.

Goodman, M. 2004. Reading Fair Trade: Political Ecological Imaginary and the Moral Economy of Fair Trade Foods. *Political Geography*, 23, 891–915.

Goodman, M. 2005. *Articulating Alternative Moral Economies?: The Socio-Ecological Imaginary of Organic and Fair Trade Foods*. PhD, University of California Santa Cruz.

Goss, J. May 2010. *RE: International Cultural Studies Capstone Forum*. Type to Conran, M.

Goss, J.D. 1993. Placing the Market and Marketing Place: Tourist Advertising of the Hawaiian Islands, 1972–92. *Environment and Planning D: Society and Space*, 11, 663–88.

Graburn, N. 2010. Secular Ritual: A General Theory of Tourism. *In:* Gmelch, S.B. (ed.) *Tourists and Tourism: A Reader*, Long Grove, Illinois: Waveland Press, Inc.

Gray, N. and Campbell, L. 2007. A Decommodified Experience? Exploring aesthetic, Economic and Ethical Values for Volunteer Ecotoruism in Costa Rica. *Journal of Sustainable Tourism*, 15, 463–82.

Greene, E.C. 2007. Global Peace Travels: Exploring Creative Ways of Using Travel and Cultural Exploration to Promote Peace. *Global Peace Travels* [Online]. Available from: http://globalpeacetravels.blogspot.com/.

Guiney, T. and Mostafanezhad, M. 2015. The Political Economy of Orphanage Tourism in Cambodia. *Tourist Studies*, forthcoming.

Gupta, A. and Ferguson, J. 1997. *Culture, Power, Place: Explorations in Critical Anthropology*, Durham: Duke University Press.

Guthrie, G.M. and Zektick, I.N. 1967. Predicting performance in the Peace Corps. *The Journal of Social Psychology*, 71, 11–21.

Guttentag, D.A. 2009. The possible negative impacts of volunteer tourism. *International Journal of Tourism Research*, 11, 537–51.

Haenfler, R., Johnson, B. and Jones, E. 2012. Lifestyle Movements: Exploring the Intersection of Lifestyle and Social Movements. *Social Movement Studies*, 11, 1–20.

Hafen, P.J. 1997. Zitkala Ša: Sentimentality and Sovereignty. *Wicazo Sa Review*, 12, 31–41.

Hailey, J. 1999. Ladybirds, Missionaries and NGOs. Voluntary Organizations and Co-operaties in 50 Years of Development: A Historical Perspective of Future Challenges. *Public Administration and Development*, 19, 467–85.

Hale, S.E.A. 2004. The Third Way and Beyond: Criticisms, Futures, Alternatives. *The Sociological Review*, 52, 424–6.

Hall, C.M. and Page, Stephen (eds) 2000. *Tourism in South and Southeast Asia: Issues and Cases*, Woburn, MA: Butterworth-Heinemann.

Hall, S. 1996. Cultural Studies and the Politics of Internationalization: An Interview with Stuart Hall by Kuan-Hsing Chen. *In:* Morley, D. and Kuan-

Hsing, C. (eds) *Stuart Hall: Critical Dialogues in Cultural Studies*, New York: Routledge.

Halpenny, E.A. and Caissie, L.T. 2003. Volunteering on Nature Conservation Projects: Volunteer Experience, Attitudes and Values. *Tourism Recreation Research*, 23, 25–33.

Hampton, M.P. 1997. Unpacking the Rucksack; A New Analysis of Backpacker Tourism with Reference to South East Asia. *Tourism Heritage Managment*, University Press: Indonesia.

Hardt, M. and Negri, A. 2000. *Empire*, Cambridge: Harvard University Press.

Hart, S. 2007. *Capitalism at the Crossroads: Aligning Business, Earth, and Humanity*, Philadelphia: Wharton School Publishing.

Harvey, D. 2000. Cosmopolitanism and the Banality of Geographical Evils. *Public Culture*, 12, 529–64.

Harvey, D. 2005. *A Brief History of Neoliberalism*, New York: Oxford University Press.

Hearn, A. 2012. Brand Me "Activist." *In:* Mukherjee, R. and Banet-Wiser, S. (eds) *Commodity Activism: Cultural Resistance in Neoliberal Times*, New York: New York University Press.

Heins, V. 2008. *Nongovernmental Organizations in International Society: Struggles Over Recognition*, New York: Palgrave Macmillan.

Hewison, K. 2000. Resisting Localism: A Study of Localism in Thailand. *The Pacific Review*, 13, 279–96.

Hewison, K. 2003. The Politics of Neoliberalism: Class and Capitalism in Contemporary Thailand. *Working Paper Series*, Hong Kong: City University of Hong Kong.

Hewison, K. 2005. Neoliberalism and Domestic Capital: The Political Outcomes of the Economic Crisis in Thailand. *The Journal of Development Studies*, 41, 310–30.

Higgins-Desbiolles, F. 2003. Reconciliation Tourism: Tourism Healing Divided Societies! *Tourism Recreation Research*, 28, 35–44.

Higgins-Desbiolles, F. 2005. More Than an "Industry": The Forgotten Power of Tourism as a Social Force. *Tourism Management*, 27, 1192–208.

Higgins-Desbiolles, F. 2008. Justice Tourism and Alternative Globalisation. *Journal of Sustainable Tourism*, 16, 345–64.

Higham, J. 2000. Thailand: Prospects for a Tourism-Led Economic Recovery. *In:* Hall, M. and Page, S. (eds) *Tourism in South and Southeast Asia: Issues and Cases*, Boston: Butterworth Heinemann.

Hindle, C. (ed.) 2007. *Volunteer: A Traveller's Guide to Making a Difference*, Oakland: Lonely Planet Publications.

Hitchcock, M., King, V. and Parnwell, M. 2009. Introduction: "Tourism in Southeast Asia" Revisited. *In:* Hitchcock, M., King, V. and Parnwell, M. (eds) *Tourism in Southeast Asia: Challenge and New Directions*, Honolulu: University of Hawaii Press.

Hochschild, A.R. 1979. Emotion Work, Feeling Rules, and Social Structure. *American Journal of Sociology*, 85, 551.

Hochschild, A.R. 1983. *The Managed Heart: Commercialization of Human Feeling*, Berkeley: University of California Press.

Hoffman, E.C. 1998. *All You Need is Love: The Peace Corps and the Spirit of the 1960s*, Cambridge: Harvard University Press.

Huffington Post. 2011. Sean Penn: In Haiti "For The Rest Of My Life." *Huffington Post* [Online]. Available: http://www.huffingtonpost.com/2011/01/06/sean-penn-in-haiti-for-the-rest-of-my-life_n_805137.html.

Huhndorf, S. 2001. *Going Native: Indians in the American Cultural Imagination*, Ithaca: Cornell University Press.

Huntington, S.P. 1993. The Clash of Civilizations?. *Foreign Affairs*, 72, 22–49.

Huntington, S.P. 1996. *The Clash of Civilizations and the Remaking of the World Order*, New York: Simon and Schuster Paperbacks.

Hutnyk, J. 1996. *The Rumour of Calcutta: Tourism, Charity and the Poverty of Representation*, London: Zed Books.

Illouz, E. 2007. *Cold Intimacies: The Making of Emotional Capitalism*, Cambridge: Polity Press.

Jackiewicz, E. 2004. Tourism Without Threat? Experts from Rural Costa Rica. *Annals of Tourism Research*, 32, 266–8.

Jankaew, K., Atwater, B.F., Sawai, Y., Choowong, M., Charoentitirat, T., Martin, M.E. and Prendergast, A. 2008. Medieval forewarning of the 2004 Indian Ocean tsunami in Thailand. *Nature*, 455, 1228–31.

Jeckell, B. and Macneil, J. 2004. More Stars Join Tsunami Relief Efforts. *Articles* [Online]. Available: http://www.billboard.com/articles/news/64587/more-stars-join-tsunami-relief-efforts.

Jenkins, R. 2005. Globalization, corporate social responsibility and poverty. *International Affairs*, 81, 525–40.

Kaldor, M. 2003. *Global Civil Society: An Answer to War*, Cambridge: Polity Press.

Keyes, C. 1987. *Thailand: Buddhist Kingdom as Modern Nation-State*, Boulder: Westview Press.

Knudsen, B.T. and Waade, A.M. (eds) 2010. *Re-Investing Authenticity: Tourism, Place and Emotions*, Toronto: Channel View Publications.

Lacher, G.R. and Nepal, S.K. 2010. Dependency and development in northern Thailand. *Annals of Tourism Research*, 37, 947–68.

Lassiter, L. 2005. *The Chicago Guide to Collaborate Ethnography*, Chicago: The University of Chicago Press.

Lawson, V. 2007. Geographies of Care and Responsibility. *Annals of the Association of American Geographers*, 97, 1–11.

Legg, S. 2011. Assemblage/apparatus: using Deleuze and Foucault. *Area*, 43, 128–33.

Leonard, E. 2013. Christina Aguilera Takes Emotional Trip to Rwanda. *People Magazine* [Online]. Available: http://www.people.com/people/article/0,20738 743,00.html.

Let's Go Publications, I. 2010. *Volunteering* [Online]. Cambridge: Let's Go Publications, Inc. Available: http://www.letsgo.com/5052-usa-travel-guides-hawaii-beyond_tourism-volunteering-c [Accessed 09/27/10].

Li, T.M. 2007. Practices of assemblage and community forest management. *Economy and Society*, 36, 263–93.

Lipman, C. 2006. The Emotional Self. *Cultural Geographies*, 13, 617–24.

Lough, B., McBride, A. and Sherraden, M. 2009. Perceived Effects of International Volunteering: Reports from CCS Alumni. St. Louis: The Center for Social Development at Washington University in St. Louis and Cross-Cultural Solutions.

Lutz, C. 1986a. Emotion, Thought, and Estrangement: Emotion as a Cultural Category. *Cultural Anthropology*, 1, 287–309.

Lutz, C. and Abu-Lughod, L. (eds) 1990. *Language and the Politics of Emotion*, Cambridge: Cambridge University Press.

Lutz, C. and White, Geoffrey M. 1986b. The Anthropology of Emotions. *Ann. Rev. Anthropology*, 15, 405–36.

Lyons, K., Hanley, J., Wearing, S. and Neil, J. 2012. Gap Year Volunteer Tourism: Myths of Global Citizenship? *Annals of Tourism Research*, 39, 361–78.

Lyons, K. and Wearing, S. 2008a. Volunteer Tourism as Alternative Tourism: Journeys Beyond Otherness. *In:* Lyons, K. and Stephen, W. (eds) *Journeys of Discovery in Volunteer Tourism: International Case Study Perspectives*, Cambridge: Cabi International.

MacCannell, D. 1973. Staged Authenticity: Arrangements of Social Space in Tourist Settings. *The American Journal of Sociology*, 79, 589–603.

MacCannell, D. 1976. *The Tourist: A New Theory of the Leisure Class*, New York: Schocken Books.

MacCannell, D. 1992. *Empty Meeting Grounds: The Tourist Papers*, New York: Routledge.

MacCannell, D. 1999. *The Tourist: A New Theory of the Leisure Class*, Berkeley: University of California Press.

McElhaney, K.A. 1998. *Student outcomes of community service learning: A comparative analysis of curriculum-based and non-curriculum-based alternative spring break programs.* The University of Michigan.

McFarlane, C. 2009. Translocal assemblages: space, power and social movements. *Geoforum*, 40, 561–7.

McGehee, N. 2002a. Alternative tourism and social movements. *Annals of Tourism Research*, 29, 124–43.

McGehee, N.G. 2008. *Volunteer Tourism: Sustainable Innovation in Tourism, or just "'Pettin' the Critters"?* [Online]. Available: http://www.besteducationnetwork.org/ttvii/pdf/McGehee.pdf [Accessed 03/22/2008].

McGehee, N.G. 2012. Oppression, Emancipation, and Volunteer Tourism: Research Propositions. *Annals of Tourism Research*, 39, 84–107.

McGehee, N.G. and Norman, W.C. 2001. Alternative Tourism as Impetus for Consciousness Raising. *Tourism Analysis*, 6, 239–51.

McGehee, N.G. and Santos, C. 2005a. Social Change, Discourse and Volunteer Tourism. *Annals of Tourism Research*, 32, 760–79.

McIntosh, A. and Zahra, A. 2007. A Cultural Encounter through Volunteer Tourism: Towards the Ideals of Sustainable Tourism?. *Journal of Sustainable Tourism*, 15, 541–56.

MacKinnon, J.B. 2009. *The Dark Side of Volunteer Tourism* [Online]. Topeka, Kansas: Ogden Publications, Inc. Available: http://www.utne.com/Politics/The-Dark-Side-of-Volunteer-Tourism-Voluntourism.aspx?page=2#ixzz187 OW8fNO [Accessed 12/14/10].

McKinnon, K.I. 2006. An Orthodoxy of "The Local": Post-Colonialism, Participation and Professionalism in Northern Thailand. *The Geographical Journal*, 172, 22–34.

McLaren, D. 2003. *Rethinking Tourism and Ecotravel*, Bloomfield, CT: Kumarian Press, Inc.

Macmillan, R. and Townsend, A. 2006. A "New Institutional Fix"?: The "Community Turn" and the Changing Role of the Voluntary Sector. *In:* Milligan, C. and David, C. (eds) *Landscapes of Voluntarism: New Spaces of Health, Welfare and Governance*, Bristol: The Policy Press.

Magnet, M. 1999. What Is Compassionate Conservatism? *The Wall Street Journal* [Online]. Available: http://www.manhattan-institute.org/html/_wsj-what_is_compassionate_con.htm [Accessed 02/05/2010].

Mai, O.C. 2010. *Chiang Mai Facts* [Online]. Chiang Mai: Open Chiang Mai. Available: http://www.openchiangmai.com/chiangmai_facts.php [Accessed 08/02/2010].

Manzo, K. 2008. Imaging Humanitarianism: NGO Identity and the Iconography of Childhood. *Antipode*, 40, 632–57.

Marcus, G. 1998. *Ethnography through Thick and Thin*, New Jersey: Princeton University Press.

Mathers, K. 2010. *Travel, Humanitarianism, and Becoming American in Africa*, New York: Palgrave Macmillian.

Mattingly, C. 2010. *The Paradox of Hope: Journeys through a Clinical Borderland*, Berkeley: University of California Press.

Mersmann, A., Havranek, C. and Ferguson, K. 2010. *500 Places Where You Can Make a Difference*, Mississauga, ON Canada: John Wiley and Sons Canada, Ltd.

Milligan, C., Atkinson, S., Skinner, M. and Wiles, J. 2007. Geographies of care: A commentary. *New Zealand Geographer*, 63, 135–40.

Milligan, C. and Conradson, D. 2006a. Contemporary Landscapes of Welfare: The Voluntary Turn? *In:* Milligan, C. and Conradson, D. (eds) *Landscapes of Voluntarism: New Spaces of Health, Welfare and Governance*, Bristol: The Policy Press.

Milligan, C. and Conradson, D. (eds) 2006b. *Landscapes of Voluntarism: New Spaces of Health, Welfare and Governance*, Bristol: The Policy Press.

Mintel 2008. Volunteer Tourism International. London: Mintel Group Ltd.

Mohan, G. and Stokke, K. 2000. Participatory development and empowerment: the dangers of localism, *Third World Quarterly*, 21, 247–68.

Mosse, D. 2013. The Anthropology of International Development. *Annual Review of Anthropology*, 42, 227–46.

Mostafanezhad, M. 2013a. The Geography of Compassion in Volunteer Tourism. *Tourism Geographies*, 15, 318–37.

Mostafanezhad, M. 2013b. "Getting in Touch with your Inner Angelina": celebrity humanitarianism and the cultural politics of gendered generosity in volunteer tourism. *Third World Quarterly*, 34, 485–99.

Mowforth, M. and Munt, I. 2009. *Tourism and Sustainability: Development and New Tourism in the Third World*, New York: Routledge.

Students Volunteering for a Spring Break They Won't Forget. 2007. Television Broadcast. Directed by MTV. USA.

Mukherjee, R. and Banet-Weiser, S. 2012. *Commodity Activism: Cultural Resistance in Neoliberal Times*, New York: NYU Press.

Muzaini, H. 2006. BACKPACKING SOUTHEAST ASIA: Strategies of "Looking Local." *Annals of Tourism Research*, 33, 144–61.

Nash, D. 1981. Tourism as an Anthropological Subject. *Current Anthropology*, 22, 461–81.

Nash, D. 2001. On Travelers, Ethnographers and Tourists. *Annals of Tourism Research*, 28, 493–6.

Nash, J. 2007. *Practicing Ethnography in a Globalizing World: An Anthropological Odyssey*, New York: Alta Mira Press.

Nations, E.O.T. 2010. *Thailand—Economic development* [Online]. Available: http://www.nationsencyclopedia.com/Asia-and-Oceania/Thailand-ECONO MIC-DEVELOPMENTS.html.

Nimmonratana, T. 2000. Impacts of Tourism on a Local Community: A Case Study of Chiang Mai. *In:* Chon, K.S., Ohashi, Taiji and Inagaki, Tsutomuki (eds) *Tourism in Southeast Asia: a New Direction.* Binghamton, NY: The Haworth Hospitality Press.

Nsabimana, N. 2013a. The #BullshitFiles: Christina Aguilera feeds war-torn Rwanda. *Africa Is a Country* [Online]. Available from: http://africasacountry.com/the-bullshitfiles-christina-aguilera-feeds-rwanda/ [Accessed 10/13/13].

Ong, A. 1998. Flexible Citizenship among Chinese Cosmopolitans. *In:* Cheah, P. and Bruce, R. (eds) *Cosmopolitcs: Thinking and Feeling Beyond the Nation.* Minneapolis: University of Minnesota.

Pain, R. and Smith, S.J. 2012. *Fear: Critical Geopolitics and Everyday Life*, Farnham: Ashgate Publishing, Ltd.

Palk, S. 2010. Why do so many women go on volunteer vacations? *CNN: International* [Online]. Available: http://edition.cnn.com/2010/TRAVEL/06/02/more.women.in.voluntourism/index.html [Accessed 01/02/2013].

Pattullo, P. and Minelli, O. 2006. *The Ethnica Travel Guide*, London: Earthscan.

Pedwell, C. 2012a. Affective (self-) transformations: Empathy, neoliberalism and international development. *Feminist Theory*, 13, 163–79.

Pedwell, C. 2012b. Economies of empathy: Obama, neoliberalism, and social justice. *Environment and Planning D: Society and Space*, 30, 280–97.

Pezzullo, P. 2007. *Toxic Tours: Rhetorics of Pollution, Travel and Environmental Justice*, Tuscaloosa: The University of Alabama Press.

Phongpaichit, P. and Baker, C. 2002. *Thailand: Economy and Politics*, New York: Oxford University Press.

Pieterse, J.N. 1998. My Paradigm or Yours? Alternative Development, Post-Development, Reflexive Development. *Development and Change*, 29, 343–74.

Pieterse, J.N. 2000. After post-development. *Third World Quarterly*, 21, 175–91.

Poon, A. 1989. Competitive Strategies for a New Tourism. *In:* Cooper, C.P. and Lockwood, A. (eds) *Progress in Tourism, Recreation and Hospitality Management*, London: Belhaven.

Pratt, M.L. 1992. *Imperial Eyes: Travel Writing and Transculturation*, New York, Routledge.

Rabbitts, F. 2012. Child sponsorship, ordinary ethics and the geographies of charity. *Geoforum*, 43, 926–36.

Raymond, E. 2008. "Make a Difference!": The Role of Sending Organizations in Volunteer Tourism. *In:* Lyons, K. and Stephen, W. (eds) *Journeys of Discovery in Volunteer Tourism: International Case Study Perspectives.* Cambridge: CABI International.

Raymond, E. and Hall, M. 2008. The Development of Cross-Cultural (Mis) Understanding Through Volunteer Tourism. *Journal of Sustainable Tourism*, 16, 530–43.

Raymond, E.M. and Michael Hall, C. 2008. The Potential for Appreciative Inquiry in Tourism Research. *Current Issues in Tourism*, 11, 281–92.

Rhoads, R.A. and Neururer, J. 1998. Alternative spring break: Learning through community service. *Journal of Student Affairs Research and Practice*, 35, 83–101.

Rieffel, L. and Zalud, S. 2006. International Volunteering: Smart Power. *Brookings Policy Brief Series.* Brookings Institute.

Rigg, J. 1991. Grass-roots development in rural Thailand: A lost cause? *World Development*, 19, 199–211.

Rigg, J., Law, L., Tan-Mullins, M. and Grundy-Warr, C. 2005. The Indian Ocean tsunami: socio-economic impacts in Thailand. *Geographical Journal*, 171, 374–9.

Riska, G. 2010. NGOs IN THE GMS Involvement Related to Poverty Alleviation and Watershed Management Thailand. Bangkok: Poverty Reduction and Environmental Management in Remote Greater Mekong Subregion (GMS).

Robbins, B. 1998. Introduction Part I: Actually Existing Cosmpolitanism. *In:* Cheah, P. and Robbins, B. (eds) *Cosmopolitics: Thinking and Feeling Beyond the Nation.* Minneapolis: University of Minnesota Press.

Rosaldo, R. 1989. *Culture and Truth: The Remaking of Social Analysis*, Boston: Beacon Press.

Ruiz, R. 2008. Eight Hot Spots For Volunteer Travel. *Forbes.com.*

Safina. Jan 13, 2009 2009. Falling in love … … .with Chiang Mai. *AirAsia Blog: Just Plane Thoughts* [Online]. Available from: http://blog.airasia.com/index. php/falling-in-love-with-chiang-mai [Accessed 08/02/2010].

Scheyvens, R. 2010. Tourism and Development in the Developing World. *Tourism Management*, 31, 292–3.

Scott, S. 2010. *Stories of Service Blog* [Online]. Washington D.C.: Commission for National and Community Service. Available: http://www.serve.gov/ stories_detail.asp?tbl_servestories_id=338 [Accessed 2/2/2010].

Searles, D.P. 1997. *The Peace Corps experience: challenge and change, 1969– 1976*, Lexington: University of Kentucky Press.

Sheldon, P.J. and Park, S.-Y. 2011. An exploratory study of corporate social responsibility in the US travel industry. *Journal of Travel Research*, 50, 392–407.

Shetty, S., Subbarao, K., Tzannatos, Z., Rudra, K. and Poshyananda, T. 1996. Thailand Growth, Poverty and Income Distribution. Country Operations Division, Country Department, East Asia and Pacific Regions: World Bank.

Shrestha, N. 2002. Becoming a Development Category. *In:* Schech, S. and Haggis, J. (eds) *Development: A Cultural Studies Reader*, Oxford: Blackwell Publishing.

Simpson, K. 2004a. Doing Development: The Gap year, Volunteer-Tourists and a Popular Practice of Development. *Journal of International Development*, 16, 681–92.

Sin, H.L. 2009. Volunteer Tourism—"Involve Me and I Will Learn"? *Annals of Tourism Research*, 36, 480–501.

Sin, H.L. 2012. Post-Ethical Tours: Corporate Social Responsibility in Tourism. *In:* Minca, C. and Oakes, T. (eds) *Real Tourism: Practice, Care and Politics in Contemporary Travel Culture.* New York: Routledge.

Singh, A. 1997. Asia pacific tourism industry: Current trends and future outlook. *Asia Pacific Journal of Tourism Research*, 2, 89–99.

Singh, S. and Singh, T.V. 2004. Volunteer Tourism: New Pilgrimages to the Himalayas. *In:* Singh, T.V. (ed.) *New Horizons in Tourism: Strange Experiences and Stranger Practices*, Cambridge: Cabi Publishing.

Smith, D.M. 1997. Geography and ethics: a moral turn? *Progress in Human Geography*, 21, 583–90.

Smith, N. 1984. *Uneven Development: Nature, Capital, and the Production of Space*, Oxford: Blackwell.

Solomon, R. 2004. *In Defense of Sentimentality*, New York: Oxford University Press, Inc.

Solutions, C.-C. 2008. *Volunteer Voices* [Online]. New York: Cross Cultural Solutions. Available: http://www.crossculturalsolutions.org/volunteervoices. asp [Accessed 09/10/2008].

Solutions, C.-C. 2010. *Cross-Cultural Solutions: Excellence in International Volunteering* [Online]. New York: Cross Cultural Solutions. [Accessed 04/ 20/2010].

Sparke, M. 2007. Geopolitical fears, geoeconomic hopes, and the responsibilities of geography. *Annals of the Association of American Geographers*, 97, 338–49.

Spencer, R. 2010. *Development Tourism: Lessons from Cuba*, Burlington, VT: Ashgate Publishing.

Springer, S. 2010. Neoliberalism and geography: expansions, variegations, formations. *Geography Compass*, 4, 1025–38.

Spurr, D. 1993. *The Rhetoric of Empire: Colonial Discourse in Journalism, Travel Writing, and Imperial Administration* Durham: Duke University Press.

Steger, M. 2009a. *Globalisms: The Great Ideological Struggle of the Twenty-First Century*, Maryland: Rowman and Littlefield.

Steger, M. 2009b. *Globalization: A Short Introduction*, New York: Oxford University Press.

Stoler, A. 2002. *Carnal Knowledge and Imperial Power: Race and the Intimate in Colonial Rule*, Berkeley: University of California Press.

Stoler, A. L. 2006. *Haunted by Empire: Geographies of Intimacy in North American History*, Durham: Duke University Press.

Stronza, A. 2001. Anthropology of Tourism: Forging New Ground for Ecotourism and Other Alternatives. *Annual Review of Anthropology*, 30, 261–83.

Stronza, A. 2005. Hosts and Hosts: The Anthropology of Community-Based Ecotourism in The Peruvian Amazon. *NAPA Bulletin*, 23, 170–90.

Sturken, M. 2007. *Tourists of History: Memory, Kitsch, and Consumerism from Oklahoma City to Ground Zero*, Durham: Duke University Press.

Sturken, M. 2012. Foreward. *In:* Mukherjee, R. and Banet-Weiser, S. (eds) *Commodity Activism: Cultural Resistance in Neoliberal Times*, New York: New York University Press.

Sumner, A. 2013. Poverty, Politics and Aid: is a reframing of global poverty approaching? *Third World Quarterly*, 34, 357–77.

Swain, M.B. 2009. The Cosmopolitan Hope of Tourism: Critical Action and Worldmaking Vistas. *Tourism Geographies*, 11, 505–25.

Tedlock, B. 1991. From Participant Observation to the Observation of Participation: The Emergence of Narrative Ethnography. *Journal of Anthropological Research*, 47, 69–94.

Tefler, D. and Sharpley, R. 2008. *Tourism and Development in the Developing World*, New York: Routledge.

Teo, P., Chang, T.C. and Ho, K.C. (ed.) 2001. *Interconnected Worlds Tourism in Southeast Asia*, Oxford: Pergamon.

Tester, K. 2001. *Compassion, Morality and the Media*, London: Open University Press.

Tester, K. 2010. *Humanitarianism and Modern Culture*, University Park, PA: Pennsylvania State University Press.

Thailand, T.A.O. 2008. *Tourism Authority of Thailand* [Online]. Bangkok: Thai Government. Available: http://www.tourismthailand.org/ [Accessed 08/15/2008].

Thomas, A. 2000. Development as Practice in a Liberal Capitalist World. *Journal of International Development*, 12, 773–87.

Thongchai, W. 1994. *Siam Mapped: A History of the Geo-Body*, Honolulu: University of Hawaii Press.

Tirasatayapitak, A. and Laws, E. 2003. Developing a new Multi-Nation tourism region: Thai perspectives on the Mekong initiatives. *Asia Pacific Journal of Tourism Research*, 8, 48–57.

Torgovnick, M. 1997. *Primitive Passions: Men, Women, Women and the Quest for Ecstacy*, New York: Alfred Knopf.

Tourism, I.I.F.P.T. 2007. *International Institute for Peace Through Tourism* [Online]. Available: http://www.iipt.org/.

Travelocity.com. 2007. *Travelocity: Go Zero* [Online]. Travelocity.com. Available: http://leisure.travelocity.com/Promotions/0,TRAVELOCITY|3689|vacations_main,00.html [Accessed 06/23/2008].

Turner, A. and Ash, J. 1975. *The Golden Hordes: International Tourism and the Pleasure Periphery*, New York: St. Martin's Press.

UNESCO. 2010. *UNESCO Chair in Cultural Tourism for Peace and Development (360), established in 1999 at the Russian International Academy for Tourism (Russian Federation).* [Online]. Moscow: UNESCO. Available: http://www.unesco.org/en/university-twinning-and-networking/access-by-region/europe-and-north-america/russian-federation/unesco-chair-in-cultural-tourism-for-peace-and-development-360/ [Accessed 1/3/2011].

UNHCR. 2013. *2013 UNHCR country operations profile—Thailand* [Online]. Bangkok: United Nations High Commissioner for Refugees. Available: http://www.unhcr.org/cgi-bin/texis/vtx/page?page=49e489646.

Uriely, N., Reichel, A. and Ron, A. 2003. Volunteering in Tourism: Additional Thinking. *Tourism Recreation Research*, 28, 57–62.

Urry, J. and Larsen, J. 2011. *The Tourist Gaze 3.0*, London: Sage.

Vadit-Vadakan, J. 2005. The Role of Ethics and NGOs in an Emerging Market. *In:* Ward, T. (ed.) *Development, Social Justice and Civil Society*, St. Paul, Minnesota: Paragon House.

Var, T., Schlüter, R., Ankomah, P. and Lee, T.-H. 1989. Tourism and world peace: The case of Argentina. *Annals of Tourism Research*, 16, 431–4.

Vasquez, E. 2010 Do Celebs Like Jolie Inspire Voluntourism? *CNN: International* [Online]. Available: http://edition.cnn.com/2010/TRAVEL/08/10/celebrity.humanitarian.travel/index.html.

Viravaidya, M. 2005. Why NGOs in LDCs Need a UN High Commissioner for Civil Society. *In:* Ward, T. (ed.) *Development, Social Justice and Civil Society*, St. Paul, Minnesota: Paragon House.

Vivas, E. 2010. *World Social Forum, ten years on* [Online]. Worldwide: International Viewpoint: News and analysis from the Fourth International. Available: http://www.internationalviewpoint.org/spip.php?article1813 [Accessed 07/22/2010].

Vogler, C. 2004. Much Madness and More of Sin: Compassion, for Ligeia. *In:* Berlant, L. (ed.) *Compassion: The Culture and Politics of an Emotion*, New York: Routledge.

Vrasti, W. 2011. "Caring" Capitalism and the Duplicity of Critique. *Theory & Event*, 14, 1–14.

Vrasti, W. 2012. *Volunteer Tourism in the Global South: Giving Back in Neoliberal Times*, New York: Routledge.

Wallace, T. 2005. Tourism, Tourists, and Anthropologists at Work. *NAPA Bulletin*, 23, 1–26.

Wearing, S. 2001. *Volunteer Tourism: Experiences That Make A Difference*, Cambridge, Cabi Press.

Wearing, S. 2002. Re-Centering the Self in Volunteer Tourism. *In:* Dann, G. (ed.) *The Tourist as a Metaphor of the Social World.* London: Cabi Publishing.

Wearing, S. 2003. Volunteer Tourism. *Tourism Recreation Research*, 28, 3–4.

Wearing, S. 2004a. Examining Best Practice in Volunteer Tourism. *In:* Stebbins, R. and Graham, M. (ed.) *Volunteering as Leisure/Leisure as Volunteering.* Cambridge: Cabi Press.

Wearing, S. and McDonald, M. 2002. The Development of Community-Based Tourism: Re-Thinking the Relationship Between Tour Operators and Development Agents as Intermediaries in Rural and Isolated Area Communities *Journal of Sustainable Tourism*, 10, 191–206.

Wearing, S., McDonald, Matthew and Ponting, Jess. 2005. Building a Decommodified Research Paradigm in Tourism: The Contribution of NGOs. *Journal of Sustainable Tourism*, 13, 424–39.

West, P. 2008. Tourism as Science and Science as Tourism. *Current Anthropology*, 49, 597–626.

Westerhausen, K. and Macbeth, J. 2003. Backpackers and empowered local communities: natural allies in the struggle for sustainability and local control? *Tourism Geographies: An International Journal of Tourism Space, Place and Environment*, 5, 71–86.

Wexler, L. 2000. *Tender Violence: Domestic Visions in an Age of U.S. Imperialism*, Chapel Hill: The University of North Carolina Press.

Wilson, A. 2004. *The Intimate Economies of Bangkok: Tomboys, Tycoons, and Avon Ladies in the Global City*, Berkeley: University of California Press.

Woodward, K. 2004. Calculating Compassion. *In:* Berlant, L. (ed.) *Compassion: The Culture and Politics of an Emotion*, New York: Routlege.

Wyatt, D. 1982. *Thailand: A Short History*, New Haven: Yale University Press.

Yoda17. 2007. Volunteer Tourism: Who Really Gains?. Available from: http://digg.com/environment/Volunteer_Tourism_Who_really_gains [Accessed 04/20/2010].

Yuthamanop, P. 2011. Income Inequality in Thailand. *Learning* [Online]. Available: http://www.bangkokpost.com/learning/learning-from-news/270964/income-inequality-in-thailand.

Zahra, A. and McIntosh, Alison 2007. Volunteer Tourism: Evidence of Cathartic Tourist Experiences. *Tourism Recreation Research*, 32, 115–19.

Zavitz, K.J. and Butz, D. 2011. Not that alternative: Short-term volunteer tourism at an organic farming project in Costa Rica. *ACME*, 10, 412–41.

Index